SOCIAL WORKERS THEIR ROLE & TASKS

The report of a Working Party set up in
October 1980, at the request of the
Secretary of State for Social Services, by
the National Institute for Social Work under
the chairmanship of Mr Peter M. Barclay

Published for the
NATIONAL INSTITUTE FOR SOCIAL WORK by
BEDFORD SQUARE PRESS | NCVO

Published by the
BEDFORD SQUARE PRESS of the
National Council for Voluntary Organisations
26 Bedford Square London WC1B 3HU

ISBN 0 7199 1080 3

First published 1982
Reprinted with corrections 1982
Reprinted 1982
Reprinted 1985
Reprinted 1989

Designed by Tony Cantale

Photoset by D. P. Media Limited, Hitchin, Hertfordshire
Printed and bound in Great Britain by
Biddles Ltd, Guildford and King's Lynn

Contents

Introduction   vii
Explanation of terms used   xii

PART ONE   **THE PRACTICE OF SOCIAL WORK**
Chapter 1   What social workers in field settings do   2
Chapter 2   Social work staffing and social problems   24
Chapter 3   What social workers are needed to do   33
Chapter 4   Social work in residential and day services   52
Chapter 5   Social work and the voluntary sector   73

PART TWO   **THE CONTEXT OF SOCIAL WORK**
Chapter 6   The economic context   96
Chapter 7   Social policy and the development of social work   102
Chapter 8   Interactions with other services   113
Chapter 9   Issues of organisation and management   126
Chapter 10   The influence of values, methods, skills and knowledge   145

PART THREE   **CLIENTS, COMMUNITY AND SOCIAL WORK**
Chapter 11   Views of social work   158
Chapter 12   Maintaining standards and protecting clients' rights   177
Chapter 13   Towards community social work   198

Appendix A   A case for neighbourhood-based social work and social services   219
Appendix B   An alternative view   236
Appendix C   List of works referred to in the text   263
Appendix D   List of members of the Working Party   267
Appendix E   List of respondents   268
Appendix F   List of areas visited by members of the Working Party or its Secretariat   276
Appendix G   List of principal statutory enactments relevant to the tasks of social workers   277
Appendix H   List of papers available from the National Institute for Social Work   278

Index   279

We list in Appendix C works referred to in the text.
Specific references to evidence we received are
accompanied in the text by the number of the relevant
submission in the list at Appendix E. But the Working
Party's thinking has been influenced throughout by the
particular insights and the general tenor of the whole
volume of evidence it received.

Introduction

1 Too much is generally expected of social workers. We load upon them unrealistic expectations and we then complain when they do not live up to them. Social work is a relatively young profession. It has grown rapidly as the flow of legislation has greatly increased the range and complexity of its work. In order to cope with demands which Parliament has imposed on social services authorities, large departments have grown up in which social workers find it difficult to come to terms with the complex pressures which surround them. There is confusion about the direction in which they are going and unease about what they should be doing and the way in which they are organised and deployed. When things go wrong the media have tended to blame them because it is assumed that their job is to care for people so as to prevent trouble arising. They operate uneasily on the frontier between what appears to be almost limitless needs on the one hand and an inadequate pool of resources to satisfy those needs on the other. Not surprisingly, for these and many other reasons, demands for an independent enquiry into their work have grown increasingly insistent during the last few years.

2 The National Institute for Social Work was approached in the late summer of 1980 on behalf of The Right Honourable Patrick Jenkin, then Secretary of State for Social Services. Would the Institute promote, at Government expense, an independent and authoritative enquiry into the role and tasks of social workers? The Institute readily agreed. The proposal was announced at the Social Services Conference in September of the Local Authority Associations and the Association of Directors of Social Services and the working party met for the first time in December 1980.

3 Our terms of reference were as follows: 'To review the role and tasks of social workers in local authority social services departments and related voluntary agencies in England and Wales and to make recommendations.' To make clear our approach, we interpreted these terms of reference, in a note of guidance we issued for those who wished to submit evidence, as requiring us 'to provide an

account and clarification of what social workers do, appraised against an explicit view of what they are needed to do'.

4 In selecting members of the working party an attempt was made to ensure that many different viewpoints from within and from outside social work would be represented. A list of members appears in Appendix D.

5 We knew our working party was expected to have only a brief existence and we therefore set outselves a year for our work. Regular meetings were completed within this period but the necessary editorial work and final drafting and printing have required a further period before publication.

6 Agreement to such a relatively short period for such a complex undertaking was severely criticised at the time but the decision seemed justifiable on the following grounds:

a) We were not starting from scratch. We were to build on work which had previously been carried out by, among others, the Personal Social Services Council, the British Association of Social Workers, the Residential Care Association, the Joint Steering Group on Accreditation and the Association of Directors of Social Services. A further study by the Local Authorities Social Services Study Group was still operating at the time our enquiry was announced.

b) It was desirable to cut to a minimum the period during which anxieties felt by some about the purpose of our work were added to the sense of uncertainty, which we have already mentioned, about what social workers should be doing and should not be doing. In this instance, it seemed that a relatively short period of concentrated activity would be preferable to the more leisurely time-scale allowed for in most similar exercises.

c) We were not expected to provide the ultimate answer to the underlying uncertainties about the future of social work. These uncertainties, we noted, were not unique to social work but were rather a characteristic of our times, mirrored as they were by uncertainties widely felt about the role of workers in other fields – which had led, for example, to the setting up of the Royal Commission on the Legal Profession and to widespread debate on teaching and on policing. Our objective was much more modest, namely such a clarification as we could encompass of exceedingly complex questions which should attempt to do no more than to provide a helpful basis for discussion in the future by social workers, their employers and trainers, and the wider public.

7 Our limited time-scale placed those who wished to give evidence under severe pressure. Our guidelines, issued in January

1981, called for evidence by Easter. The remarkable response – over 350 bodies and individuals sent submissions in time for consideration by the working party – proved invaluable and demonstrated the importance which those in and beyond the social work world attached to the enquiry. We list those who thus contributed evidence in Appendix E. Many others, whom it has not been possible to mention individually, have since sent in papers or have otherwise helped our work in different ways. Several witnesses have at our request given oral evidence. We are grateful to the Association of Directors of Social Services for providing up-to-date factual information, which would not otherwise have been available, on length of time in post and age of social workers, the result of a questionnaire circulated at our request to its members. Other organisations and Government Departments went to great lengths to provide material on issues which were of particular concern to us. We are grateful to them all.

8 Members of the working party and of its secretariat paid several visits to different parts of the country specifically for the purposes of our enquiry and we list in Appendix F the places to which we went. We much appreciated the warm welcome and helpful arrangements made for us on these occasions which were of great value, in particular to those of us not working either in local authorities or in social work practice.

9 We met as a full working party or in sub-groups on twenty-four occasions and in addition we held two longer residential sessions at the Civil Service College, Sunningdale.

10 We should have liked to have commissioned new research, particularly of clients' views of social workers. However, we were advised early on that it would not be possible, within the time available, to do so on a satisfactory basis. Nevertheless, we have had the benefit of the part-time research assistance of Mr Gordon Craig – who built on the early work which Professor Harry Specht kindly carried out for us, reviewing in general terms research material currently available on users' views of social work and social services. Mr Craig's work for the Committee on non-accidental injury enquiries is being published as a separate document by the National Institute for Social Work, as is a further paper in which he presents a review of studies of public and clients' attitudes.

11 We pay tribute to the work of our Secretary, Mr Bob King, of Mr Peter Righton, formerly Director of Education at the National Institute, who has shouldered a considerable drafting burden and of Miss Carol Whitwill, their personal secretary and helper. We are also

grateful to Dr Ian Sinclair, Director of Research at the Institute who has supervised the research input and provided welcome help and advice. It was invaluable to have the resources of the National Institute behind us and to have the ready support of its principal, Mr David Jones, throughout our work.

12 The report in its final form will be seen as the work of many hands; only by sharing the drafting among a number of people could the task have been achieved in the time. We have to accept the fact that the end product is neither as polished nor as terse as we would have wished. Nevertheless we trust that it will prove to be of help to those to whom it is addressed – local authorities (both their elec..ed members and officers), voluntary organisations employing social workers, universities, polytechnics and colleges responsible for their training, the Central Council for Education and Training in Social Work, the Government at whose request the enquiry was undertaken, and finally to social workers themselves.

13 The topics which we cover indicate our view of the nature of social work. It is not an activity which can stand alone; it must be set in the context provided by social policies, organisational structures and the nature of other professions and services. We have therefore attempted to provide such a context within which the reader can set our examination of the role and tasks of social workers.

14 We make clear in Chapter 3 that we believe social work comprises two major strands – counselling and social care planning. The latter has two aspects. It may be related directly to solving or ameliorating an existing social problem which an individual, family or group is experiencing. But social care planning also includes what we call indirect work, to prevent social problems arising by the development and strengthening of various kinds of community groups and associations, and to enable informal as well as formally organised resources to be brought to bear upon them when they do.

15 Within personal social services agencies counselling is carried out largely by social work practitioners but social care planning is undertaken both by practitioners and by social work managers.

16 Thus we consider that both practitioners and managers in personal social services agencies are engaged in social work. Our report, however, deals in the main with the role and tasks of practitioners. We leave it to others, who may have the time which we have not, to explore more fully the role and tasks of social work managers and to make clear the implications for them of what we see as the practitioner's.

17 Those who look in this report for a detailed list of particular roles and particular tasks appropriate to the social worker, will look in vain. We have been warned by numerous respondents not to impose a blueprint on a scene which is very complex, varies greatly from one local authority to another and is moving all the time. We have heeded that warning; instead we have thought it more helpful to set the job of a social worker in a broad context and to leave it to others to develop the details as they seem most appropriate to local circumstances and local priorities.

18 In spite of all the complexities and uncertainties surrounding the functions of social workers, we are united in our belief that the work they do is of vital importance in our society, as it is in other modern industrial societies. It is here to stay, and social workers are needed as never before. But it is important that we use a scarce and costly resource – the trained social worker – in a creative and effective manner. With this thought in mind we have drafted our report.

Explanation of terms used

1 One of the problems which faced us, both in discussion and in writing this report, was how to achieve consistency and clarity when using key words and phrases. In the evidence we received, in written and spoken form, we found some words used in a variety of senses. We set out here our working definitions of some essential terms.

2 We have decided to use the term **client** to describe those who seek, or have imposed upon them, the services of social workers, of social services departments or of voluntary social services organisations. We considered three possible options: 'consumer', 'user' and 'client'. 'Consumer' we disliked because of its general association with the acquisition of material goods. It also suggests that a person has nothing to give or contribute to the process that is social work. For some time we preferred 'user' because it appeared to us a relatively neutral term, with a wide range of applicability. But it does not carry the important notion that social work is a personal service to meet individual needs, still less that some who receive it are subject to measures of control. We therefore decided to retain the term which is in current use, 'client', despite the negative reactions it may provoke as implying an undesirable degree of dependence and perhaps of stigma.

3 **Community** is a word with many meanings. What we mean is best illustrated from the standpoint of an individual person living in a particular locality. He is likely to share some things in common with, and to feel some loyalty towards, a number of other people within a particular geographical area – his family, his immediate neighbours, relatives and friends readily accessible; employers and fellow-employees if he works in the area, local shopkeepers and schoolteachers; publicans and others who cater for his leisure. More remote, but important for his peace of mind, are local representatives and officials who determine his rates, clear his rubbish, sweep the roads, and make decisions which affect his environment.

4 With this constellation of people (and many more), he will usually have developed relationships varying from the very intimate

to the very distant; he will be in sympathy with some and at odds
with others; to some extent what he does and the life-style he adopts
will be influenced by their views, as his views will influence some of
them. He is part of many networks of relationships whose focus is a
local area. He may think of these networks as close or loose, as refuges
or as traps; he may be an active participant in local affairs, or a
recluse; he may bless these networks or curse them. But whatever his
position in or attitude to the networks, if he falls on hard times,
becomes handicapped or is confronted by acute personal crisis, he
will be vitally affected by the extent to which the networks can be a
resource to him by way of information, practical help, understanding
or friendliness. It is these local networks of formal and informal
relationships, together with their capacity to mobilise individual and
collective responses to adversity that constitute the first sense in
which we use the word **community**. Similar, though perhaps more
constricted, networks will surround someone who lives in a
residential home or other institution.

    5 Community of interest: the same person is likely, in
addition to his local connections, to have a number of relationships
that matter to him with people and institutions outside a
circumscribed geographical area. He may share with such people a
particular social disadvantage or handicap, or a common interest
based on work, leisure activities or attendance at the same doctor's
surgery or hospital out-patients. He may have a range of interests or
beliefs that link him with others who share them all over the country
and abroad. He may visit friends and relatives at a considerable
distance. The allegiances he feels to people or groups outside a local
area may well be as important, or more important, emotionally than
those within it. We use the term 'communities of interest' to describe
these networks of relationships.

    6 We define our use of the term **community social work**
below in paragraph 23.

    7 Community work is variously defined by different people
wishing to use it for their particular purposes. As an occupation, as
distinct from a voluntary activity of citizens, however, it is generally
accepted as embracing both direct work with community groups and
work at the inter-organisational and planning level. It is undertaken
with communities, which may be large or small, and based on
geography or community of interest. Its basic concern is to enable
their members collectively to overcome problems and improve their
conditions of life while at the same time enhancing the sense of
common feeling, solidarity and competence of the community. In

seeking to do this a worker will enable the community to express and articulate its problems and identify ways of resolving these and fulfilling the aims of the group. This work is most readily understood in terms of direct work with groups and organisations within the community or in encouraging their formation. Examples of such groups are a tenants' association, a mothers' and toddlers' group, a 'festival' committee. But community work also takes the form of involvement in planning and influencing policies for the benefit of the community concerned. Work of this kind can be an element in social work and we use the term community work primarily in this sense. It does not encompass the whole of social work, which includes counselling (see paragraph 9) and elements of social care planning (see paragraph 11) which relate to working with individual clients, families or groups. Nor does social work embrace the whole of community work. Many important tasks with which community workers are involved lie well outside the direct concerns of social work and the personal social services, and are more appropriately undertaken by other sectors such as environment, education, employment, leisure, housing or industry. The effectiveness of these services, and of community work undertaken in relation to them, is of critical importance to the success of social work and of the community work undertaken by social workers.

8 Community workers are generally employed within organisations, whether voluntary agencies, local authorities (in chief executives' departments or in planning, housing, education or social services departments) or other statutory bodies. A few are directly employed by local community groups. The evidence we received indicated that few identify themselves as social workers, who are regarded by them as essentially providers of counselling to individuals or families.

9 By **counselling** we mean the process (which has often been known as 'social casework') of direct communication and interaction between clients and social workers, through which clients are helped to change, or to tolerate, some aspects of themselves or of their environment.

10 We use the term **personal social services** (which is commonly used in a rather wider sense) to describe those services for which local authority social services committees have responsibility and similar services provided by voluntary organisations. Where the context makes our meaning clear, however, we use **social services** in this sense rather than the wider sense noted below.

11 Social care planning covers plans designed to solve or

alleviate existing problems and plans which aim to prevent the development of social problems in the future or to create or strengthen resources to respond to those which do arise. It may embrace:
- planning and organising a response to a client's existing problems and arrangements for the client's future;
- planning and organising, and monitoring and evaluating, the delivery or development of social services for a particular population (whether defined by geographical area or by a common disadvantage or handicap), by a worker's own agency, alone or collaboration with others, whether statutory or voluntary agencies, mutual aid groups, volunteers or informal carers;
- sharing in joint planning with other statutory or voluntary services, bringing the experience of social workers and other personal social services staff to bear upon their policy planning;
- creating or strengthening voluntary organisations or mutual aid groups, recruiting, training and supporting volunteers, supporting informal caring networks, with a view to their responding to existing or future problems or preventing problems developing;
- training, supervising and managing social work and other social services staff.

12 The expression **social services** usually means all those statutory and voluntary services currently regarded as essential for survival and personal development in a civilised society. These include housing, social security, health, education, employment and leisure services. We sometimes use the term in this wide sense.

13 **Social services workers** is the term we use for a range of staff employed in local authority social services departments or voluntary agencies to help people in their own homes or in day centres or residential homes. They carry various designations including 'home help organiser', 'care assistant', 'home help' and 'family aide'. They undoubtedly carry out social work in the informal sense (see paragraphs 14–15 below) and many will also undertake formal social work (see paragraph 22) when the circumstances demand it, whether or not under the supervision of a social worker. Some confusion may arise from the inclusion of the term 'social work' in the designation of some of these post-holders (in particular, 'social work assistants'). They are distinguished from social workers in that they provide a specific service, often undertaken following a social worker's assessment.

14 **Social work** is sometimes used in a very wide sense to cover anything done to help a fellow being in trouble by anyone who does

not owe a duty as a relative or close friend. People in many walks of life who have no special qualifications or experience may see themselves, or be said by others, to be doing 'social work' in the course of their duties or outside them. It can cover practical help like shopping for an elderly neighbour, or giving advice, or in some general way befriending.

15 A phrase that illuminates one aspect of it is 'caring for strangers'. It may have an element of challenge to the person helped – to find ways of overcoming difficult circumstances or private sorrows. It may have an element of control also, restraining or dissuading someone from doing something harmful to self or others, cautioning someone against possible consequences, bringing home to someone the hurtful effects of things he has done. This is all informal work, not formally organised or planned. We have no wish, and certainly have no power, to stop people using the term 'social work' in this wide sense.

16 It is sometimes argued that this is all there is, or ought to be, to social work. Those who hold this view find it difficult to see why there should be a paid occupation of social work.

17 But just as there are health problems which call for something more than the informal 'doctoring' people do for themselves, and educational demands which call for more than the informal 'teaching' parents give their children, so there are practical, emotional and behavioural problems which call for more than a good-neighbourly, common-sense response.

18 And just as Parliament has given to health and education authorities functions and powers in their respective fields which may fundamentally affect people's lives and for the purpose of which they must employ responsible staff, so it has given social services authorities far-reaching functions and powers to provide help to people with practical or emotional or behavioural problems. For these functions also staff need to be employed both by the local authorities and by voluntary agencies who undertake similar work.

19 Parliament, reflecting the general climate of opinion, has moreover so framed the law as to require social services functions and powers to be exercised with regard for the dignity and the personal characteristics and circumstances of the individual and for the individual's right, subject only to safeguarding him and others from harm, to make decisions for himself. This is reinforced by the way in which agencies have framed their policies. These conditions require something other than a purely rule of thumb approach. They may face staff with complexities of legal, ethical and emotional problems through which common sense, goodwill and a code of procedure alone cannot find a way.

20 Just as there is, therefore, a specialised and formal aspect of doctoring and teaching, so there is a specialised and formal aspect of social work.

21 While it is Parliament and the employing agencies (back to the time of the earliest employment of social workers (almoners) by hospitals, and probation officers by police court missions), who have created and extended this formal aspect of social work, its practice within these agencies has established it as a discipline in its own right, transferable, as we are now seeing, to private, independent practice. Training designed for it is regulated under statutory provisions, and training and practice interacting with each other have established a generally recognised, though far from definitive, range of appropriate methods, knowledge and skills.

22 Our report as a whole seeks to clarify and describe more fully what we mean by this formal aspect of social work. We distinguish in Chapter 3 'counselling' and 'social care planning' as its two components. We use the term 'social work' sometimes in its wider sense but, as the context will often make clear, sometimes for its formal aspect. Only where necessary in order to avoid misunderstanding do we use the clumsier expression 'formal social work'.

23 In Chapter 13 we describe what we have termed **community social work**. By this we mean formal social work which, starting from problems affecting an individual or group and the responsibilities and resources of social services departments and voluntary organisations, seeks to tap into, support, enable and underpin the local networks of formal and informal relationships which constitute our basic definition of community, and also the strengths of a client's communities of interest. It implies, we suggest, a change of attitude on the part of social workers and their employing agencies. The detailed activities in which community social workers engage may include an increased measure of activities of the kind carried out by community workers but they will continue to have statutory duties and other responsibilities to individuals, families or groups which do not fall within the remit of community workers.

24 **Social workers**: the vast majority of people who undertake informal social work are not social workers in the sense of being paid to do a particular job, and we do not include them in our definition of social worker. We have to restrict ourselves, in the first instance, to paid employees of local authority social services departments or related voluntary organisations, who are either designated as social workers in their employment contracts or who carry out duties within which formal social work predominates, whether in the field, in day or residential services, or in hospitals or on other attachments.

25 Clarity would be served by restricting the designation 'social worker' to holders of the Certificate of Qualification in Social Work or its equivalent. But with an occupation in which many of those employed are at present not so qualified, such a restriction of usage seemed to us premature.

26 Nor did we think it appropriate to restrict the designation to those involved in direct work with other people. Even in its broad informal sense social work may include working by indirect means, organising services, arranging for others to provide them, or putting people in touch with each other or with organisations. Formal social work covers the same range of activities. In social services departments and voluntary agencies, many staff who do not spend most, or even any, of their time in direct work with clients, are engaged in such indirect social work. They are usually working as managers (for example, 'area managers', 'team leaders', 'officers-in-charge' of residential homes) and the term 'social worker' may not be included in their job designation. In our view what they do indirectly for clients is as much a part of formal social work as is (for example) the direct services of counselling, and we include such managers (if this activity forms a major part of their duties) within our definition of social worker.

27 For the purposes of this report, therefore, a social worker is any employee of a local authority social services department or related voluntary agency, who spends the major proportion of his working time in formal social work, irrespective of how this time is distributed between direct and indirect service. We concentrate primarily in our report on those social workers engaged in face-to-face work with clients. It is therefore important to stress at the outset that we regard many managers in personal social services organisations as social workers.

PART ONE

THE PRACTICE OF SOCIAL WORK

Chapter 1

What social workers in field settings do

Introduction

1.1 In this chapter we attempt to give the reader a picture of what social workers in field settings are doing day by day in England and Wales now. We compose the picture from the evidence we received, the experience of committee members, particularly those involved in direct practice, and from the available research reports. We start by describing typical days in the lives of two social workers and use these accounts to illustrate some of the roles and tasks of social workers and the kinds of people with whom they work. Most of the chapter describes the work of local authority social workers. We do however make some references to social work practice in voluntary agencies.

1.2 Both the social workers whose days we describe are employed by a local authority and accountable, via the director of social services, to the social services committee. The first works as one of a group of four social workers, two social work assistants and a clerk, who are accountable to a team leader and who occupy their own office in the part of the local authority's area for which they are responsible. They cover a population of about 19,000 people and all carry so-called 'generic' caseloads. That means they all have some children and families, some elderly and some mentally or physically disabled people as their clients, although most of them have a bias towards a particular client group. The social worker with whom we are concerned, Mr Carr, is especially interested in adolescents and has a number in his caseload. He is now paid on level 3 of the pay scale agreed by the National Joint Council, which means he is expected to take considerable responsibility for his own work and to carry cases involving high risks. He has been in this team for a year. He qualified four years ago and spent three years in another team in the same authority.

An area team social worker's day

His day starts at 8.45 reading letters and catching up with messages which came yesterday while he was away most of the day at juvenile court. While he reads he listens to another social worker in the office who is seeking help from colleagues about what to do for an elderly lady who has been wandering around her street at night in a nightdress and whose neighbours are complaining about a smell of gas coming from her flat. They say the 'welfare' should do something but the lady concerned does not want to be considered for an elderly persons' home, has refused day care, and has no relatives that the social worker can discover. This particular area has no street wardens but another social worker has contacts with the local church.

Mr Carr joins in and suggests a proper discussion with the complaining neighbours and any others, as well as with the old lady. He then rings a children's home to arrange to meet a 16 year old boy there tomorrow to discuss his plans for leaving care and perhaps going to live with his now remarried mother. Next he 'phones a social worker in another county in response to a call from her. She is out but a colleague says it's about Mary B who used to be in care and known to Mr Carr. She is now married and her new-born child is failing to thrive.

Mr Carr rings the Electricity Board about the fuel bill of a family who came to the office three days ago when Mr Carr was on duty. They have had a notice of disconnection and have two young children and no money to pay the bill at once. The man with whom Mr Carr wants to negotiate an extended repayment scheme is out. Mr Carr arranges a time to talk to him. The matron of a local day nursery rings to say that Tony, a 6 month old baby on the at risk register, has not been brought in today nor was he in yesterday. Mr Carr says he is visiting the home today and will check on what is happening. As Mr Carr is leaving the office the finance section of the department ring about failure of the parents of a child in care to pay their contributions. Mr Carr promises to investigate and asks them to stay any action until he gets back to them. Before he can get out of the door a Mrs Southgate rings to say no one has come to see about a bath aid for her mother as Mr Carr had said they would when he talked to her two months ago. He promises to look into it and ring her back. He then dashes for the door so as to get out to his planned home visits. These are all on a particular housing estate.

Mr Carr goes first to Ms Cross, a very young anxious single parent who had been referred by the health visitor because she was finding it hard to manage her 3 year old daughter Tina consistently. Last week Ms Cross and Mr Carr worked out a plan for dealing with the daughter's wetting. Ms Cross was very pleased because this had worked well. The daughter was less disruptive this week and allowed her mother and Mr Carr to talk about ways of handling the child and Ms Cross' own loneliness. Mr Carr suggested she might join Gingerbread, or a young mothers' group run by two of his colleagues. Ms Cross seemed to like the latter idea and Mr Carr left saying he would talk to his colleagues. He and Ms Cross also agreed she would continue to manage her daughter's toilet training and would start regular sit-down meals instead of letting the child eat whatever she could snatch as she ran around.

Mr Carr's second visit is to Mr and Mrs Nichols. Mrs Nichols is aged 78 and her husband 77. She has been becoming increasingly mentally infirm and now needs almost constant attention. Mr Nichols, with daily assistance from a home help, has struggled to look after her and himself, but while he is mentally unimpaired he suffers from arthritis which makes moving slow and painful. The Nichols have two married children, one of whom is in Australia and who comes home for a month each year to be with her parents. The other, a son, lives in another part of Britain but comes for weekends when he can, and makes sure his parents do not suffer any financial hardship. Mr Nichols senior has in the past resisted any idea that he could not carry on caring for his wife at home, but has now told his general practitioner that he does not know whether he can manage now that his wife wanders about all night and seems not to need any sleep. Mr Carr is calling at the general practitioner's request, but has met Mr and Mrs Nichols before. He had written a letter saying he was coming and Mr Nichols had telephoned to confirm the appointment.

During quite a long visit, Mr Nichols told Mr Carr about his increasing problems. Mrs Nichols was present and fluctuated between what seemed to be irrelevant comments and extremely penetrating remarks like 'You're not come to put me away, young man.' She was agitated and distressed much of the time, apparently pleading with her husband to feed the puppy. They had not had a puppy for twenty years.

Mr Carr listened to Mr Nichols and then outlined the various possibilities to him. It seemed to Mr Carr that Mr Nichols was saying he wanted his wife to go into residential care, and was not particularly interested in the possibility of day care or additional support services at home, not just because they would not ease the night-time problem, but because he was exhausted and worn out with the incessant demands of a person who was only the wife he knew in brief unpredictable flashes, and that he wanted to make a clean break from her. Mr Carr suggested that he might try to find temporary care for Mrs Nichols while Mr Nichols said he wanted to think things over and consult his son. Mr Carr arranged to call back in a week and to talk to the general practitioner about Mrs Nichols' night wakefulness.

Walking back to his car, Mr Carr met a former client who wanted to know how to claim an attendance allowance for looking after her now totally bed-bound mother. Mr Carr told her quickly and, pushing away his thoughts that he should check if there were other ways of helping her, drove on to his next visit which was to the Harris family.

This family made Mr Carr feel useless because they always seemed to have some unanswerable excuse for their difficulties. This was another single parent family, mother and two boys of 14 and 10, both poor school attenders. Usually one of the boys was ill but sometimes it was the mother who was ill and on occasions the maternal grandmother who lived nearby. The Harrises had had a very disturbed and upsetting eighteen months. Mrs Harris left her husband (the boys' stepfather) because of his violence and he had tried to follow them. Mr Carr realised that the whole family had been very afraid of meeting Mr Harris if they went out and Mrs Harris had been depressed and the boys, especially George the elder, had worried about leaving her alone. In fact over the three months he had known them, Mark the younger boy, had returned to school fully, but George was still attending very erratically. On the previous visit he had found George at home looking after his grandmother who was off sick for a day or so; this despite the fact that Mrs Harris was not herself working and was always complaining of not having enough to do. On this visit Mr Carr was pleasantly surprised to find that Mrs Harris and George had actually been up to school together to work out with the Head a way of helping George attend more fully, working this up gradually; although Mr Carr had previously tried to persuade them to have such a meeting and had made arrangements with the Head and the Education Welfare Officer either George or his mother had always refused. Mrs Harris explained that she suddenly felt she wanted to do this on her own, and that a single mothers' group which she was attending in the area office had also encouraged her to act more decisively. Although Mr Carr had encouraged Mrs Harris to go to this group to get some support and perhaps make some friends he had thought it was not proving particularly helpful. But George now said that his mother had made a friend in the neighbourhood at the group; this led to a discussion of friends during which Mr Carr was able to help Mrs Harris see how much she was giving George a double message; that he should go out, go to school and so on and yet also that the world outside was full of dangerous and delinquent people, so home was the safest place. Mr

Carr suggested as he left that George let him know how the plan for gradual attendance worked out; he could drop into the office to do this. He arranged to visit the family in another month.

Mr Carr left the Harrises feeling slightly more hopeful than normal. He decided to drop in on an elderly peoples' lunch club which he had helped a group of volunteers to start. Once there he was told about the wickedness of 'them' in social services headquarters for refusing to install telephones for two members of the club and for cutting down transport to bring people to it. Mr Carr explained about the local authority cuts and said he would tell his team leader.

On his way back to the office Mr Carr called for his regular appointment with Tony's parents. This is the child about whom the day nursery matron rang this morning. Mr Carr could get no reply at the flat. When he got back to the office he rang the nursery and found that the baby Tony was still not there and that the mother of another child said Tony's parents had gone away but she didn't know where to. Mr Carr repeated this to his team leader and she said she would call round at the parents' flat on her way home since Mr Carr had an Intermediate Treatment group that evening. (Intermediate Treatment is the name given to a range of activities for children which provide more than just supervision of the child at home but do not mean removal from home. Courts can make an Intermediate Treatment requirement. It often takes the form of evening groups or weekend camps.)

Mr Carr did a bit of paperwork and reflected with pleasure that he had managed to carry out all the visits he had planned. Not infrequently an emergency can throw out his entire day. He realised that had the matron reported that Tony was bruised rather than missing he would have been unlikely to have seen any of his other clients today. Mr Carr then went home for an early meal before going out to his Intermediate Treatment group. He picked up two volunteers and one of the boys who is subject to a supervision order and went to the church hall where the group meets each week. It is run by four volunteers and two social workers and usually has about twelve boys aged fourteen to sixteen, all subject to supervision orders. This particular evening there was a talk from a community policeman, table tennis and pool and a planning session for a coming camping weekend.

After this group the social workers and the volunteers adjourned to the pub to discuss the session and plan next week's. Mr Carr wrote brief notes of this discussion for the office record.

1.3 The second social worker, Miss Taylor, qualified five years ago and has been in her present position in a hospital social work department for two years. She provides a social work service to the patients of the paediatric department and two of the surgical clinics. On the day we report she was concerned largely with paediatric work. She describes it in her own words:

A hospital social worker's day

'I arrived at 9.15 for a fortnightly social workers' meeting. On this occasion the hospital administrator and the records officer joined the meeting to discuss problems of hospital transport and how to use it to get some of the long stay children out of the ward. We social workers also wanted a way found to tell patients in advance of their attendance about claiming for fares to the hospital. At present this takes up social work time unnecessarily. The meeting also discussed how to respond to a local initiative to set up a stroke support group for patients and their families. It was agreed that a social worker should offer to join the group meetings.

After the meeting I went back to my office and immediately Dr Oliver 'phoned from the paediatric out-patient clinic to ask if I would see a family with him. I joined the doctor and the family – a mother and father and a 13 year old girl who suffered from diabetes and who was no longer keeping to her diet. After a brief introduction Dr Oliver left and within a few minutes 'phoned in to say to me that he wondered whether this family should be referred to a psychiatrist. I spent about three-quarters of an hour with the family and came to the conclusion that there were many family problems which seemed to result in the daughter's difficulty in keeping to a diet and the parents' finding it impossible to help her to do so. I suggested a psychiatric referral to the family. They were at first very doubtful protesting that none of them were mad and that their daughter had a physical illness. I discussed what I saw as the fears behind their protesting and assured them that psychiatrists see many families with problems who are certainly not mad. The family agreed to a referral and I said Dr Oliver would arrange it and explained the procedure to them. I also told the family about the Diabetic Society and gave them the address where they could make contact. I said that if they wished I would arrange a meeting with the dietician for them. This seemed important to the daughter who was complaining that her diet was very boring.

As soon as this family left I was called in by Dr Parsons who had with him parents who had just been told that their son Ian needed to be admitted to the ward at once for investigations. They were extremely anxious and distressed, saying they could not let him stay today and pressing Dr Parsons for reassurance that he was not seriously ill. I suggested that I spent some time sorting things out with them and while they moved to another room I discovered from Dr Parsons that he thought it possible that the boy might have leukaemia and that he thought the parents feared this too. I spent half an hour with the parents during which they told me what they feared and eventually agreed that Ian must stay and sought my help with how to tell him. In the end the parents and I told Ian together and I then suggested they should see me the next time they visited, which all three agreed would be tomorrow, and that I would see Ian once he was settled in the ward.

I went back to my room and made a few 'phone calls and wrote to three charities asking for help for accommodation costs for parents of a child with kidney disease. A mother came in from the clinic asking about fares; she was really in quite a state because her supplementary benefit is paid by giro and she is attending another hospital with another child and has still, after three months, not got back fares for other than the first two visits. I 'phoned the social security to inquire (this was actually two calls because they passed me on to another office). They said that they would be paying the fares; had

a somewhat heated conversation but they did actually give a day and I wrote a letter for the mother to send with her H11 form and asked her to let me know if she hadn't received the money in a week (the date the social security had given).

I went up to the children's ward calling en route on the accommodation officer to ask her if she was being successful in finding anything for Yvonne's parents, Yvonne needing surgery in two days. On the way up to the ward met Mrs Spencer, mother of a child on the ward who stopped to tell me at length and very anxiously, about all her renewed fears. How her ex-husband won't pay any attention to Pat's diet. In fact I have seen him, there is no evidence that he does neglect the diet, but this couple are continuing a marital quarrel and use Pat's diet as part of it. On the ward Sister caught me to tell me how difficult Mrs and Mr Lyons were being on the ward; fighting loudly in public and upsetting everyone else. The previous evening she had finally had to ask them to stop it. I decided I should probably see them together, maybe with Dr Oliver if he agrees. Sister also asked me to see a new patient; a child with severe renal illness who may need to be considered for a kidney machine; these families always have to have a very full social assessment as well as a medical one.

Met Mrs Newton on the ward who told me how well the weekend had gone, and how they had been able to take John out to the park for a little, he was so well. Then I went on to talk to Susie, a 9 year old whose parents rarely visit. Susie is obviously afraid that they may abandon her completely (and at times I share this worry); she is a very sad little girl, but she easily irritates staff and other children by her demands and want of attention.

Went for a late lunch before returning to the ward for the weekly round; this is the psycho-social round where the family and social problems are more discussed than medical ones. During it we agreed that Dr Oliver and I would see the Patels together. I would also see the Whites and assess how they are likely to deal with Colin's diet at home. Dr Oliver also referred to the new family, the Jones' whom Sister had mentioned that morning and we agreed that he would introduce me to the parents after the round. I reported back on my 'phone conversation with the local social worker for Susie's family and on the multiple problems of that family; but it does seem that it is these rather than their rejecting Susie which keeps them away. Staff nurse said that they had in fact 'phoned during the weekend and had spoken to Susie. Dr Oliver thought that Marie, a diabetic girl whose insulin was out of control was being very difficult in school as well as on the ward. I explained that this was not what her headmistress said, she was only worried about Marie going into coma at school. I know that the ward staff find Marie a very difficult little girl to manage, but although she can be difficult at home and school, it does seem clear that she is at her worst on the ward; maybe she is frightened. Dr Oliver agreed to meet with Marie's Head as well as the parents to discuss whether she needs a special school: the Head wants to do this.

Went down to the office (after seeing Marie and her mother briefly to tell them about the appointment with the Head and after being introduced to the Jones' whom I arranged to see at more length tomorrow). Phoned Marie's school and wrote a note on Susie and the Lyons. I then saw my social work student who is doing a four month placement at the hospital which is nearly over. He had been spending most of his time in the last week covering the geriatric ward where the social worker was on holiday. He had engaged in numerous negotiations with the area teams and home help organisers to arrange domiciliary care for patients who were about to be discharged. He had also had several fairly lengthy discussions to explore the networks of care which exist or might be developed to help their elderly relatives on their return home and we had agreed to make one of these the focus of our discussion today. As it turned out however, the student had come straight from seeing an elderly man whose wife had just died and much of the session was taken up with talking about how this man was feeling and how the student might try to be alongside him through the first stages of mourning. I began to draft a report for the college on this student.

Before going home I went back to the ward to see Ian. His parents had left about an hour ago and Ian was sitting alone apparently avoiding advances from the other children or the staff. Initially he turned away from me and wouldn't talk but as I was leaving he suddenly burst out telling me how frightened he was and how he didn't want to upset his mum and dad by telling them because they would be more worried. We talked for some time and agreed that when his parents came tomorrow Ian and I might be able to share with them what he had told me because they wanted to help him. On the way out I told the staff nurse how upset and frightened Ian was and how hard he was trying to be brave and not show it.'

Two examples from voluntary agencies

1.4 The Scott family, consisting of a mother and four children, aged 14 to 8, had been referred to the voluntary agency because it was feared the mother would have another nervous breakdown. She had received psychiatric treatment in the past. The housing conditions where they lived then were bad and the family income came from supplementary benefit. The eldest girl had been cautioned for stealing and her mother had been afraid to let her out in the evening because the house where they then lived was in the city's red light area. One of the boys banged his head against the bedroom wall at night and this violent rocking collapsed his bed and continually woke his brother and sister who shared the room. The other boy wet his bed every night. The mother had complained about the house. The only water supply was in the kitchen which had only a small water heater. There was no bathroom and only an outside toilet. One of the bedrooms was too damp to use and there was nowhere for the children to play or entertain their friends. The social worker and the mother had agreed that what was most needed was re-housing. It had taken five months of negotiation with the local authority before the family was offered their present three-bedroomed heated flat. After the move, the 14 year old was allowed out at night and there was space to play in. The mother's anxiety and depression ceased. The younger boy never wet the bed again. The social worker got a legless bed for the older boy and it was placed in the middle of the room. At the suggestion of the social worker, the boy was told he could rock as much as he liked as it would no longer disturb anyone. On the final visit the social worker learned that the bed rocking had now virtually ceased and the mother thinks all is well with the family.

1.5 A second family, the Mortons, have continuing problems. They had come to the agency on the advice of a friend because they had financial and housing difficulties. It transpired that Mr Morton had been diagnosed as terminally ill three years ago. There was a large family of children but only one remained at home. The social worker had assessed Mr and Mrs Morton as having chronic financial problems and considered that the poor housing was causing depression to all members of the household. Together they tackled these practical issues. The social worker recognised that Mr Morton was deeply distressed at having to give up work. This related to his own loss of role in the family and community and also to his inability to continue being a very generous grandparent.

Mr and Mrs Morton's difficulty in accepting Mr Morton's illness had led Mrs Morton to encourage the family to joke continually about him. This deeply offended his dignity. The social worker had been able to help Mrs Morton to share her distress openly and so free her husband from ridicule, and had also tried to help the child to manage his feelings about living with a dying father.

The varying contexts of social work

1.6 These accounts show that to understand what social workers do it is necessary to recognise the varying contexts within which social work activity takes place.

1.7 Although Mr Carr and Miss Taylor might both have been employed by the same local authority they worked in different settings, one in an outposted sub-team of an area office and the other in a hospital. These are only two of many settings within which local authority social workers are employed. We could have given examples of social workers in a specialist team concentrating either upon a particular client group such as the elderly or families and children, or upon a phase of the work such as intake or long-term work. Other local authority social workers are located in health centres, child guidance clinics and schools. An even wider range of settings are apparent when one includes social workers employed by voluntary agencies.

1.8 The range of tasks which social workers carry out seems to remain the same whatever the setting but the amount of time given to particular tasks varies greatly between settings. Social workers in many area teams and social work departments in general hospitals, will undertake more negotiation, mediating and planning than those working in a child guidance team or in some other psychiatric settings where the focus will be upon therapy.

1.9 The amount of social work time available also affects the kind of work individual social workers do. We noticed on our visits that the number of social workers for apparently similar populations varied. If under pressure the counselling activities are likely to be reduced or even cut out altogether while statutory visiting, especially of children at risk, will be given priority.

1.10 It may also vary between apparently similar settings. A social worker in an area team may spend more time in direct work with clients than social workers in another team where caseloads are small and a great deal more time is spent working with volunteers, self-help and voluntary groups.

1.11 The setting however provides only one part of the context for social work. Another part comes from the legislative framework within which social services departments must operate and in particular from the statutory duties required of social workers. Mr Carr in his visit to Tony's parents and in his work with the Intermediate Treatment group was carrying out statutory duties laid upon his authority.

1.12 The organisational context, as it relates to resources, also affects the social work role. Mr Carr received the brunt of criticism from elderly citizens at the luncheon club because his department were, in effect, rationing the allocation of telephones and the provision of transport. Miss Taylor's student was involved in negotiating with the department for meals on wheels and home helps for patients whom the hospital wished to send home.

1.13 Further aspects of the context of social work are provided by the views held by society about the particular client groups with whose problems social workers are supposed to work. In our examples the office discussion about the elderly lady wandering at night showed an appropriate questioning as to how the department should exercise responsibility. On the other hand the team leader would be unlikely to hesitate to remove Tony (the baby who had not been brought to the day nursery) from home if she had cause for concern about his welfare.

Types of caseload

1.14 Research studies give some indication of the client groups most likely to be referred to social services departments. In general clients tend to come from the neediest and most socially deprived areas (Goldberg and others, 1977; Goldberg & Warburton, 1979). The largest group is of elderly people; other groups strongly represented are families in which there are neglected, abused or delinquent children; offenders; physically handicapped people; and emotionally distressed people.

1.15 Not all those who are referred to social services departments are seen initially by social workers and many will be offered one of the services organised by the department such as home helps or meals on wheels, but will not be allocated to a social worker. Studies in 'Seatown' suggested that while the elderly and physically handicapped constituted the largest part of the intake of one local authority area, they made up a minority of social workers' caseloads.

1.16 Social workers are likely to have many children and families among their clients. It is often reported that social workers are especially anxious and concerned about families in which children may be abused because of the liability they are perceived by the public to carry in instances in which children have died or been seriously injured. It is also suggested that social workers may have a preference for the intensive counselling which they see as more necessary with children and their parents than with elderly people.

1.17 Studies comparing caseloads of social workers of differing seniority tend to indicate that senior social workers and qualified social workers carry proportionately more cases of children in care, families with multiple problems or people with mental handicap or illness, whereas unqualified, inexperienced or assistant social workers carry proportionately more cases of physically handicapped and elderly people.

Social work tasks

1.18 A sub-group of the Working Party attempted to categorise social work activities. They began by distinguishing direct from indirect social work. Direct social work is that undertaken with the aim of easing or ending some existing social problem for a specific client, whether an individual, a family or a group. It often includes work with others for the ultimate benefit of the client. Indirect work consists of work which is not focussed upon a specific client: thus it includes general tasks of management and planning and work which aims to prevent the development of future problems or to create better social services for future clients.

1.19 Direct social work tasks include assessment, giving practical services and advice, surveillance and taking control, acting as intermediary and counselling. Assessment can be broken down into a number of discrete activities. These will include noting the problems of which the client or the referrer complains, forming an impression of the client and the client's situation, collecting additional information, thinking out the nature of the problem and deciding what action the social worker or the social services can take, and communicating this to the client. Surveillance is necessary when someone, usually a child or an elderly person, is thought to be at risk, and when these fears are justified social workers may have to take control.

1.20 Acting as intermediary, or mediating, covers putting clients in touch with local networks, volunteers, voluntary and statutory agencies and sometimes helping them to get what they need from such services. Counselling refers to discussions between client and worker where the aim is to help the client change, or adapt to, some aspect of his life or relationships, taking the client's feelings into account.

1.21 These tasks are seldom performed singly; an episode of work with a particular client might well include them all.

1.22 Indirect social work, not focussed on a specific client, may include giving information and negotiating with other services and agencies. It also may involve planning and management tasks, supervising and training staff, developing and supporting voluntary effort and community networks. It is not solely a management activity but may be combined with direct work.

1.23 Setting out tasks in this way tends to make them appear mechanical and dehumanised. In fact, the aim of social workers will always be to create a relationship with their clients so that the tasks are accomplished in partnership by people who share some measure of trust and understanding. Both direct and indirect work as described here include activities which later in this report we call 'social care planning'.

1.24 We can use these categories to explore further the work undertaken by Mr Carr and Miss Taylor, but it may be useful first to note a time dimension. Many referrals made to social workers are dealt with by them in a very short period of time. In contrast, a small number of cases become long term; although few, they take up a great deal of social workers' time.

Short-term work

1.25 One research study found that with 25% of referrals, work was completed on the first day, and 47% of cases had been closed within a week. Another study found that 39% of referrals were closed immediately. Some of these clients could have their needs met quickly, others are referred on to more appropriate agencies and some turned away because their needs are not judged to merit high enough priority for them to be given a scarce resource (perhaps a day nursery place or social work counselling).

1.26 The phrase 'short-term work' however is often taken to mean any work completed within three months. Many intake teams set such a limit for their work. Cases which may require more time are likely to be transferred to long-term teams in those area teams which divide their staff in this way.

1.27 Short-term work takes place in area teams, in hospitals, voluntary agencies, day centres and residential establishments. Sometimes it is the social worker who determines the length but the work may be short because the client stops coming to the office, is out when home visits are arranged, is discharged from hospital or absconds from a residential home. The client may have got the help sought: the social worker may close the case because there seems no more that can usefully be done.

1.28 Research studies of short-term work in area offices suggest that most clients are usually female and their problems usually those which affect elderly people or mothers who are not well off and have young children. There is relatively little overt statutory work (for example compulsory admissions under the Mental Health Act), but much concern about fuel debts, housing problems, and old people in need of services. The younger clients make fewer demands on services (although they may be seeking day nurseries or short-term admissions into care for their children). They bring problems of family relationships (for example teenagers getting beyond control).

Clients are increasingly people who have at least once before come or been referred to social workers.

1.29 All planned short-term work involves an element of assessment. We saw Miss Taylor undertaking several pieces of assessment during the out-patient clinic and on the ward and her student had been similarly engaged in the geriatric ward. Assessment may be a major part of the work when, for example, an elderly person is being assessed to see what domiciliary services she needs or a short-term fostering is being arranged for a child whose single parent has to go into hospital. With people who come with other kinds of problems, social workers may undertake only limited parts of a full assessment unless the client returns a second or third time.

1.30 Some research evidence (328) suggests that assessments are not always as thorough as they might be. The researcher found that while social workers identified two problems per client, the clients themselves identified three on average. She suggests that a part of the reason for this may be shortage of resources, that social workers, knowing the pressures on them, are reluctant to uncover relationship problems which make heavy demands on time. Perhaps Mr Carr's reluctance to get engaged in longer discussion with the lady who asked him about a disability allowance was not just that he was already late on his visits, but because he feared that emotional difficulties were all too likely to be developing. This evidence poses an interesting contradiction to the view that social workers are only interested in helping with problems of personal relationships and pay too little attention to the material difficulties presented by clients.

1.31 Many people are sent or come to social services departments and voluntary agencies seeking information or practical help. Their needs may be ones which can be met by the agency, either immediately by the social worker or after an assessment by some other part of the agency such as the day services or home help section of a social services department. Mr Carr would have been filling the role of information giver when on duty in the office where he would be providing an immediate service to callers. Miss Taylor gave a good deal of information to one of the families she met in out-patients. They had not asked for information, but she had assessed that their worries might be lessened by information about the Diabetic Society and by the facts about the kind of families who are seen by psychiatrists.

1.32 Often people coming to a social worker need to be referred to some other government or voluntary agency and many need assistance in negotiating with other agencies for what they want.

Social workers spend a good deal of time acting as mediators between clients and the fuel boards, the Department of Health and Social Security and housing departments. We saw Mr Carr attempting to mediate with the Electricity Board and Miss Taylor with the social security office.

1.33 Social workers also engage in short-term counselling with some clients. A three month period is long enough for client and worker to engage in a brief exploration of, for example, the problems in a marriage or between an adolescent and his parents. Where clients are anxious to change and accept some responsibility for their part of the problem, short-term counselling can be very successful. Both Mr Carr and Miss Taylor undertook a considerable amount of counselling during their day. Most of Mr Carr's work was with longer term clients but Miss Taylor's work was nearly all short term and involved helping clients to express their fears and thus to free themselves to act in ways more helpful to their children, or the children themselves to tolerate their own painful situations.

1.34 Most short-term work probably takes place with individual clients but social workers frequently establish groups which have a limited number of meetings. We learned of groups for young people and children who might be at risk of breaking the law and which were intended to introduce them to leisure pursuits which they might develop later. We have also been told of time-limited groups for those who had experienced bereavement and for single parents. In all such groups social workers would be likely to be providing information, mediating between members and undertaking some counselling.

Long-term work

1.35 About 8% of those who come to social services departments become long-term clients. The actual length of time they remain in contact with the department varies greatly from several months to a number of years. They fall into two major groups. Those suffering from chronic physical or mental conditions and families where children may be in some sense 'at risk' in their physical or psychological or social development. We discuss these groups separately.

Chronic conditions or states to be endured

1.36 Sometimes clients may be suffering from an underlying condition which cannot be changed. This does not necessarily mean that social work is inappropriate nor that it is necessarily continuous although clients may remain in contact with the agency over a number of years. Social workers can sometimes help clients to endure and live with states that are physically or mentally extremely distressing. Such help may protect the client from the secondary ills which can accompany such states. People suffering from chronic conditions are likely to require social services as well as social work help and it is this group which receives the largest amount of residential, day and domiciliary services from social services departments. People with chronic conditions are likely to suffer from increasing disability over time and so their need for services requires constant monitoring and re-assessing.

1.37 Social workers are involved in assessment, in arranging practical help, in acting as intermediary with relatives and other services and in counselling. They must frequently co-ordinate a variety of helpers and services and may at times provide information and counselling for the people who provide the day-to-day care for elderly or handicapped clients. These are often relatives but may also be volunteers or staff in residential and day care establishments.

1.38 Some of the work undertaken by Miss Taylor's student would be very likely to lead to such long-term work.

1.39 Assessment and re-assessment is likely to be a recurrent activity with such clients. Social workers have a responsibility to help clients and their families decide how long they can go on living in the community, to explore with them various options and to help negotiate for what is wanted when a client (and family) has reached a decision. The range of resources available may be limited but there is often some choice and the clients need to understand what a particular choice entails. For example, an elderly person may elect to have domiciliary services rather than sheltered housing, but this choice may make a move to a residential establishment necessary later and at a time in life when the client is less able to cope with the upheaval.

1.40 While the provision of practical services and advocacy and assessment may be the most obvious components of the social work task with the elderly, the care and surveillance role also allows for counselling and support. A good example is the following account which we received in evidence:

1.41 'Mr Evans was 87 with limited mobility due to obesity and severe arthritis. A widower for many years he lived alone, seeing his daughter from time to time only when he was able to make the forty miles bus journey. He used the social worker's quarterly visits to talk about his life and his own death. "If I try to talk to my daughter or anyone else, they only tell me not to be morbid and that I've got years to live yet. But with my age and health it stands to reason that's nonsense. I know you

won't shut me up about my death or
talk such nonsense." Mr Evans could
therefore share his feelings about his

life and death and feel he was not
alone in preparing for the reality of
death.' (115)

Work with families and children

1.42 Work with families and children will involve social workers in
all the activities we have already seen as necessary with other client
groups.

1.43 Mr Carr's day contained examples of what was probably
long-term work with families. Tina's mother might well need long-
term mediation and counselling, although it is also possible that her
needs would be met by the young mothers' group which might be the
start of a social network which would support her in future. The
Harris family had been receiving counselling for some time and this is
likely to continue for at least several months.

1.44 The social worker working with the Scotts had obviously
been in touch with them for several months. She had apparently
accepted Mrs Scott's definition of their problem as being one of
housing. Meeting this need involved considerable mediation and
advocacy. Once it was successfully achieved many of the other
difficulties resolved spontaneously. On others, the mother was able
to use the social worker's advice or counselling to get some improvement. It is not clear from the example how much the problem which
concerned the referrer, namely the mother's depression, was
improved by the material change which the social worker helped her
achieve, and how much by the social worker's acceptance of her own
diagnosis of the primary problem. What is illustrated is the significant
difference which may occur in a family's behaviour and relationships
if a material change is achieved.

1.45 It is clear from our evidence that social workers seldom
occupy only one role with a client or family or a group. They move
between assessment, advice, mediation and counselling. The two
examples which follow illustrate this interplay of roles. The first came
from a group of social workers who are employed by a local education authority.

1.46 'Peter, aged 8, had been
causing concern at school because of
lack of progress and uncooperative
and aggressive behaviour, and at
home because he had been stealing
from a local shop and was defiant
and sulky. His mother was angry

with him but asking for help and the
head teacher of the school contacted
the Child Guidance Service.

The social worker visited the
mother at home. She was a young
West Indian woman with two other
children aged five and two and a

half. Peter's father had abandoned her soon after his birth and she had separated from the father of the other two children about a year before. She lived alone with the three children on the tenth floor of a tower block. Her parents were dead and her grandparents, who had brought her up, lived in Jamaica.

The mother's attitude to Peter was more rejecting than to her other children. She was restrictive with all three, but especially with Peter; she complained of getting very low and depressed, feeling all three children were on top of her all the time because of living in a tower block. The social worker helped the mother, both by recognising her strengths, by helping her negotiate with the housing department for a transfer, and by tackling Peter's behaviour and relationship with his mother. This was done mostly by behaviour modification techniques which were taught to the mother; at the same time she was encouraged to give him more positive and affectionate attention. Checking with the school on Peter's ability to cope with his work revealed that he needed to wear glasses and was not doing so. The mother was encouraged and helped to talk to the school staff about Peter, and they in turn were able to reassure her that she was a good mother. Peter's stealing stopped and both mother and he became more affectionate to each other although mother was still overly critical especially when she was depressed. Mother developed more trusting relationships with the school staff.' (55)

1.47 The next example, from an area team, illustrates the various activities which may be included in very long-term direct social work with families and children.

1.48 'Mary was a rather dull, very anxious girl who had spent much of her childhood at special boarding schools. Her parents had high expectations and were deeply disappointed in their daughter. From about the age of 16 she behaved in a rather promiscuous way, having two pregnancies and abortions. She then became pregnant again by a West Indian man whom she hoped would support her. She was determined to keep the baby. Her parents, who were violently anti-black, threw her out of the house. Mary was referred to social services.

Her determination to keep the child and bring it up herself was unshakeable, even though the father was clearly not in fact offering any support or relationship. The social worker arranged a mother and baby home and James was born uneventfully. From the outset it was clear to those around her that Mary was finding it extremely hard to manage the ordinary practicalities of looking after a baby, and this was made more difficult by her own very high standards set for herself and for the baby. Mary's parents continued to refuse to support her.

The social worker then arranged for Mary to go to a small residential home for girls and their babies. Mary happily remained there for two years which was the maximum possible. She learnt to look after James on the physical level and was closely attached to him and he to her, although she continued to have little idea of what to expect of him.

After two years the social worker arranged a special needs flatlet for Mary and James and also a day nursery placement for James. Practical help was also given to Mary to help her set up her home. On the material level, Mary continued to function adequately and did not incur significant debt. However, she became quite depressed, largely through her isolation. The social worker tried to get her involved with various local groups: Gingerbread, mother and toddler groups and so on. These never succeeded. Mary's volatile temper and her anxiety made it hard for her to stay in a group or for the members to tolerate her. She even had to be banned for a while from the day nursery mothers' group after causing an uproar in it. Similarly her anxiety made it hard for her to hold down a job, although she tried on a number of occasions.

As James grew older, Mary found it increasingly difficult to manage him. He responded to her inconsistency by becoming very aggressive both at home and in the nursery. As battles between James and his mother increased both social worker, Matron and Mary became concerned about Mary's violent slapping. However, Mary was able to use help offered at a special day unit for young children and the relationship with James improved somewhat. He and his mother remained closely attached to each other, although James by the age of 4 years was more often overtly critical of his mother.'

The social worker in this case was facing a dilemma; how to provide long-term support, care and protection to this family. She was aware that there were on the whole more, and more intensive, supporting facilities available for young children than for older ones. While the risk of Mary's injuring James was in fact very slight, it was necessary to provide considerable support in order to allow James to develop his capacities. Mary remained virtually friendless, despite many attempts to link her with both formal and informal networks.

1.49 This example shows how it may be necessary for the social worker to assume responsibility for controlling and protecting a child or children and in some cases for monitoring and supervising the way their parents look after them and bring them up. Mr Carr had such responsibilities towards Tony (the baby not at the nursery). While numerically such cases are small they take up a great deal of social work time and, as our evidence made clear, place a very considerable burden of anxiety upon social workers at all levels in the organisation.

1.50 Social workers are involved with many children and families where children are the subject either of a supervision order or a care order. Such cases are by definition long term and can only come to an end when the order runs out or is discharged.

The boys with whom Mr Carr was engaged in the evening were all subject to supervision orders, some with an Intermediate Treatment requirement. Mr Carr is obliged to see these boys and they him. He will be assessing, advising, mediating and providing counselling for them but within the context of a compulsory order.

1.51 Social workers are responsible for children who are in care of the local authority and where the social services department is *in* *loco parentis*. So long as they remain in care social workers will have the responsibility for seeing that these children's needs are met at the various stages of their lives. Sometimes their major role will be as mediators with foster parents or residential staff who provide the actual parenting. Where living arrangements break down the social worker plans with and for the child, and needs to keep in mind the child's future as well as the present. Most children in care require counselling to come to terms with their often disturbing lives and to find a way for themselves into adulthood. Social workers may provide such help themselves or arrange it on behalf of a child or they may link the child up with adults or peers who can offer what is needed in a way the child or young person can accept.

1.52 Some work with families and children takes place in groups. Such groups may, for example, be for parents whose children have been removed by the courts, for parents who have abused their children or for young people who are leaving care. They form part of long-term work although the groups themselves are likely to be time-limited. Most of the examples of direct long-term work may seem to have emphasised face-to-face discussions between the client and the social worker. In part this may reflect our choice of Mr Carr and Miss Taylor and the particular days they had. Other social workers, and Mr Carr and Miss Taylor on other days, may spend more time assessing, advising, mediating and counselling, not with clients themselves but other people who are essential to the client's well-being. These include relatives, neighbours, volunteers, staff in voluntary and statutory agencies and self-help groups.

Indirect work

1.53 It is clear that social workers spend some of their time in work which is not directly related to the problems of a particular client, but which is intended to assist groups of citizens to deal with their own problems, to create networks in localities or amongst those with similar social or medical problems, to sponsor self-help, and to support individual and group attempts to offer help to those with social problems.

1.54 Several kinds of indirect work are listed in one research study (Stevenson and Parsloe, 1978). They include:

● Liaison/education – some social workers take specific responsibilities for liaison with, for example, general practitioners, schools, army camps, etc. These tasks help both parties to receive and make appropriate referrals, and may involve the social workers in spending time simply getting to know what a potential resource does. Some social workers are involved in education, for example in running seminars for medical students, or in training social work students and staff of their agency.

● Creation and support of new resources – social workers may be given special responsibility for recruiting or supporting volunteers, foster parents, good neighbours, etc. In addition, they can create and maintain toy libraries, welfare rights information banks, and resource books of various kinds.

● Running groups/providing informal advice for people who are not clients – social workers organise groups for a variety of people including depressed isolated mothers, long-stay psychiatric patients about to be discharged, and so on. They may also take part in summer camps for the handicapped, or in starting 'ring around' schemes for old people who have had a telephone installed by the local authority. They provide advice informally to people they meet on their rounds, and more formally through advice sessions at luncheon clubs, etc.

● Planning – social workers take part in a variety of groups designed to plan services and establish criteria for who should get them. They may help with lunch clubs and other forums for professional workers in their areas designed to enable these professionals to consider issues of common concern.

1.55 This research was undertaken between 1974 and 1977. It is our impression that indirect work may since have increased as departments have seen the organisational stresses of rapid expansion removed, staff turnover has fallen and social work managers and practitioners have found some breathing space to consider ways of improving existing services and preventing some problems from developing.

1.56 We have been given a number of examples of indirect work. One social worker we met told us that she was advising the staff of a small sheltered home for former long-stay psychiatric patients about daily routines to foster the independence of residents. We heard of area teams working with tenants' groups who wished to improve the quality of life for those living in particular buildings and with groups of parents who wanted to share the burdens and pleasures of having a handicapped child with others in a similar position.

1.57 We quote more fully another example of indirect work undertaken by a group of hospital social workers who became aware that stroke patients and their families had a multiplicity of needs, the response to which was often complicated by the large number of medical and paramedical staff involved in treatment and the varying degree of referral to and response from hospital social work departments. It was not clear that the level of service being offered was the best possible (245).

1.58 Method. The team undertook to analyse the problems of the client group, to study the literature and draw on experience of all those involved in care of the group, including doctors, nursing staff, occupational therapists, physiotherapists, home help organisers, staff of day centres, homes for the elderly, aids centres, rehabilitation facilities, stroke clubs, national organisations providing relief and advice, and the Department of Health and Social Security. A detailed survey of thirty-six patients and their families was carried out and ten in-depth studies made. A report was prepared recommending:

● A study day for medical, nursing, paramedical and social work staff and home help organisers.

● Preparation of a booklet containing relevant financial provisions, social service provisions, health and medical services, employment, leisure facilities and helpful organisations for stroke patients and their families.

Resources. The main tasks eventually devolved onto the team leader, a social work assistant and a student, but all members of the team were involved in various tasks, as and when they could be fitted in, and in the study day. £50 to cover the cost of publishing the booklet was raised by dint of a great deal of effort.

Results. The team now have an outline working format understood and shared by medical and nursing staff, occupational therapists, physiotherapists and community resources. The booklet is widely used and appreciated. A physician hopes to have a post of nurse approved to help stroke patients and their families. Knowledge of experiences has been shared, roles clearly identified and understood by each discipline.

1.59 The social workers add in their evidence to us: 'It was appropriate that the initiatives for this project should come from the social work team. We have the opportunity of an oversight of the patient and his family and by our training are able to identify areas of stress, emotional, physical and economic stress, and to exercise appropriate intervention. We also have a vital role to play in seeing that communications between all personnel and agencies are functioning appropriately in the interests of the client group.'

1.60 Indirect work tends to expose other needs. We were told of one social services area team which had run a summer project for families newly arrived from Bangladesh. Some of the women who attended asked for an opportunity to meet regularly in order to break the social isolation they were feeling and to learn more English.

Other needs were revealed and the social worker concerned developed long-term commitments to mediate on their behalf with various bodies, such as the housing department and the local racial harassment group.

1.61 Another form of indirect work is the recruitment of people who are willing to provide a service to the clients of a statutory or voluntary agency. Social workers recruit and select foster parents and volunteers and may provide support and training for them. The trend towards fostering new client groups, in particular elderly people and difficult adolescents, has led to more work with foster parents both individually and in groups, primarily by specialist social workers from statutory or voluntary agencies.

1.62 These various forms of indirect work involve social workers in similar roles to those they fill when doing direct social work, but in addition they may be involved in supervision and professional development of staff and students.

1.63 In Miss Taylor's case we saw her involved in a supervision session in the afternoon where she took direct responsibility for the professional development of a future social worker. Since all social work students are required to spend half of their training time in placements, experienced social workers like Miss Taylor play an important role in this task.

General conclusion

1.64 From our descriptions of the work undertaken by social workers drawn from the evidence we received (and this Chapter is largely descriptive), our firm conclusion is that there are many things being done by social workers which it would be to the serious detriment of clients to have left undone; and that, if social workers did not do them, many of them would not be done.

SUMMARY OF CONCLUSIONS

1. Social work may be classified as direct (including assessment, practical help, surveillance and control, counselling, management, mediation, support of voluntary effort) or indirect (including supervising staff and volunteers, training, planning, management, mediation, community development) (1.18–22).

2. Social workers seldom occupy only one of those roles with a client or family or group (1.21).

3. If social workers did not undertake the tasks these roles require many of them would be left undone and this would be to the detriment of those affected (1.64).

Chapter 2

Social work staffing and social problems

Introduction

2.1 In this chapter we present estimates of the number of people engaged in formal social work in England and Wales, and examples of social problems which affect individuals and families, some of which result in their coming, or being referred, to social workers.

How many social workers?

2.2 Formal social work is carried out by the staff of statutory and voluntary agencies and by some workers in the private sector. There are no official statistics providing a comprehensive account of the numbers and deployment of workers in all three sectors. Available figures for the statutory agencies are the most reliable, but are not complete in their coverage and have to be treated as informed estimates. On the voluntary sector we have relied on information from the National Council for Voluntary Organisations and the Central Council for Education and Training in Social Work; their estimates are derived from a study carried out by the Personal Social Services Council and the National Council for Voluntary Organisations. There are no statistics for the private sector, but it is safe to assume that the number of qualified social workers employed in field, residential and day care settings is negligible. The figures throughout refer to England and Wales for 1980.

    2.3 The paucity of basic statistical information is a long-standing deficiency which was noted by the Birch Report *(Report of the Working Party of Manpower and Training for the Social Services)* in 1976. Problems arise in considering trends from the lack of consistency in the definitions used in earlier attempts to collect data. The figures

24

which we present, for example, are different in several respects from those given in the Birch Report, which used a wider definition of residential and day-care staff. The Birch figures also included an estimate of staff in the private sector.

2.4 There is not, and never has been, any restriction on the use of the title 'social worker'. As the Leaper Report (*Setting a Target Date*, Personal Social Services Council, 1980) commented in March 1980, there is no legal enactment which reserves functions and titles relating to social work practice in the United Kingdom. 'Anyone can call himself a social worker and undertake activities which he describes as, or the public believes to be, social work. Equally there is nothing in law which prevents the appointment of an unqualified worker to a post which may at present be designated as social work.'

2.5 It is much easier to quantify the number of social workers in 'field' settings and in headquarters of local authority social services departments than in their residential or day services, where the distinction between social workers and other staff is unclear in the statistics (as it is in practice). We therefore treat these two groups separately. The estimates for 1980 by the Central Council for Education and Training in Social Work indicate that there are approximately 15,700 field social workers engaged in front-line social work, a further 5,000 who are team leaders or area or divisional managers, and 4,000 in headquarters management or advisory posts. Over 70% of those engaged in front-line social work are now qualified, holding the Central Council's Certificate of Qualification in Social Work or one of its predecessor qualifications; the comparable figure for those in management posts is over 90%. The proportion of qualified staff at front-line level has increased rapidly over the last few years and this trend is likely to continue, as approximately 3,500 students obtain the Certificate of Qualification each year and the majority of them go into local authority fieldwork. If headquarters' staff are excluded, over 80% of these social workers work in area offices, 15% work in hospitals, 1% in medical general practices or child guidance clinics, and a further 2% in other settings.

2.6 Surveys suggest that about 65% of these field social workers (again excluding headquarters' staff) are aged between 25 and 45 years (Age Concern, 1981; Association of Directors of Social Services, 1981). Those aged below 25 years account for approximately 3% of the total, and about 20% are within the 25 to 30 years age range; 73% have been in post for at least two years, and 40% have been in post for more than five years (Association of Directors of Social Services, 1981). The conventional view that most field social workers are very young and inexperienced is not, therefore, supported by this evidence.

2.7 If all management staff are excluded, there is approximately 1 local authority field social worker for every 3,200 of the population. This ratio may be compared with those for general practitioners – 1 to 2,100 – and for police constables – 1 to 550.

2.8 The Central Council's estimates for residential and day services staff include all 'care' staff other than care assistants. They exclude non-care staff. Approximately 28,300 care staff are employed in social services departments' residential services, and roughly 4,300, or 15%, of these hold a social work or social services qualification, including the Certificate in Residential Social Work, the Certificate in the Residential Care of Children and Young People, the Certificate in Social Service and the Certificate of Qualification in Social Work. It is probable that no more than 3.5% hold the last-mentioned certificate. In day services there are approximately 7,500 managing or care staff: qualifications they hold include the Diploma in the Teaching of Mentally Handicapped Adults and the Certificate of the Nursery Nurses Examination Board; it is estimated that about 30% of them have such a qualification. A very small number hold one of the other qualifications mentioned above.

2.9 The most recent information on paid social work staff in voluntary agencies is again taken from the estimates of the Central Council. There are probably about 3,700 field social workers, of whom 2,200, or 60%, are likely to be qualified, holding either the Certificate of Qualification in Social Work or one of its predecessor qualifications. This estimate includes all staff up to and including the most senior level. Roughly 9,200 care staff are estimated to be employed in voluntary residential homes, of whom about 17% hold qualifications similar to those held by social services departments' residential staff. In voluntary day services there are about 1,000 managing or care staff of whom about 10% are estimated to hold qualifications similar to those held by local authority day services staff.

2.10 We recognise that by no means all the managing and care staff working in day or in residential services would think of themselves as social workers. We give their numbers here because we believe their posts involve them in what we have identified as formal social work, even though this may not be the predominant form of activity in which they are engaged.

The kinds of problems that may come to social workers

2.11 When trying to get a picture of the problems social workers are asked to tackle a researcher is usually left with national or regional statistics on the one hand, or descriptions and personal anecdotes of particular families and areas on the other. Neither really helps the social worker or layman to get a grasp of the size and nature of the problems in terms he can understand. What is more, the relation of problems to resources is made no clearer. For this reason our researchers tried to provide a picture which, while it could not attempt to encompass all the circumstances or origins of social problems, might illustrate the number and variety of potential claims there might be on social workers' attention from a population of 10,000 at any one time or over a period of a year.

2.12 This picture is set out below and some of its features are illustrated on page 29. The figures quoted represent neither the actual experience of any particular place at any particular time, nor a set of national averages (though they are generally related to these). They simply indicate a possible state of affairs, consistent with the available information. We have, in describing them, frequently used the word 'may' to emphasise their approximate nature and their status. Some of the figures will understate and some overstate what would be likely to be found in any actual population of this size. Taken together, and with all the provisos which have to be attached to them and to the information drawn upon, they demonstrate, on a scale which the mind can compass, some of the circumstances and incidents which might eventually lead people to come, or to be referred, to social workers. These circumstances and incidents are not mutually exclusive: some of those affected will certainly be affected by more than one of them.

2.13 In treating this picture as realistic, we take account of the differences in the sources of information used for it. Some of the information is provided by national statistics regularly collected centrally; some of it by research studies undertaken in particular areas at particular times. Some of it relates to events or conditions the incidence, or prevalence, of which is known to fluctuate widely from time to time and vary greatly from place to place; some of it to conditions of which, because they are subject to great uncertainties of definition and assessment, widely varying figures may be presented in different sources.

2.14 On present staffing patterns, the population of 10,000 might be served by three social workers, a team leader, and a social work assistant (as can be seen from our earlier figures this would give a ratio of staff to population more generous than average). Clearly these workers would not be involved with, or even aware of, the majority of the people affected by the problems we illustrate. Many of these people would not seek out social work help, advice or intervention, or want it if it were offered. Even if they sought it, social workers might not be able to make any useful response to some of their problems. A minority, on the other hand, would have social work intervention thrust upon them by order of a court or in exercise of statutory powers and duties.

2.15 Of those who did seek help or advice, many would turn not to social workers, but to others – for example, to doctors, health visitors, housing officers, teachers, policemen, local office staff of the Department of Health and Social Security, clergy, staff of Citizens Advice Bureaux, Marriage Guidance Councils and other voluntary organisations, or to neighbours, relatives or friends. Some of them might be sent on to see social workers, for others an alternative response would be provided by those they consulted.

Financial and housing problems

2.16 Many people experience financial or housing problems. Among 10,000 citizens, one in ten may well be living at or below the level of financial need recognised for purposes of supplementary benefit. This number may include 250 children. More than 100 people may have been unemployed for over a year. Gas and electricity disconnections may be running at forty or so a year. Five hundred people may be living in housing which is either technically unfit for habitation or in need of extensive repair; rather more, some of them elderly and handicapped, in houses which lack either a bathroom or an inside lavatory. There may be ten or twelve people unintentionally homeless at any time.

Families

2.17 Problems associated with marriage and families are common. In one year, 25 marriages may end in divorce; up to 30 children may be affected. The area may have 150 single-parent families with 250 children. There may be 125 births and 25 abortions during a year. Two children may be adopted. Of the children in the population, 150 may display moderate to severe behavioural problems of one kind or another at any one time. Child abuse, despite the publicity it receives, is relatively infrequent. One case each year of identified abuse might be expected, but there may be several children at any one time on the 'at risk' register.

2.18 Twenty children may be in the care of the local authority at any one time, ten or eleven being received into care, and as many

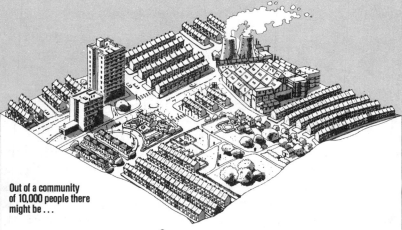

Out of a community
of 10,000 people there
might be . . .

**600 people
aged 75 and
over**

**1000 people
at or below the
Supplementary
Benefit level**

**150 children
with appreciable
behaviour
problems**

**Over 500 people
living in houses
which lack one
basic amenity**

**200 handicapped
people needing
day-to-day help**

**10 children
under
supervision**

**20 children
in care**

**150 single-parent
families**

**Over 100
long-term
unemployed**

**10 physically
handicapped
schoolchildren**

**20 people
discharged from
psychiatric
hospitals in a year**

**20 mentally
handicapped people
living at home:
most attending
training centres**

**25 elderly people
in residential
homes**

**18 indictable
offences a year of
which young people
under 17 are found
guilty**

Some of the 10,000 citizens
will appear under more than one of
these groupings.

discharged from care, in the course of a year. Ten of those in care may be subject to care orders made by a court in an attempt to ensure their proper development, health or education. Others will be in care at the request of parents who were unable to provide for them. Ten other children may be subject to supervision orders at any one time.

Elderly and physically handicapped people

2.19 A population of 10,000 can be expected to include about 1,500 who are over the age of 65, and 600 over 75. Of those over 65, about 600 might be living alone. 'Mental disturbance' would be surprisingly common among them, although estimates of its incidence would vary greatly with the definitions adopted. One estimate would give 300 elderly people with some form of dementia or suffering from anxiety or depression. The local authority will be supporting 25 elderly people from the population in some form of residential accommodation.

2.20 Defining degrees of physical handicap is particularly difficult, but some 200 people may be handicapped severely enough to require at least some support to cope from day to day. A majority of these handicapped will be elderly people over the age of 65. Two younger physically handicapped people may be attending a local authority day centre, and two or three others may be found in local authority or voluntary residential homes. But the vast majority of the handicapped will live in the community. Of these, some will be benefiting from various practical services, 70 of them may receive aids or adaptations to housing during a year, and 20 or more have telephone rental paid. Among school-age children, 10 may display some form of appreciable handicap, 2 of them may be deaf or hard of hearing and 1 blind or partially-sighted.

Mentally handicapped people

2.21 Thirty adults and six or seven children of the population may show an appreciable degree of mental handicap. Ten of these may be in hospital, and five or six in homes or hostels. The remainder will be living at home, most of them attending adult training centres or special schools.

Mental illness

2.22 Rather more than 100 of the adult population may have contact with specialist psychiatric services in any year. Twenty or more people may be admitted as in-patients to psychiatric hospitals during a year, and about as many discharged back into the community, some of them after more than one stay. Most people affected by mental illness, however, do not go into hospital; on one estimate and definition 225 out of those over 18 might have a serious mental illness at any one time. Ten people may attempt suicide during a year, and one succeed. A sizeable number will have drink problems and one or two will be misusing drugs.

Health problems
2.23 While minor health problems are unlikely to have social consequences, we note that 10,000 people will probably make, between them, 40,000 visits to their general practitioners and 9,000 visits to general hospital out-patient or emergency departments during a year. Ten may be patients in general hospitals at any one time.

Offenders
2.24 The area may produce about 100 indictable and 350 summary offences of which someone is convicted in the course of a year; 18 of these being indictable offences, and 10 summary offences, of which young people under 17 are found guilty. There may, in addition, be about 20 cautions given by the police to such young people. At any one time, about eight people from the area may be in prison.

The social work response
2.25 Some of the problems illustrated here are predominantly social in character; others, such as sickness or poverty, are likely to be accompanied by social problems. Not all the people included in this picture would consider that they had a social problem and often relatives and neighbours would take the same view. (For example, many elderly people are clearly a problem neither to themselves nor to others.) But many of those who would come or be referred to social workers would come from those affected by problems we have illustrated. Some would see social workers in voluntary agencies or in hospitals or other special settings. The majority, however, would come to social workers in social services departments' area teams. How many are likely to get this social work service, and how intensive would it be?

    2.26 Out of this population a team operating like the one in 'Seatown', studied by Goldberg and her colleagues (1979), would see between 500 and 600 people in a year. A team with the 'Seatown' ratio of staff to population would have available roughly 6,000 working hours in the course of a year, after allowing for leave, sick leave, time while posts are unfilled, and bank holidays. On this estimate, and to judge from studies of how social workers use their time, they would be able to spend an average of about three hours with each client and his family in a year. In practice they would concentrate their time most heavily on a small number of clients, particularly those at risk of coming into care, and spend relatively little time on those seen at intake or on the routine monitoring of elderly and physically disabled people. The team consisting of a team leader, three social workers, and an assistant, which we discussed earlier, while 50% better off in terms of staff time, would nevertheless be able to give comparatively little time to each client. We have already seen in Chapter 1 some examples of how they might spend this time.

SUMMARY OF CONCLUSIONS

1. Comprehensive statistics of the numbers of social workers are not available: we have to rely on estimates (2.2–10).

2. Approximately two-thirds of the front-line social workers in field settings are qualified; the view that most are very young and inexperienced is not borne out by the available evidence (2.5, 6, 9).

3. One in six or seven of care staff in residential homes holds a social services qualification (2.8, 9).

4. Local authority social workers are unlikely to see more than a small proportion of those who might have a claim on their attention and are able to give comparatively little time to most of those they do see (2.14–26).

Chapter 3

What social workers are needed to do

Introduction

3.1 In this chapter we suggest that social workers are needed as planners of social care and as counsellors and we explain why they should fill these roles. We consider what light legislation and clients' views can throw upon what social workers are needed to do and explore some of the implications of our belief that social care planning is an appropriate task for social workers. After acknowledging the need for social workers to act as agents of social control and rationers of resources, we consider some things social workers should not do.

What social workers are needed to do

3.2 Our understanding of the nature of social problems and the evidence we have had leads us to believe that social workers are needed to carry out two different but interlocking activities.

3.3 The first is to plan, establish, maintain and evaluate the provision of social care. We call this social care planning and see it as an activity which needs to be practised at all levels of social services organisations. The director of social services or the head of a voluntary agency must be concerned with discovering, and where necessary establishing, networks for the whole geographical area or client group for whose social care he has responsibility. It is usually at this level that structural problems are clearest and must be confronted. At an intermediate level, the head of a residential home or day centre or a unit leader in a voluntary agency must be concerned with the planning and delivery of social care to a group or locality or a particular range of clients. Finally, social workers in statutory and voluntary agencies and in residential, field or day services, will be planning with their clients – be they groups, individuals or families – provision of care to suit their particular needs.

3.4 The second activity which social workers are needed to provide is that of face-to-face communication between clients and social workers, in which social workers are helping clients to tolerate, or to change, some aspect of themselves or of the world in which they are living. As we note in Chapter 10, this activity is now very often called counselling, and the client may be an individual, a family or a community group.

3.5 In suggesting that these activities are two aspects of what we call social work, we are not wishing to make any exclusive claims for social workers. As we have made clear in our definition of social work, many other people, both as part of their job and as volunteers, engage in such activities. Lately there has been considerable growth of many forms of counselling, much of which is provided by volunteers. Bereavement and abortion counselling are just two examples. Similarly, at least at the individual and family level, social workers are not alone in planning social care networks. Most parents, and especially mothers, spend a considerable amount of time, energy and imagination in piecing together, from what is available, a web of activities and opportunities to meet the social needs of their family. Likewise tenants' groups and community associations will often be attempting to improve the quality of life and relationships in their area. None the less, in the context provided by our present social legislation, the public are entitled to expect that all who call themselves social workers will be available and able to engage in both these activities if necessary, and will certainly accept a responsibility to ensure that both social care planning and counselling are provided, even if not by them. Similarly, we consider that senior social work managers in local authority social services departments have an ultimate and unavoidable responsibility for the planning of social care networks for their areas.

Why social workers?

3.6 It may be asked why these two activities should be undertaken by social workers. The answer lies in history, and tradition, in the nature of our society and its legislation, and in the expectations which we all, as citizens, have about the kind of care which should be provided for those who, for whatever reason, cannot provide adequately for themselves. As we shall argue in Chapter 7 where we describe three possible approaches to social policy, whether social workers are employed and what they are expected to do will be determined largely by political decisions at a national level. There is no uniform set of roles and tasks that will inevitably fall to social workers. The needs we describe could be ignored, diagnosed differently, or met in other ways; but our society has developed a welfare state approach. However imperfect it is, it requires not only that people's basic needs should be met where necessary by statutory social services, but also that they should be met in such a way that each person's individual dignity and worth are respected. To translate this objective into action demands a rejection of the idea that one part of a person in need can be isolated from other parts, that the person can be separated from other people and treated in a vacuum, or that the material and structural aspects of a problem can be separated from the emotional. An attempt must be made to see people and their needs as a whole and to take account of their views about what services, if any, are to be provided.

3.7 Social workers themselves say in evidence to us that they acknowledge the value of individuals and recognise their right to self determination. Further, the nature of social work knowledge, as one of those who sent us statements made clear (23), 'is concerned not just with a depth of understanding of a specialised and narrow area but with a comprehension of some of the ways in which different areas interact with and affect each other. . . The objective in view is the acquisition of a synthesis of knowledge which approaches more closely the totality of the client in his situation than any narrower approach can do.'

3.8 In arguing that social workers are appropriate people to provide the integrated response of social care planning and counselling which we have described, it may seem that we are assuming that they have a monopoly of virtue, wisdom and the ability to see the 'whole man'.

3.9 This is not our position. We are at pains to point out throughout our report that social workers have a monopoly neither of concern nor of solutions. Many people in our society act in ways which support the value and independence of individuals, and some other groups – those concerned with holistic medicine, and some religious groups are examples – attempt to see people in the round. What we are suggesting is that the public has the right to expect that those bearing the title 'social worker' will always be bound to attempt to put into practice in their work a respect for persons and to see other people in all the complexity of their life, relationships and environment.

3.10 Naturally, social workers may frequently fail in these endeavours, which are, by any standards, extremely difficult. Social workers and social work organisations may not always treat people with respect. They may not often enough protest at the lack of control people have of their own destiny, at structural and organisational injustices and inequalities, at inappropriate forms of care in residential establishments, at squalid waiting rooms in area offices and so on. These are just a few of the criticisms we have received which show social workers falling short of their ideals. None the less we believe that the principles which social workers stress and their attempts to put them into practice remain an important protection to their clients against insensitive or arbitrary action and blinkered attempts at solutions.

3.11 This responsibility for taking as much as possible of the complexity of another's life into account is something which social workers are clearly needed to do as long as no one else in the social services field has this as a prime responsibility. Placing it upon a particular group of workers allows others to concentrate on their particular contributions.

What kinds of social care should social workers plan and provide?

3.12 The kind of service social workers are to be involved in planning and providing is once again a matter of social policy and political decision. One answer comes from legislation. It is, however, an extremely complicated one. The activities of local authorities, as social services authorities, are controlled by more than thirty separate Acts of Parliament which, together with subsidiary legislation, contain a great many detailed statutory provisions, some mandatory and some permissive. While many of these provisions are concerned with social services rather than social work, they provide the legal boundaries within which the social care planning and counselling of social workers in social services departments must take place. Action which cannot be justified by some part of this legislation would lay the local authority open to a charge of acting *ultra vires*. (A list of the principal statutory enactments is included at Appendix G.)

3.13 Some of this legislation bites directly, or, where they are providing services as agents of local authorities, indirectly upon voluntary agencies. Otherwise their work will depend on the policy of the agency which will in turn be tied to its objectives as a charity.

3.14 However, all social provision, both voluntary and statutory, depends ultimately upon there being sufficient political will, public support and economic resources for a particular kind of service. Priorities and commitments change over time and social workers must be ready therefore to adapt the services they provide. Another way of discovering what formal response there should be to social problems is to ask the public and clients of the social services.

Views of the public and of clients

3.15 As we note in Chapter 11, the evidence is that the public are reasonably satisfied with what social workers do and it may be assumed that they consider they are needed to do what they do now. However, the concepts of the 'public' and 'satisfaction' are so vague as to be of limited help in our enquiry.

3.16 The views of clients are perhaps more important and certainly more complicated. A large number seem well satisfied on two counts: they appreciate the way in which social workers deal with them, and they are relieved to know that the social services are there when they may need them.

3.17 On the other hand, there is another clearly identifiable group who consider that social workers fail to provide the material things or practical help and advice which they desperately need and compound this inadequacy by a failure to understand their clients' position or to fight for what their clients need. In addition, they feel that social workers sometimes attempt to offer counselling when what is needed is money, equipment or welfare rights advice.

3.18 The more extreme of these critics can see no need for social workers at all. We have no doubt that some self-help groups can provide what their members need better than social workers and we hope that social workers see their role as including help to clients to form or maintain such groupings. Some of the criticisms we received however, suggested, not that others could do better what social workers were doing, but that social workers lacked special knowledge of the particular problems of certain clients. Examples came from groups of parents with handicapped children. We are convinced that social workers should be encouraged to add to their general knowledge particular areas of expertise and specialist knowledge and return to this point in Chapter 10.

3.19 Another factor which seemed to underlie some of the criticisms was that social workers have legal authority to intervene in some circumstances when parents or relatives do not wish them to do so. We consider that such authority is necessary and discuss it in more detail later in this chapter.

3.20 We consider that clients' needs, the legal mandate, political will, economic resources, and public opinion all serve to determine what kinds of social services should be provided for whom. At present we believe the appropriate contribution of social workers to social service provision lies in the two activities we have suggested, social care planning and counselling. We now return to explore these in more detail.

Social care planning

3.21 It has been suggested by some of those who sent us their views that social services departments have taken a reactive stance towards social problems, dealing with those needs which are forced upon their attention but failing to develop overall plans which link the voluntary, volunteer, statutory and private services in an area into a coherent plan.

3.22 There is a great deal of truth in this suggestion, but we would not wish it to be overlooked that social services departments, in their eleven years of life, have been expected to develop entirely new structures, to meet greatly increased demands resulting from legislation and demographic trends, and, more recently, to find ways of managing under severe financial constraints.

3.23 In times of such constraints it is, however, more than ever necessary that social services departments carry out a role in social care planning, which no one other agency is expected to undertake. While the voluntary sector will have a vital role to play with particular families, groups and areas, only the local authority departments have the responsibility and coverage for coherent social care planning. They need to discover and bring into play the potential self-help, volunteer help, community organisations, voluntary and private facilities that exist.

3.24 One piece of evidence (275) developed the notion of social care planning and examined some of its overall practical implications. We have incorporated much of its thinking into our report. We were not told of any agencies which had developed such overall plans but several respondents spelt out how a plan might be developed for a particular client group. The elderly and young offenders were two examples, and we quote the latter.

3.25 The University of Lancaster Centre of Youth, Crime and Community state (49) how their staff have worked with local authorities to help them formulate appropriate policies for dealing with juveniles offending in their areas. The work involved some or all, of the following elements:

● formulating policies and procedures about shifting resources towards Intermediate Treatment and establishing standard criteria for suggestions made in reports to the courts, with particular attention to the statutory conditions to be satisfied for a care order to be made because of an offence;

● establishing Intermediate Treatment facilities and developing staff skills in assessing young offenders and setting objectives for their supervision;

● advocating change of emphasis in reports to the courts to give greater weight to the nature and circumstances of the offence and what any proposed social work supervision would actually mean; and promoting liaison between magistrates, teachers, police and social workers;

● making social workers more aware of the ineffectiveness of residential or custodial placings in dealing with deliquency and the frequency with which such a placing leads on to detention centre and prison;

● establishing recording and monitoring systems so that trends can be quickly identified.

3.26 This example shows the way in which social care networks need to operate at all levels of an organisation and how planning and direct services interrelate.

3.27 This is an example of social care planning at the level of a particular client group. Social workers will spend much of their time trying to put social care planning into practice with individual clients, be they individuals, families or groups. This involves creating, with a client, a system or network of care, tailored to his particular situation.

3.28 This is a complicated, skilled task and one which has, in our view, received too little recognition. It has been dismissed as 'work with the environment' or 'work with other than the client' as if client and environment were not part of an inseparable interacting universe with built-in capacities for mutual support and help.

3.29 An example from the evidence sibmitted to us (72) shows the nature of this social planning at an individual level:

'Mr Angus, aged 93, had hitherto lived alone in a self-contained ground floor flat, but was admitted to hospital as an emergency case after a fall. He was not suffering from a specific illness but had a weakening of his leg muscles and experienced difficulty co-ordinating his movements as a result of his age. He was unhappy in hospital and resented the regime to which he was subjected, but his keenness to return home was tempered by the fear of further falls – a fear which he himself regarded as irrational. His grandson was working abroad and he had no other family in this country, though he had many friends who expressed a willingness to help him. After a full assessment the hospital social worker put into operation an ambitious plan which involved the provision of as full-time coverage of care for Mr Angus as possible by the use of a wide network of statutory and voluntary services. The grandson returned temporarily home and agreed to augment the provisions made by the state by paying for some part-time help. The social worker arranged physiotherapy for Mr Angus, and, subsequently, a necessary wheelchair to increase his independence at home. The friends, meanwhile, organised shopping and library rotas. The social worker throughout provided support, information and encouragement for everyone involved, since this mosaic-like plan involved considerable professional co-ordination as well as dependability from the care-givers. On occasion she provided timely reminders to the helpers of the importance of their work. But after the assessment the social worker herself had little direct contact with Mr Angus, though his knowledge of her presence and ultimate responsibility for the arrangements were of considerable reassurance to him.'

3.30 The kind of social care network which the social worker in this example was able to provide depends not only upon departmental policies which are clearly spelt out, and upon a capacity to assess the plan with the individuals concerned, it also demands a knowledge of the resources of the community, and in some circumstances the capacity to bring into action a latent or unused willingness to provide neighbourly help. If social workers are to arrange social care networks for particular clients, they will need a considerable knowledge of local communities and skill in exploring communities of interest which may be important to a particular client. Departments may wish to employ some social workers who already have local knowledge as well as providing time for others to acquire a knowledge of community strengths and to assist communities to develop helping networks. This means social workers must – for example – recruit volunteers or see that they are recruited, know what voluntary organisations work in the area and what they can and might provide, meet street wardens and home helps to learn about existing helping networks and any which might be created if introductory links were made . . . and so on.

3.31 This kind of development task is one which social workers need to undertake in a spirit of genuine sharing. A colonising or patronising attitude towards communities is unlikely to promote good social care networks, and could well undermine the networks already existing.

3.32 There is a belief that social workers have, at times, a condescending attitude towards volunteers and some of our evidence lent support to this view, although a major study by Holme and Maizels

(1978) does not. We recognise, too, that some volunteers may fail to meet the standards of reliability which work with people under stress requires. However, we consider that the role of social workers includes a responsibility to create and maintain shared working relationships with volunteers as well as with neighbours and relatives, if the needs of clients are to be met. These relationships will only be constructive where there is a genuine respect of each person or group for the other. We return to the contribution of volunteers in Chapter 5.

The need for counselling

3.33 To many it may seem strange that we consider we need to justify the direct counselling role of social workers. It has after all been the activity which at least social workers themselves have traditionally regarded as the hallmark of their calling; and which several of our respondents consider to lie at the core of social work.

3.34 We believe it is essential that social workers continue to be able to provide counselling and we use the word to cover a range of activities in which an attempt is made to understand the meaning of some event or state of being to an individual, familiy or group and to plan, with the person or people concerned, how to manage the emotional and practical realities which face them. Such work is always part of assessment and may be a large or small part of future meetings between client and social worker.

3.35 The following quotation from evidence (143) given to us illustrates some aspects of counselling and shows how counselling and social care planning are in reality inextricably intertwined:

'Mrs Bell is a woman in her mid-30s, married with three children aged 13, 9 and 6. Her husband is an electrician and Mrs Bell had a part-time job until her illness.

Mrs Bell was admitted to hospital and acute leukaemia was diagnosed. She was very ill, developed septicaemia, was barrier nursed and the doctors were unable to bring her into remission. She was referred to the social worker for two reasons:

● The doctors thought Mrs Bell might die, so there might be family and social problems and the social worker might be able to offer bereavement counselling and practical help.

● The doctors wanted the social worker to assess whether emotionally Mrs Bell could take more treatment.

Social work intervention I
● Mrs Bell was very ill, upset, depressed, and would not communicate with anyone or do anything. Different and confusing messages were being conveyed to her. Her husband had been told, "it was all in her mind and she should pull herself together", yet the doctors thought there might be psychiatric reasons behind her failure to come into remission (Mrs Bell had received electro-convulsive

therapy for depression after the birth of her first child).

● The social worker's initial assessment was that withdrawal was Mrs Bell's way of coping with her situation: she felt very ill, did not want to be bothered with anyone and had "given up".

● The social worker's goal was to help Mrs Bell to have something to live and fight for. She wanted to build up some kind of trust with Mrs Bell and to make and use a relationship with her. However, this was very difficult, Mrs Bell completely rejected her for a long time and would not communicate.

● Eventually, the social worker found a way of communicating with Mrs Bell by talking about her family and suggesting that they made something together for the children. Mrs Bell became interested in the idea of making glove puppets, she began to talk about her family and eventually she began to respond to treatment.

Social work intervention II
Once Mrs Bell was brought into remission, she and her family needed help in handling the ambiguities and uncertainties of her chronic sickness:

● To work with Mr Bell who was not coping with the situation:

(i) The social worker asked the doctors to explain to Mr Bell the nature of his wife's illness – that her problem was not psychiatric but physical, and she would not be able to do much when she returned home and should not be pushed to do "too much".

(ii) The social worker enabled Mrs Bell to become more independent of her mother, who was living permanently in their home, had "taken over" and wanted to treat Mrs Bell as a complete invalid. The worker also helped Mr Bell to accept limited help three days a week from his mother-in-law.

(iii) She encouraged Mrs Bell's participation in a group.

● To help all the members of the family to handle the uncertainties of Mrs Bell's illness: explaining the illness to the children in ways which they understood, accepting that Mrs Bell could do more some days than others.

● To negotiate invalidity benefit for Mrs Bell. The family was now in a poverty trap because Mrs Bell had to resign from her part-time job and Mr Bell could not participate in overtime because of his wife's illness.

● To support Mrs Bell and family to lead a normal life. Mrs Bell was becoming socially isolated because she was afraid to go out and her friends were avoiding her because they thought she was dying and they did not know how to respond. Eventually, she began to lead a relatively normal life, meeting her friends, freed from her mother, and the children ceased reacting only to the sickness of their mother. The social worker helped the family to cope with the role reversals needed when Mrs Bell was ill, without putting her into a permanent invalid role.

Evaluation
The social worker was trusted and accepted by the Bell family and she enabled them to cope with the ambiguities of chronic sickness. They approached her when they felt they needed help.'

3.36 In describing social work we have suggested that social workers are needed to help people to tolerate *or* to change their social and emotional circumstances. We consider it essential that both these tasks are recognised since there is great pressure on social workers, especially at a time of scarce resources, to deny the importance of helping people to tolerate certain states of being in which they find themselves.

3.37 It is hard to describe this aspect of social work without being accused of supporting the unacceptable, or papering over the failures of social policies and promoting a so-called 'pathology view' of social problems. We are not suggesting that people are personally and individually responsible for their poverty or bad housing. We see such problems as largely structurally determined. What we are suggesting is that structural pressures affect how people feel about themselves and how they relate to each other. We believe social workers can help people with this aspect of their problems.

3.38 Similarly the emotional pain of bereavement and feelings of loss which are inevitable in any society can be tolerated and accommodated so that, while it affects one's life, it does not become destructive or debilitating. Inadequate housing can be tolerated in ways which are less, rather than more, destructive of family relationships, without pressure for rehousing being reduced. Most elderly people unable to care for themselves will eventually find ways of tolerating their lost independence so that they can have some pleasure and security in their new situation.

3.39 Achieving such accepting tolerance is a difficult process and one in which help may be needed. It can be provided by many kinds of people but, if friends, relatives, workmates or volunteers fail, or the client does not wish to use them in this way, social workers are needed.

The implications of promoting community networks

3.40 In discussing the planning of social care networks we have assumed that they are necessary to alleviate existing problems. While we believe this to be the case we also consider that social services departments, through their social workers, have a responsibility for creating, stimulating and supporting networks in the community which may prevent the occurrence of some social problems and be available to help those who will have problems in the future. The need for social workers to engage in such social care planning which does not arise directly from existing problems has been a theme in our evidence. It is given various names such as indirect work and community development.

3.41 Most respondents were not arguing that this task should be seen as an alternative to the more traditional counselling service which social workers have provided to those with specific and complex social and psychological difficulties. Rather, promoting community self-help was seen as an undeveloped aspect of the social worker's role which has been undervalued by management and frequently ignored in training.

3.42 We strongly agree with this view. Our own position about the nature of social work leads us to believe that social workers have a responsibility for developing social care networks in general as well as in relation to particular clients or groups.

3.43 We recommend that the managements of social services field, day and residential teams consider how to encourage and support their social workers in this indirect work. It will require imagination and planning to combine this role with responsibility for a case-load (which is the usual form of work allocation in local authority area teams) or with the day-to-day care of full-time or day residents. Not least of the difficulties is that the time-scale for the two kinds of work is different. However, once the importance of this aspect of social work is recognised we believe appropriate management strategies can be developed. They are essential, since if social workers are left with a general directive to undertake community development but without changes in the way work and accountability are allocated, they will have no choice but to continue to react to the most insistent demands made upon them. These, as all the studies of social services departments' teams show, come from what social workers call 'statutory work' and take the form of individual cases for which the department has some legal responsibility.

3.44 Two possible management strategies have been suggested to us. One, which owes much to the thinking of Professor Hadley, is the development of patch teams and the other, suggested by Professor Stevenson (1981), is a community development sub-group within an area team. Each might allow social care planning, in both senses in which we are using the word, to be developed: planning to deal with existing social problems and planning to lessen the likelihood of future problems. They are probably only two of many schemes which managers will be able to devise to suit the needs of their localities or of particular client groups.

3.45 We have been told that social work training has concentrated too exclusively upon direct counselling-type support work with individuals and groups. We recommend that the Central Council for Education and Training in Social Work consider how it can assist training courses to develop the social care planning aspect of social work, without detracting from the training needed by social workers to fill their other direct counselling role.

3.46 We have had some evidence which outlined some of the attitudes and skills required to develop this community approach which was described as 'teamwork on a basis of equal but different' (15). 'It is crucial that the social worker should be a competent broker and negotiator, that his knowledge of available sources of help in the community is extensive and accurate, and that he is prompt and reliable where administrative tasks are concerned. He must be trusted by all concerned and able to summon specialist help when this is needed . . .'

3.47 These skills, knowledge and attitudes are the same whether a social worker is acting to help members of the community develop their capacity to provide for each other or is working with a particular client to set up a network of provision to meet his or her particular needs. What is necessary, however, if adequate individual caring networks are to be established, is that social workers also have the time, and are required to spend it, in more general social care planning, which is not necessarily geared to an individual 'case'.

3.48 The way in which social workers' time is divided between this more general social care planning and planning and counselling in relation to particular clients will depend upon the particular setting in which they work. We can imagine that some social workers in specialist settings, particularly in voluntary agencies, child guidance clinics, some psychiatric teams and some residential homes and day centres may spend a very high proportion of their time on direct counselling whereas others in day services or area teams may be more concerned with developing links with volunteers, voluntary agencies, relatives and neighbours.

Interagency relationships; negotiation and advocacy

3.49 So far we have concentrated on community links. These may or may not include contacts with other statutory agencies. These, however, form a considerable part of the work of many social workers and deserve to be mentioned separately.

3.50 Much of our evidence suggests that at least some work undertaken on behalf of clients with other agencies is necessary only because the other agencies are failing to provide prompt and adequate service. Social workers, it is said, carry the burden of failures in social policies.

3.51 While we would not deny that there is some truth in this complaint, we consider that some clients may always need help to manage the extreme complexities of the welfare state and to put their case to other officials. This is a task which could be carried out by others, but it follows from our view of social work that social workers who are creating networks of care, with and for clients, will be one of the groups of necessity involved with other services, and that they will need skills in negotiation and advocacy if their clients' needs are to be met. Evidence from Family Service Units (320) stressed the importance to clients of their social workers' negotiating on their behalf. One quotation from a client makes the point: 'They have got me things I could never get, grants and things I never even thought of for the kids. You know, extra money on the social security to go to the laundry, and he got me extra money for extra sheets because they wet the bed. I couldn't get them because every time I went up they wouldn't do anything.'

Social workers as rationers and gatekeepers

3.52 Failure to provide service is a feature not only of other services but also of the social services, and in their case too it is often the result of inadequate resources. Social policy may advocate nursery places for the children from disadvantaged families or day care and home helps for elderly people, but demand far outstrips supply. As a result, social workers are needed to ration scarce resources. This is most obvious in the case of area team social workers in local authority teams but residential and day care staff also have to ration the resources available to their clients and social workers in voluntary agencies have to decide who meets the eligibility standards established for their service. In short, social workers have a role as rationers and gatekeepers. They say 'no' on behalf, mostly, of taxpayers and ratepayers and where financial cuts bite they are having to deny increasingly needy people.

3.53 We do not accept the argument that this is not a part of the social work role, although we sympathise with social workers' distaste for it and consider that the public should recognise in this instance, as in others, what social workers do in their name. We consider this should be done by social workers because we believe that what services there are should be given to those in greatest need. Assessing need is a problematic activity at the best of times, but is one in which social workers are experienced and for which social work students are trained. In addition, the approach social workers adopt should mean that they carry out the necessary assessment in as humane a way as possible and taking many factors into account.

3.54 Social workers act as gatekeepers for the services of their own department and one of these services is social work time. Some of our respondents have suggested that certain client groups are more likely than others to receive services from a social worker. The example always quoted of a group who do not receive their fair share of social work is elderly people. In some areas it seems all elderly clients are allocated to social work assistants and they continue to provide all the services the client receives even where there might be a need for a full assessment or for counselling help to reach a decision about alternative living arrangements.

3.55 We have selected these two needs because we consider that both require the time of a social worker. We realise that each agency may have a slightly different list of situations which, on the face of it, require social work help. We were given several by our respondents and the following serves as an example:

- Life or liberty are at risk.
- A major change of living situation may be involved.
- Counselling may be needed when private sorrows or relationship problems are escalating into life crisis proportions.
- The client, family or group seems unable to make use of available resources.
- A network of resources needs to be established and monitored.

3.56 If an elderly person has problems of these kinds, we consider they are as much in need of social work help as a child might be. We cannot accept what in effect is rationing by age.

3.57 We are not suggesting that many of the needs of the elderly should not be met, as they are, by family members, social work assistants, volunteers and neighbours. All we are saying is that the elderly are as entitled as members of other age groups to social work help when social care networks or counselling are needed and will not be provided unless a social worker is involved.

Social workers and social policing

3.58 For similar reasons, we consider that social workers should continue to carry out, in strictly defined circumstances, what some respondents called 'social policing'. The law requires local authorities to investigate possible instances of children being harmed by their parents and we consider it appropriate that such investigations should be undertaken by social workers. We recognise that such investigations, and the surveillance which may follow from them, are disliked by many clients and are open to abuse. None the less, we cannot believe they would be better conducted by civil servants or by the police. We also consider that they require the same skills in planning and counselling as other tasks performed by social workers.

3.59 We have been told by some of those we met and who talked to us that these 'social policing' powers may often poison the relationship between social workers and parents and that some single parents feel obliged to talk to social workers because they fear they might be charged with neglecting or abusing their children if they do not. Such statements are deeply worrying, and we suggest that social workers must do everything they can to make sure that clients in such vulnerable situations know their legal rights and are introduced to all possible kinds of community and mutual support schemes. However, once social workers have done all they can to ease what is by definition a very tense and difficult situation, they may still have a responsibility to supervise a child or children which they must not ignore.

3.60 The role of social workers in non-accidental injury cases is a particularly difficult one and it has been made even more so by the attitude taken by parts of the media. It seems that in some peoples' eyes, social workers cannot do right; they either fail to protect children from injury or, when they act to prevent a child being injured, they are accused of interfering with parental rights.

3.61 It is our view that, if society wishes social workers to act in this role, the public need to be aware that they are asking social workers to be brokers in lesser evils and to act on the basis of their best judgement. Inevitably they will sometimes be wrong. Children will continue to die from injuries inflicted by their guardians in circumstances where social workers are involved and they will die because as a society we value parents' rights so highly that we weigh them in the balance against childrens' lives. Sometimes the social workers who have to measure the balance will misread the situation and make the wrong prediction.

3.62 Social workers may have responsibility for deciding whether care proceedings should be started when a child is at risk or, as the law stands at the time of writing, whether a child in care may go home on trial. However, they very rarely make such decisions alone. Almost always medical and nursing personnel are involved and often others such as police and teachers. A great deal of work has gone into developing procedures for collecting and sharing information between professionals. We hope such work will continue so that these extremely difficult decisions will be made on the best available information and the responsibility for them be shared. At present it seems to us that other professionals are sometimes too ready to leave the decision to social workers and that social workers carry an unfair share of the blame when things go wrong.

3.63 It is not only in relation to children that social workers have a social policing role. They are also involved in the compulsory admission to hospital of people suffering from mental disorders. Again we consider this is an appropriate role for them. We welcome the plans outlined in the White Paper, *The Reform of Mental Health Legislation*, that social workers who are required to undertake this task should be specially trained. We consider this will make them more likely to approach this task with confidence and with the concern for the potential patient and his relatives which a trained and experienced social worker is able to combine with the use of compulsory powers.

3.64 Non-accidental injury cases and compulsory admissions are what come to most people's minds when the term social policing is used. There are however many other aspects of what social workers are needed to do which involve elements of control. For example the establishment of social care networks for young offenders often involves requiring adolescents to meet with their social workers or to join Intermediate Treatment groups. If these young people refuse the social worker can take them back to court.

3.65 There are those who consider that all social work with delinquents should be on a voluntary basis. Most of the committee do not take this view and see control as an appropriate part of social work provided it is exercised as part of a social plan for the person concerned.

What social workers should not be doing

3.66 It is apparent from the evidence we received and from the experience of members of the committee that there are many ways in which scarce social work manpower is not being used to the best advantage.

3.67 If social workers are to take on a more general responsibility for social care planning they will have to be freed from work which others could or should do. Such changes are likely to have the added benefit of improving the morale of social workers.

3.68 We suggest that social services committees and social work managers should consider what social workers in their organisations are doing which they should not be under three headings:

Tasks which could be performed by other staff and/or volunteers. For example:
- Routine clerical work.
- Arranging transport or payment for transport for clients.
- Assessing routine requests for assistance.
- Assessing the need for and issuing aids for the disabled.

● Much routine provision of practical aid and advice, surveillance and monitoring.

We have discussed elsewhere the need for more clerical support
and for a rational division of tasks between social workers and aides
and assistants.

The greater part of the work of an area team is concerned with the
provision and administration of practical and material services. Social
workers should only be involved in a small part of that total work:
that part which requires their particular skills in assessing, counselling and planning.

We recognise that listing particular tasks as suitable for social
workers is of limited use since their appropriateness may depend
upon the context within which they are undertaken. It may, for
example, be entirely appropriate for a social worker to drive a parent
to see his child in a community home and to collect rent from the
same parent each pay day, if these activities are part of a plan to
rehabilitate a family and where the attempt to build a relationship
between social worker and parent needs to start from practical help.

**Things which would be more appropriately done by other
agencies.** For example:
● Systematic provision of information and advice.
● Routine assessment of housing need.
● Rent collection.
● Debt collecting for fuel/water boards.

**Things which should not be done by social workers or by
anyone else.**
It was suggested in our evidence that there might be two circumstances in which social workers were doing unnecessary or unpro-
ductive work:
● Where social work is given without clear objectives, without
an adequate assessment of the need or an agreement with the client
about the sort of help which is acceptable. Social workers tend, it was
suggested, to keep cases open longer than necessary and to continue
to try to work with clients who are unlikely to respond to the help
offered.
● Social workers were sometimes asked, or expected, to monitor
or provide support to clients with chronic problems to allay the
anxieties of other professions or services, or the anxiety of their own
agency to avoid criticism, even though there is little likelihood of
improving the client's lot or of staving off a crisis.

There are admittedly circumstances in which social workers ought to perform a monitoring role, often for long periods with little tangible result, because the clients present a risk either to themselves or to others, but this work needs to be justified first and foremost on the ground that it will reduce the risk.

SUMMARY OF CONCLUSIONS

1. Social workers are needed to plan, establish, maintain and evaluate social care and to provide counselling (3.3–5).

2. Social problems need to be seen as having a practical or material and an emotional component (3.6).

3. Social care planning and counselling are not performed only by social workers but all who call themselves social workers must be able to carry out both activities (3.5).

4. Social workers should be able to develop special knowledge and skill (3.18).

5. To undertake social care planning social workers require knowledge of the relevant local communities and communities of interest (3.30).

6. Social care planning requires a partnership with volunteers and voluntary agencies (3.30–32).

7. Social care planning includes both plans to meet existing need and to prevent future needs arising (3.40).

8. Social work managers must find ways to allow social workers to undertake social planning in the preventive as well as its reactive sense (3.43).

9. Social work training should encompass social care planning as well as counselling (3.45).

10. Rationing scarce resources is part of the social work task (3.52).

11. Rationing by age is unacceptable (3.56).

12. Social workers should when necessary carry out 'social policing' (3.58).

13. Social work employers and managers have a responsibility to establish what work social workers are doing which should be done by others or not at all (3.68).

Chapter 4

Social work in residential and day services

Introduction

4.1 The purpose of this chapter is to describe the role of residential and day services in the whole pattern of social care, and then to draw out the implications for the role and tasks of social workers in day and residential services.

4.2 Most clients of social workers live in their own homes. But many others live, by their choice or someone else's, elsewhere. This may often be in a hospital (run by a health authority), in a home or hostel (managed by a local authority social services department or a voluntary agency), or in a foster-home. Some of them, because they are very old and confused, or suffering from very severe physical or mental handicap, will never make, or return to, a home of their own.

4.3 Historically there was a great gulf between those in Poor Law institutions and everyone else. Even today there is often a big organisational divide between residential and fieldwork in social services departments. Perhaps even more telling, many social workers in the field regard it as one of their primary objectives to keep people out of residential establishments wherever possible. Yet a person who leaves home for another place remains the same person, with the same human needs and the same emotional links with family or local community. The services provided to people living in their own homes and those provided to people living permanently in residential establishments are not fundamentally different in kind. They represent, indeed, two extremes of a continuum of provision – between which we can identify a wide range of services that are provided neither wholly in a person's own home nor exclusively in a residential setting. There are two major categories of service in this range:

● Special centres, private family homes, or facilities shared with the public at large, attended regularly or occasionally by clients of social services, who come to them for all or part of the day, but who return to their own homes to sleep: these are described as 'day services'.

● Places – including private family homes (usually called foster homes) – where clients live instead of in their own homes, for shorter or longer periods, and under a variety of temporary or intermittent arrangements (e.g. full-time, weekdays only, week-ends only); these, together with places where clients live permanently, are the 'residential services'.

4.4 These services are scarce resources, and the needs of clients do not always correspond with what is available. Usually they provide separately for each major group (children, elderly or physically handicapped people, mentally handicapped adults or children, mentally ill people), but there are some overlaps and some mixed provision. Most, but not all, of these services are provided by social services departments or voluntary agencies. Among the exceptions, special schools for handicapped and maladjusted children and some child guidance services are the responsibility of education authorities; sheltered and special housing and housing for homeless people is provided by housing authorities. There is private provision of nursing homes, homes for elderly people and lodging houses – and so on.

4.5 Such day and residential services fulfil a number of different purposes and use a wide variety of methods to achieve them. We discuss primarily residential services in this chapter, but what is described is not exclusive to residential care. In our view, the clearest difference between residential and day services is that in one the residents spend the night, and in the other they do not.

4.6 We have included private family homes in the lists in paragraph 4.3 because it is our view that people placed (fostered) with families should be considered as recipients of day services or residential services just as much as those placed in centres or homes. To see child-minding, for example, alongside day nurseries and playgroups, as one of a range of day services for children, is to recognise the important contribution this range of services makes to the meeting of local community needs. To think of children (or adults) living with foster-families as receiving one form of residential care, diminishes the sharp differentiation often made between fostering and residential care and puts the relationship between them in what we believe to be a more helpful perspective.

4.7 If we view the personal social services as distributed along a continuum in the way we have described, we may expect there to be tasks for social workers to carry out for and with clients at whatever point on the continuum they are situated. Just as people who remain in their own homes may be aided by a social worker's planning of social care, or by direct counselling to help them change (or tolerate) some aspect of their life or environment, so may people who spend all or part of the time away from their homes. Many members of the staff of residential and day units are indeed undertaking the role and tasks of social workers, including both the social planning and counselling components. Yet a great deal of the evidence submitted to us seemed to take it for granted that the role of social workers was confined to what is generally called 'fieldwork'. Indeed, only one tenth of the evidence made reference of any kind to residential services, and a rather lesser proportion to day services.

4.8 We regret this imbalance and believe that social workers have an important part to play in both day and residential care: a part important enough for us to devote to these services a chapter on their own.

Day and residential services – the present situation

4.9 The scale of day and residential provision in England and Wales can best be illustrated from the most recent figures available to the Working Party. By far the largest client group in residential homes is formed by elderly and physically handicapped people – 136,000 on 31 March 1980, of whom 126,000 were aged 65 and over. Places for a further 22,000 elderly people were available in day centres.

4.10 On the same date 10,000 adults and 1,400 children lived in homes or hostels for mentally handicapped people and nearly 3,500 adults in homes or hostels for mentally ill people. There were 45,000 places available in training centres for mentally handicapped adults, 10,000 in centres for younger physically handicapped people and 5,000 in centres for mentally ill people. A further 14,000 places were available in day centres catering for mixed groups.

4.11 As regards day and residential services for children and young people, on 31 March 1979, 36,000 were boarded out with foster parents, and 35,000 were living in community or voluntary homes. On 31 March 1980, 51,000 places were available in local authority or other day nurseries and 67,000 with registered childminders providing substitute home care.

4.12 These services are expensive to run and it can cost many thousands of pounds to keep one person in residential care for a year.

Together they account for nearly two-thirds of the annual social services budgets of local authorities and employ over half of their social services staff.

4.13 The standard of residential care, including fostering, has often been debated in this century. Though we are aware of the continued existence of poor or unsatisfactory provision, there can be little doubt that standards have improved greatly, in certain respects at least, in the last decade. We probably saw some of the better examples of practice during our visits to different parts of the country and we certainly saw much evidence of competent, imaginative and innovative practice, the existence of which is confirmed by other records. Mary McCormack's *Away From Home* describes an imaginative array of provision for mentally handicapped people, for example, and voluntary child care organisations like Barnardo's have pioneered projects which are expanding the horizons of residential and day care. The scope of this pioneering becomes clear when it is realised that while in 1969 60% of Barnardo's units were 'ordinary homes', this is now true of fewer than 10%. Instead, the provision of homes and schools for maladjusted and educationally sub-normal children has increased (nearly 35% in 1980), together with units for the mentally handicapped (10%) and day care units (nearly 20%). Intermediate Treatment (both as a day and residential service), is demanding new approaches to assessment and supervision of offenders.

Some of the continuing problems and constraints

4.14 Stigma. There is still a stigma attached to being in residential care, and in social services day nurseries. It is partly to do with the inheritance of Poor Law attitudes, partly with the poverty, handicaps or unacceptable behaviour of some of the clients, partly with the integration of offenders and non-offenders in the same establishments, partly with the attitudes of those social workers and others who regard residential care as the (undesirable) last resort. But whatever the reasons, stigma is a painful experience. Children and young people in foster-care or residential homes, are at very serious risk of being seen by relatives, teachers and friends as 'different' from other children (whether or not they have been labelled as handicapped, maladjusted or delinquent). The children in the recent *Who Cares* survey, conducted by the National Children's Bureau, noted among other things: the expectation of neighbours that they will be worse behaved and need stricter controls than children living with their own families; the assumption often made that they must have done something wrong to be 'put away'; the greater likelihood, compared with other children, of being suspected – particularly by school teachers – of theft or vandalism.

4.15 Segregation into client groups. Just as patients in hospitals are put into different wards depending on the nature of their complaint, so people in residential and day care tend to be separated on account of their age, physical, mental or emotional problems. This means that they often lose contact with other groups and types of people and live in situations that are inherently limiting to relationships.

4.16 The predominance of short-term fieldwork assumptions. When residential services are planned or evaluated the central importance of tending and nurturing (which we discuss in paragraphs 4.43–47 below) is often overlooked. Sometimes treatment is regarded as the sole function of an establishment rather than as one component of life for those within it. Reviews of residents' progress may be dominated by fieldwork assumptions and thinking, playing down the insights of residential staff into personal issues such as religious choice.

4.17 Units are often part of large bureaucracies. Most residential and day units are run by large local authority or voluntary organisations, with hierarchical structures inhibiting flexible and spontaneous responses to needs, and giving residents the sense of being at the receiving end of a rather impersonal process. The inability of some local authorities to find a way for children in care to shop like other children of the same age, without 'order books' which label them immediately as 'in care' is a continuing scandal. Smaller voluntary organisations have all found ways of coping with this, as do foster and normal families. Though often termed 'institutional', residential establishments may now be so not because of their own nature or wishes but because of the bureacracies within which they are located. The Residential Care Association's evidence (137) put this issue forcefully: 'local authorities are often still unaware of the nature of residential social work practice, and it is perhaps questionable whether their size and structure will ever permit them to respond flexibly enough to permit residential establishments to fulfil their roles, without a major change of attitudes'.

4.18 Picking up the pieces too late. Because much effort now goes into keeping people out of residential care, it may be too late, when people are finally moved from their homes, to achieve growth, trust and relationships that could have been developed earlier – a point made to us cogently in evidence submitted jointly by five voluntary child care organisations (321). Residential staff are sometimes given impossible tasks – like seeking to develop caring relationships with a group of resentful teenage offenders; or creating life and sharing among senile elderly people.

4.19 The assumption that family life is necessarily best. Despite the emotional damage that may be caused within nuclear families, these family units are generally esteemed more highly than 'institutions' by the public and fieldworkers. The saying 'a bad home is better than a good institution', simple, yet misleading, still has its adherents. It is possibly for this reason that fostering is assumed unquestioningly to be better than other substitute placements, even though many residents in homes, including some we met, do not share this view.

4.20 Conditions of service and staff turnover militate against some residential care. The evidence we received from the Residential Care Association (137), put this point strongly. '. . . some aspects of practice in social services departments reflect staff need rather than client need. The current patterns of training and promotion are in direct conflict with clients' wishes for continuity of professional contact, and residents suffer seriously in some establishments because of high staff turnover.' It is clear that, whatever we may have gained with the disappearance of the force of dedicated spinsters who served a lifetime in residential work with little or no time off, we have lost something difficult to replace.

4.21 Over 80% untrained staff in residential work. Although they play a vitally important role in clients' lives, it is still the case that over 80% of residential staff have received no relevant qualifying training. While we appreciate the obstacles – both financial and organisational – to expanding training opportunities at the present time, we believe that bold and imaginative measures to increase the proportion of qualified staff in residential homes are now urgently necessary.

Three approaches used at present
4.22 Against this background, staff of day and residential services face a formidable challenge, in responding to the needs of the groups they serve, and in minimising or repairing the damage that may be done by unhelpful organisational, social work or public attitudes. These services vary enormously in purposes and methods; they also make very different assumptions, not always consciously formulated, about the potential and limitations of human beings. It is impossible for us to enter into the detail of this rich variety or even to

acknowledge all the distinctions. We believe, however, that we can identify three broad approaches to day and residential services, each of which is associated with one primary purpose, and one particular way of thinking about people. They are not mutually exclusive. They do not cover every example of day and residential provision. Inevitably, they risk over-simplification. In the hope, however, that description of the three approaches will throw light on the conclusions we reach later about the role of social workers in these services, we present them in order of increasing optimism and refer to them as the 'refuge', the 'control and learning' and the 'growth and development' approaches.

4.23 The **refuge** approach presupposes that those receiving the service are so incapacitated by age and infirmities, or so profoundly handicapped mentally or physically, that there can be little or no realistic hope for either the restoration of lost interests and abilities or the acquisition of new ones. People thus afflicted may also have lost (or never possessed) the power to communicate with their fellows, other than in simple and limited ways, and be incapable of making even the most superficial friendships. They may be dependent on others for feeding, dressing, toileting, washing and so on. The major purpose of residential and day services, therefore, is to provide physical care from the day of admission to the day of death or departure for hospital. Such a purpose is compatible either with a cold and callous attitude or with the most humane and warmly caring attitudes that can be imagined. We recognise that the qualities and attitudes of staff can have a massive impact on the well-being and the behaviour of these residents, but think it important to underline our view that this approach, with its limited major purpose, is a clearly suitable one for day hospitals or centres, and for residential homes, which provide for extremely confused elderly people and for those almost wholly incapacitated by mental or physical disability. As an approach it is in no way inferior, when appropriately applied, to the two we are about to outline.

4.24 The **control and learning** approach has for its major purpose changes in behaviour, or the maintenance or improvement of skills and self-dependence, in directions largely determined by the staff of day and residential units. This approach is based on the view that society has the right to decide what are acceptable standards of conduct for its members (particularly the young), and the obligation to increase as much as possible the capacities for work, leisure activity and family life of those who are disadvantaged by reason of illness or disability. It scarcely needs saying that there are differences of opinion as to what standards of conduct should be, what methods should be used to promote them, and what are the appropriate levels of independent activity for particular groups of sick or handicapped people. Within a control and learning approach therefore, such standards and levels can be interpreted either very narrowly or very broadly, and sanctions for misconduct or non-achievement may range from the mild to the severe. It does not follow that a day or residential unit based wholly or mainly on this model must be rigidly authoritarian in its regime; it may be this, but may also be extremely flexible in recognising that different individual situations call for different responses from staff, and in allowing people some degree of influence over the regime in which they find themselves.

4.25 Elements of this approach can be found, and seem to us to be appropriate, in most day and residential establishments for children and young people; but it tends to be seen at its most thoroughgoing in centres where young offenders and children with behavioural problems are present in some numbers: community homes with education, observation and assessment centres, residential special schools and day centres for handicapped youngsters, Intermediate Treatment schemes provided on a residential or daily attendance basis (or combinations of both). Foster-parents, child-minders and other community homes often adopt a rather more relaxed version of the approach, though there are wide variations. and examples of very rigid and very flexible care can be found in each form of provision.

4.26 As regards adults, the control and learning approach is predominant in those residential homes for elderly, mentally ill or handicapped or physically handicapped people in which residents have or retain some capacity to make friendships, pursue personal interests, learn or maintain skills, and make independent choices; and in day centres where the emphasis is on opportunities to acquire social and work skills, as well as to make friendships which are satisfying and enjoyable in themselves. Workshops providing sheltered employment are also examples of this approach, as are (though often in its severest and bleakest form) reception centres for the single homeless.

4.27 The third approach we have chosen to call the **growth and development** approach. This term seems to us preferable to (say) 'treatment' or 'therapy' because, while treatment with specific aims and methods is sometimes offered within day and residential centres (e.g. behaviour modification programmes, group therapy), we are sceptical about regarding the entire day or residential experience as itself a form of treatment. The different influences of a regime are too numerous (and often in conflict). The growth and development approach has as its major purpose the release of disabling inhibitions and the emergence of a sense of responsibility and independence of thought and action, provided only these do not infringe the rights of others. Behind this purpose lies the presupposition that people are entitled (within the limits just defined), to lead their lives as they prefer and make decisions and choices (including mistakes), for themselves.

4.28 While many people would give assent to the values underpinning the growth and development approach, its advocates in the day and residential services have to face two inescapable realities: first, that (as we have seen earlier) a large number of those receiving these services – particularly the very old and the very handicapped – have seriously limited capacities for development or decision making in the sense intended here. Secondly, by no means all members of the public would in practice approve efforts to help people feel less inhibited or act more independently. A good many would regard it as more appropriate (and less threatening) to encourage behaviour and attitudes that conform to conventional standards, and probably most seek to bring up their children in this way. It does not follow from this that care-givers in day and residential work are compelled to do the same with those in their care: but it does follow that they need to take note of prevalent public views. For these reasons, the growth and development approach is rarely, if ever, operated in its pure form, but rather in combination with a flexibly interpreted version of the control and learning approach. Units that ignored the need for a structure of control and accountability, or flew too far in the face of what the public will tolerate, would rapidly find themselves faced with public inquiries, if not outright closure.

4.29 Day and residential centres that follow a growth and development approach, differ from those using only a control and learning approach in one or more of the following ways:

● very high (and genuine) level of participation by the clients in deciding on the rules and activities to be followed in the centre (or the foster family);

● informality and minimal distinction of status between clients and staff (or foster parents);

● readiness to allow clients to express their real feelings although this may sometimes result in behaviour which is embarrassing, or even frightening or destructive; accompanied by practices which face them with the consequences of their behaviour, and give

them and the staff (or foster parents) a shared responsibility for
dealing with these consequences;

● open interchange between clients and staff (or foster family)
and their local community, with involvement in its life rather than
isolation from it.

Examples of this approach are found in a few community homes
and foster families for adolescents, residential special schools for
older maladjusted children, units (both day and residential) for the
mentally ill and in some family day centres we visited or about which
we were told.

4.30 We repeat that we do not regard any one approach as
intrinsically 'better' than the others. Each approach must be determined in relation to the needs and capabilities of the people being
helped. The growth and development approach, for example, could
not be adopted for the clients referred to in paragraph 4.23, and it
would clearly be outrageous for bright but disturbed younsters to be
subjected to a refuge approach, however humane. There can be good
or bad practice under any of the approaches. The point is to identify
which approach is appropriate, and to seek to achieve good practice
within it. This will hardly be practicable unless all members of staff
and social workers placing clients understand the objectives of the
home or centre and their individual role in seeking to fulfil them. The
organisation of the agency and deployment of staff in the unit also
need to be matched to the objectives.

What are day and residential services needed for?

4.31 The obvious answer to this question is far from straightforward.
We may be tempted to reply 'to provide for those who need them',
but that only raises the further question: 'who decides who needs
them and why?' Furthermore, it is not only the needs of those who
may receive the service that have to be considered. Many members of
the public who would wish people in day or residential care to be
skilfully and humanely cared for, expect at the same time that the
services will protect them from the loss and inconvenience caused by
offenders' activities, or spare them the pain and embarrassment of
extremes of visible handicap or strangeness of behaviour.

4.32 The doors of day centres or residential homes are often kept
shut, with residents safely on the inside, to protect people living
outside, while staff may prefer them to be open for their charges to
make forays into the neighbourhood as often as they want or can.
Magistrates and the police may expect community homes with education and Intermediate Treatment projects to place the accent on

'discipline' and staff may be divided between those who agree with this emphasis and those who see their work primarily in terms of treatment.

4.33 At the same time staff may be seeking to implement policies which their residents do not agree with. We are familiar with this conflict in relation to teenagers, but less aware of the problem (developed in one piece of evidence submitted to us (95)) in 'enlightened' establishments for elderly people where the staff wish their charges to be active and self-sufficient while some old people themselves may prefer to remain inactive.

4.34 Many would argue that clients' preference (including the views of parents of young children) and perceptions of their own needs should always be taken seriously when admission to either residential or day care is being considered; that there should be a continuing dialogue between clients and service-providers about needs and preferences. It should not be automatically assumed, for example, that no one would choose to enter a residential home if an alternative were available. Some old people (if not the majority), are thankful to relinquish the increasingly burdensome responsibility of keeping up their own home – even if community care is provided on a generous scale and there is a day-centre or sheltered housing a few streets away. The *Who Cares* survey and what we were told by the National Association of Young People in Care make it clear that some children are happier in a children's home than in foster care or with their own parents.

4.35 But some people, whatever their own preferences, may be so frail, confused, handicapped or young, that adequate service to or protection of them in their own homes is not practicable. Others may be able to live at home with help from relatives or friends, provided that day services or short-term residential care is available to give the helpers relief. Others, again, for example offenders or seriously disturbed youngsters, may need to be compulsorily admitted to residential care for the protection of either themselves or the public.

What day services provide

4.36 It is clear from recently-published research studies (notably Carter, 1981) that day services are well able to fulfil the aims of providing:

● Tending (see paragraphs 4.43–44) during the day-time, for the profoundly handicapped, or the deeply confused elderly, who are wholly dependent on others for continuous care, and whose families or other relatives are willing and able to undertake these tasks at night and during week-ends.

● Opportunities for learning social skills, and in certain instances work skills, by people who are physically handicapped or mentally handicapped or ill.

● Opportunities for such people and for elderly people to pursue and enjoy activities and interests for their own sake and to make friendships and enjoy social life.

● Opportunities for delinquent or disturbed youngsters to explore new interests, engage in activities rewarding in themselves, and learn acceptable patterns of behaviour.

● Care, play, fun and learning opportunities for pre-school children placed for the day by their families.

The fundamental difference between residential and day care

4.37 All these things can also, in principle, be provided by residential services. There is, however, one fundamental difference between admission to day and to residential care. Compared with attending a centre during the day at the end of which clients return to their own homes, going to live somewhere else, even for a short period, is a profoundly disturbing experience. Leaving home and family for a totally (or relatively) unknown place, with its unfamiliar fellow occupants and staff, strange food, rooms and beds, new rules (most of them unwritten) to be learned, and a new pattern of relationships between people to adjust to, makes a daunting challenge. Whether we welcome or abhor the prospect of such a radical change in our lives, it confronts us with shock at loss of what we have taken for granted (however painful this may have been), and anxiety about what we are about to face. Nothing in attendance at a day centre is quite comparable to this, and all that has just been outlined applies to entry into a foster home as much as to admission to a residential establishment.

4.38 Precisely because departure from home is fraught with the possibility of such emotional turmoil – but also because of the fear that going into residential care (especially into a non-family setting), will damage people by making them over dependent, protecting them unduly, and subjecting them to impersonal bureaucratic procedures – it is now common to hear it said that people should remain at home if at all possible. Residential provision, on this view, should be made only as a last resort, and if there is no alternative, then a substitute family is to be preferred to a residential home, and it is increasingly urged in favour of day care that it may prevent the necessity for either.

What residential care may provide

4.39 The very fact that residential care entails such a fundamental change and challenge for those admitted to it has some notable advantages as well as obvious risks. It can lead a person to a significant re-evaluation of himself and his life, give him opportunities for trying out and learning new ways of relating to people at a level deeper than is possible in day provision, and it can provide someone who has had distressing and damaging experience of his own family not only with relief but also with joy and renewed hope. In these ways a shorter or longer period in a residential home can be particularly suitable for some children and young people of school age and beyond, but also for some physically handicapped and mentally ill or mentally handicapped adults whose previous lives (whether in their families or in hospitals) have constricted rather than expanded their growth as people. For elderly people, as we have noted, entry into a residential home can have the effect of relieving them of changes and challenges (once they have adjusted to the move), which they no longer have the wish or the energy to continue facing.

4.40 Residential care (including fostering) should be aiming to provide:

● A secure base of satisfying and enjoyable experience with sufficient choices and challenges to equip people for the demands of living independently (where this is a realistic possibility).

● Experiences which reinforce each individual's feeling that he matters; having, for example, a genuine voice in decision-making.

● Relationships with care-givers that are both warmly human and skilfully adapted to the circumstances of individuals.

● Boundaries which reflect the limits there are to self-expression and the right of others to respect and choice.

● Opportunities for friendships with fellow clients and other people of a resident's choice, both within and outside the establishment.

● Opportunities to be creative and to maintain or develop skills.

● The opportunity to explore and learn from the consequences of new experiences.

4.41 Residential care is, in our view, most likely to be successful from the resident's viewpoint in the following situations:

● where as far as possible the residents enter on their stay **willingly;**

● where they are able to choose the home to which they go and have some experience of it before agreeing to enter it;

● where existing residents are prepared for the arrival of a new resident;

● where the stay and period in residence is planned and purposive;

● where the place has a staff team who agree about what they are doing and are committed to it;

● where the place has a relaxed relationship with the surrounding community;

● where the staff are secure in themselves, aware of their own limitations, and have a wide range of interests and experience;

● where a treatment method does not dominate the whole place to the exclusion of spontaneity, variety and normal life-events and reactions.

Day and residential services: the basic tasks

4.42 If day and residential services are to confer on clients the potential benefits which we have outlined above (paragraphs 4.36 and 40 respectively), we believe they have to undertake the basic tasks described in the following paragraphs.

4.43 Tending. This task must, in our mind, be seen as the primary responsibility of all who are in direct daily contact with clients in day or residential provision. It consists of all those activities necessary to ensure the physical well-being of a group of day centre attenders, children or adults with child-minders or foster families, and residents in homes and hostels. These activities include the provision of food and space for work, recreation, rest and sleep; the furnishing, repair and maintenance of premises; the management of daily routines, with their planned or spontaneous variations; the organisation and performance of chores; the supervision of bathing and toileting, or assistance with these to those who are unable to undertake them unaided; appropriate interaction (in residential care) with residents at rising and bed-time.

4.44 In social work, tending is usually undervalued. It is seen as mundane, humdrum and of less importance than activities like case reviews, case allocations, and casework generally. Yet tending is the very basis of good day and residential care. It is often in the 'daily round and common task' that real sharing, communication and understanding occurs. Each aspect of routine, each activity will convey a message, will be a symbol of the quality of care the residents are experiencing. Some tending jobs will be performed by domestic staff, and residents themselves may well (and appropriately) share in many; but it is the daily care-givers – whether mothers and fathers of families, care assistants, residential social workers, nurses, teachers or instructors – who have the day-to-day responsibility for their performance and quality. Collectively, the various tending activities not only convey clear messages to residents, but also are the focus of intense feelings related to conflicts between control and freedom, dependence and independence, self-esteem and self-disgust. The more obviously difficult (and more prestigious) basic tasks in day and residential care – enumerated below – cannot be accomplished at all unless the tending task is at least 'good enough'; and, as our evidence made clear (particularly 217), they are often undertaken as part of tending rather than separately from it.

4.45 Providing group and individual experiences that are satisfying in themselves and contribute to learning and development. Many tending activities – for example the sharing of meals, the occasion of getting up and going to bed, the joint performance of daily chores and maintenance activities, together with the associated opportunities for caring and skilled interaction between care-givers and clients, will in themselves provide some of these experiences. Organised or spontaneous leisure activities, with opportunities for individual choice, are another focus for such experiences, as are the emergence of conflicts and crises and their resolution, formal or informal 'therapeutic' meetings between care-givers and groups of clients, individual counselling sessions (often taking place subtly and informally during the course of a shared tending activity, such as bathing), special celebratory occasions, children's play, the struggles, achievements and failures of severely handicapped people in communicating feelings accurately, or making a toy.

4.46 Maintaining links between clients and their family and community networks, the local neighbourhood and relevant workers outside the family, centre or home; and between the centre or home and its managing agency. This is a vital task in keeping alive the feeling of residents that they are in touch with people who matter to them and outside interests in their lives, and are part of the community in which is set the place they live in or attend. Without its skilled and sensitive performance, there is a real risk that care-givers as well as clients will become isolated and 'institutionalised'. It entails not only work that ensures the maximum desirable and feasible movement of clients across the boundaries between their place and their various communities of interest, locally or further afield, but also 'public relations' activities with neighbours and local organisations, with the object of integrating centre or home as far as possible into the immediate neighbourhood. This includes the difficult job of opening up centre or home to the local community – by way, for example, of encouraging spontaneous or casual 'dropping in' or offering, say, workshop facilities as a resource to local people – without subjecting clients to the feeling that their privacy is infringed.

4.47 We do not consider tending, providing satisfying experiences, and maintaining links – basic and vital to day and residential services as they undoubtedly are – are necessarily formal social work tasks (though this is not to say that they are not carried out by social workers in these services). Large numbers of adults in families undertake such activities, and few of those whose paid occupation it is would think of themselves as social workers or of training for social work as relevant to it. Many make an excellent job of them on the basis of good sense and growing experience. This is not to say that they should be denied opportunities to prepare for the task through appropriate courses.

The contribution of social work to day and residential services

4.48 There are in our view, three distinct, though related, formal social work roles which may be performed in the day and residential services. All of them presuppose skill in assessment and evaluation. The first is that of **manager** – whether as head of a day centre or residential home, or as member of the middle management team in a social services department or voluntary agency. The responsibility here is either the planning and coordination of services generally in a particular area, ensuring necessary interchanges between day and residential services and field and domiciliary work, together with the supervision and monitoring of standards of practice; or leadership of a day or residential establishment, with the job of ensuring that the three basic tasks outlined above are undertaken by its staff with skill and sensitivitiy. Staff supervision and development is an important part of this role.

4.49 The second role pinpointed in evidence we received, is that of **consultant** – either to fostering or child-minding families, the adult members of which undertake direct care-giving (and in relation to whom a local authority has a monitoring duty to fulfil), or to the staff of one or more day centres or residential homes. We believe this role becomes increasingly necessary and important as day and residential units become more closely linked with surrounding neighbourhood and outside services.

4.50 In saying that these two roles may appropriately be undertaken by social workers, we do not claim that only social workers could or should undertake them. We are saying no more than that the skills and knowledge appropriate to a social worker's role in other settings equip him particularly well to do so.

4.51 The third role that seems to us to be appropriate in certain circumstances is that of **direct care-giver**. We do not think that there is more than a very limited scope for social workers to be employed as care-givers in day centres though they can play a particular role in liaison between centre and home. In the residential services, however, where absence from their own home makes clients especially vulnerable in ways we have already indicated, there are arguments for saying that all homes for children and young people should employ at least one social worker, and that in the larger homes, and homes and schools for exceptionally disturbed and difficult youngsters there should be a team (among other staff) of care-giving social workers. Social workers in this role would also be appropriate in a number of units where social learning programmes are well-established and work is being attempted with mentally ill or handicapped or physically handicapped people in accordance with a growth and development approach, and possibly in a rather smaller proportion of homes for elderly people where the majority of residents show relatively few signs of serious deterioration.

4.52 It is in residential homes where a relatively high proportion of time is devoted to the two basic tasks other than tending, that the clearest role exists for social workers as care-givers. Both tasks may include elements of the counselling aspect of social work. We give a general illustration of the demands that may arise in each of these tasks which seem to call for the skills of social workers.

4.53 Throughout life, all people stand in need of experience which helps them grow and develop, face and master conflict and risky situations, and confront change with equanimity. Care-givers can only ensure that these opportunities are provided in full measure and used effectively if they have both a wide range of social work skills and knowledge and sufficient personal resources, whether of conversation, activities or interests, to stimulate, and extend the imaginative lives of, both clients and their own colleagues. None of these skills and attributes can be divorced from 'good tending' (indeed most of them are mediated through meticulous attention to it), but neither are they confined to tending alone.

4.54 We have already referred also to provision of opportunities to maintain links across the boundaries between day centre or residential home and the outside world. This is not always easy in the face of geographical isolation or negative public attitudes. Inevitably this part of their work faces residential or day centre workers on occasion with difficult decisions about granting or witholding permission (for example to join in outside activities, or visit friends, shops, theatres or public houses); with helping clients work through the consequences of making unwise choices; with the possibility of residents risking life and limb, or the home or centre risking disapproval from neighbours who believe that people there should be more restricted in their movements than people in families.

4.55 We hold that the counselling elements outlined in the preceding two paragraphs ought to count as formal social work. Caregivers other than social workers will, of course, undertake them too – though we believe that they should do so, whenever possible, under the supervision of a social worker. Equally, social workers acting as caregivers will themselves engage in tending (as well as in the tasks for which they are specially equipped). In paragraph 4.51 we referred to the circumstances in which the appointment of social workers to the team of caregivers was particularly appropriate. For all day and residential services, however, whether or not social workers are employed as care-givers, we consider that support from social workers – whether this takes the form of direct management or outside consultancy – should be available.

The role of key-worker

4.56 People in day or residential care (but especially children and young people in residential care), are at particular risk of finding that responsibility for their lives and problems is divided between a number of people – e.g. a field social worker for links with the family, a residential worker for life in the home and no-one in particular for foreseeing and planning what is to happen after departure. It is our view that one agreed and appropriate person should concern himself with, and accept formal responsibility for, the client's needs as a whole. We give unqualified support to the concept of the **key-worker** and consider it to be a manifestly appropriate role (other things being equal) for social workers in the day or residential services.

4.57 We acknowledge that a better developed and organised continuum of services might reduce their number, but we believe that there will always be some children for whom long-term residential care is the most suitable provision, in particular a number of deeply damaged children who cannot cope with the demands of fostering, and who can best be helped by very highly skilled residential work over a number of years. In such cases care-givers in homes or schools providing this service need to have two qualities not commonly found anywhere, and extremely scarce within social work. The qualities are: a tenacity of caring commitment to particular individual children, that counts no clock and is not destroyed by rejection; and a willingness to remain in post for longer than the customary average in order to provide children with continuing and unbroken relationships over several years.

4.58 For satisfactory emotional growth and development every child needs, we think, the unconditional commitment of at least one person (usually mother or father, or both). For a child in residential care this person may be someone outside a residential establishment or foster home. Sometimes he or she will be found only within the residential setting. Every child in long-term care needs such a person and one of the tasks of the key worker is to make sure, whenever possible, that a committed adult is available to the child.

The way ahead

4.59 In the Summary of Conclusions below we make a number of recommendations that would, in our view, considerably help residential establishments and social workers in them to achieve the tasks and carry out the roles described more effectively. We see all our recommendations in the context of the argument of our report as a whole. Community social work, with its emphasis on social care planning, and the development and support of community networks will have major consequences for residential care. Instead of being seen as isolated from communities, residential establishments will be seen as part of the neighbourhood in which they are located. As was stressed in the evidence from Dr Barnardo's (81), the rigid distinctions between fieldwork and residential work, between one client group and another, between professional and friend, between staff and clients, between treatment and life experience, will need to be rethought and modified. Far from being the last resort of a last ditch service, residential and day care centres may well become focal points of community-oriented social work.

SUMMARY OF CONCLUSIONS

1. Services to people in their own homes, day and residential services are parts of a continuum of care, and this should be reflected in the way the services are organised (4.3). Child-minding and fostering should

be seen as variants of day and residential care respectively (4.6).

2. There should be no pre-supposition that care provided in a client's own home, or in a foster-home, is necessarily better than, or preferable to, care in a residential home. Sometimes an early admission to residential care, whether for a child, a handicapped adult or an elderly person, can open up opportunities for growth and development that will be impossible later on without it (4.18, 19).

3. Different approaches to the practice and organisation of day and residential services – 'refuge', 'control and learning', 'growth and development' – are appropriate according to the characteristics of particular clients and client groups (4.30).

4. Day and residential care should not only provide physical tending of high quality (4.43, 44), but also stimulate opportunities for learning, friendship and sharing in decision-making (4.36, 40, 45).

5. Day centres and residential homes are often well placed to become resource centres for the local communities in which they are situated. Subject to an over-riding concern for the convenience and privacy of permanent attenders or residents, social services agencies should explore the community resource potential of the centres or homes for which they are responsible (4.46).

6. Tending, providing satisfying experiences for clients, and maintaining their links with the community, are not in themselves formal social work tasks, though they will often be performed by social workers in day and residential services (4.44–47).

7. Managing day or residential services, or acting as consultant to them, are formal social work roles (4.48–9).

8. In certain circumstances, direct care-giving is also a formal social work role in residential homes, particularly where care-giving includes a substantial proportion of counselling – for example in homes where a 'growth and development' approach is adopted. Social workers as direct care-givers have an especially important contribution to make in homes providing long-term care for very damaged children (4.51–52, 55).

9. When social workers act as direct care-givers in residential homes, the counselling they undertake should be mediated through their own good tending practice, not superimposed upon it. Unless tending is of high quality, sophisticated counselling, whether of individuals or groups, will be of little avail (4.53).

10. Homes and day-centres which do not employ social workers as direct care-givers should have social workers available to provide support (4.55).

11. For each person in day or residential care, a social worker should be appointed as key-worker. This should preferably be a social worker employed in the day or residential services, not necessarily a field worker (4.56, 57).

12. A child's key-worker has the task of ensuring that the child has, whenever possible, the continuing and unconditional commitment of at least one adult (4.58).

13. Conditions of service of day and residential staff, including hours of duty, living-in arrangements and holiday periods, should be arranged to suit the needs of the particular group receiving care – not the other way about. For some client groups – but particularly for vulnerable children in long-term residential care – shift systems and weeks of limited hours do not permit the commitment and continuity of contact between staff and clients implied by our view of the social worker's care-giving role. This is an issue which we believe employers and Trade Unions must confront and resolve (4.20, 57).

14. The issue of training for residential staff should be comprehensively and urgently reviewed (4.21).

Chapter 5

Social work and the voluntary sector

Introduction

5.1 In any discussion about social work and the voluntary sector two difficulties frequently arise. First, there is a singular inability to achieve the right perspective on the contribution of the voluntary sector to social services: the contribution is either grossly exaggerated (lyrical paeans of praise) or seriously underestimated (the voluntary sector is simply an afterthought in service planning). Second, discussions and even reports about the voluntary sector often founder because it is not made explicit enough just what is being meant by the term 'the voluntary sector'. It is our aim in this chapter to overcome both these difficulties, and to outline in relation to our working definition of the voluntary sector the roles and tasks of social workers.

5.2 We regard the voluntary sector as comprising four main systems which seem to us to constitute a spectrum of social care ranging from the spontaneous and localised to planned services on a national scale. The four categories are:

● Informal carers: natural and neighbourhood support networks.

● Mutual aid groups: usually groups of strangers who have in common particular difficulties.

● Volunteers: individuals offering their services free to a statutory or voluntary agency.

● Formal voluntary organisations: national or local bodies who employ paid professional staff.

5.3 We are aware of definitions (e.g. Department of Health and

Social Security, 1981) other than the above. But even more important than the exactness of the definition is the need to draw attention to the range of caring within the voluntary sector so that inaccurate generalisations are not made across the whole sector. Further, in discussing partnership between the voluntary and statutory sectors later in this chapter it will be clear that the nature of that partnership will vary according to which part of the voluntary sector is involved.

5.4 In this chapter, as elsewhere, we base our views upon the evidence we received and the discussions we had with members of statutory and voluntary organisations. These included discussions within our own membership, which included people who belonged, by employment or affiliation, to both sectors. We received nearly one hundred submissions of evidence from the voluntary sector, the vast majority of which came from formal organisations and mutual aid groups.

The extent of the voluntary sector

5.5 The size of the contribution of the voluntary sector to the welfare of individuals and families is often underestimated. Although figures do not tell the whole story, the wide scope of national and regional formal voluntary organisations in their particular fields was clear from the evidence we received. To give three examples:

● Family Service Units (120) work at any one time with 1,200 families including over 3,000 children in 26 local authority areas.

● The National Society for the Prevention of Cruelty to Children (268) dealt with 39,504 children in 1979/80 and spent £4.7 million on their social work services.

● Age Concern (239) had 115,000 volunteers drawn from 1,000 Age Concern groups assisting over one million old people.

In 1975/6 the income of 65 national voluntary organisations amounted to 10% of the total expenditure of local authority social services departments.

5.6 In a recent book on the voluntary sector, Johnson (1981) summarised what evidence there was on the number of voluntary social service organisations existing in specific localities. He noted that they ranged from eight organisations for every 10,000 people in Birmingham, to fifteen organisations for every 10,000 in Glasgow. One of the problems this sort of estimate entails is the difficulty of differentiating a voluntary *social service* organisation from other types of voluntary organisation.

5.7 Various efforts have been made to assess the numbers of staff and volunteers working in voluntary social service agencies, and because of the problems of definition, it is hardly surprising that a wide range of results has emerged. The Birch Report (1976) estimated the total number of paid staff at 18,860. The Personal Social Services Council (1975) arrived at the total of 10,142 and the Central Council for Education and Training in Social Work (1980) at a total of 8,181. We give later estimates in Chapter 2 together with our definitions of the categories of staff we have in mind. The Wolfenden Committee (1978) inquired into the numbers of people undertaking voluntary work as unpaid volunteers. Sixteen million man hours were worked weekly by volunteers, of which about two-thirds were given to personal social services.

5.8 None of these figures includes parents, housewives, grandparents, friends and neighbours who provide largely unmeasured and perhaps unmeasurable quantities of unpaid help, care and support. Some efforts are now being made to assess the size of this type of voluntary care. A recent report by the Equal Opportunities Commission (1981) estimates that there are one and a quarter million carers (mostly women) in Britain. A 'carer' is defined as someone who takes on the responsibility for a person who is handicapped, sick or elderly.

5.9 Finally we noted the relatively recent growth of self-help groups which cover so many areas of concern from the very specialist such as brittle bones to the more general such as bereavement. Quantification of the number and durability of these groups is extremely difficult. What is certain is that the days when the only self-help group was Alcoholics Anonymous are now past.

Informal carers

5.10 We have stressed elsewhere in this report the vital importance of knowing, understanding and taking account of informal caring systems for any social care planning, be it for an individual or a community. There is no less a responsibility on social workers in the formal voluntary organisations to develop their roles in relation to these other systems than there is for social workers in the local authority setting. We certainly do not underestimate the skills that are required to ensure that informal carers are linked appropriately with social workers. There is always the danger at the one extreme of such carers being 'taken over' or at the other being left to struggle unsupported in caring for an elderly relative. Yet without the informal carers services would barely be viable. The study by the Department of Health and Social Security on community care (1981) makes this point: 'One of the firmest conclusions to be drawn from . . . this study is that the strength of the network of informal support available to people is often critical to the feasibility and cost-effectiveness of community-based packages of care.'

5.11 In view of the fact that we are urging greater use by social workers of informal carers it may seem premature to be hinting at limits to this. We believe it important to do so for no evidence suggests that informal caring can be limitlessly increased. Indeed some studies (e.g. Sainsbury and de Alarcon, 1974, Webb and others, 1976, Holme and Maizels, 1978, Abrams and others, 1981) have revealed an immense burden being carried, for example by families of the mentally ill, for which professional support is needed if their caring is to continue.

5.12 The roles and tasks of social workers in relation to informal carers are likely to fall within the description of facilitating, enabling, supporting and planning, all of which will require the skills associated with direct service provision such as, for example, assessment, communication or counselling. The more effective the informal network the more likely it is to recognise when the specialist role of the social worker must be called into play. To use a medical analogy, we might all help or advise a neighbour with influenza but not leukaemia.

Mutual aid groups

5.13 The variety and range of mutual aid groups is considerable. Some operate through very local networks, others have national or regional networks. Some may even employ social workers or other professionals while others are extremely guarded in the links they have with professional social workers. Their passion, partiality and specialist concern may well be their great strength – which is not always easy for those in local authorities who are compelled to have a broader perspective. The potential of their contribution should certainly not be underestimated. It would be hard to conceive for example of the development of alcoholism services without Alcoholics Anonymous.

5.14 The very growth of mutual aid groups indicates the need people have to be in contact with others who have similar problems. There is within that setting the opportunity both to give and receive advice, support and encouragement in tackling the difficulties with which an individual or family may be confronted. The very particular nature of many of these groups – for example the Brittle Bone Society (103), the Hyper-Active Children's Support Group (168), the Leukaemia Society (77) – made it evidently clear how important it was for social workers to be aware of them and emphasised the need to understand the style of each if they were to be used appropriately.

5.15 In many respects the roles and tasks of social workers in relation to mutual aid groups are similar to those referred to in connection with informal carers. It is perhaps worth noting that social workers or other professionals may in some areas have been instrumental in establishing such a group. Community work and group work skills might well be required to undertake such a task. It is one which we would wish to see encouraged. The time, energy and support that mutual aid groups at their best can provide are such valuable assets in overcoming a person's sense of despair, isolation or confusion that every opportunity needs to be taken to develop them.

5.16 When such groups are established, by whatever means, there may well be a supportive role to ensure that the group has, for example, access to any necessary technical information or that it does not founder simply because no accommodation can be found for meetings. The indirect service role here of the social worker could be of immense significance in determining whether the group really survives. The skills that are required are no less 'professional' than those used in direct service work and indeed may often be the same.

Volunteers

5.17 There seem at present to be two quite contradictory demands being made of social workers in respect of volunteers. The first is that the large number of unemployed provide exciting opportunities for voluntary organisations and others to recruit volunteers. The Department of Health and Social Security has issued proposals on this and is making available £4 million. At the same time the Department in its own report on community care states that 'time and money must be invested in matching the volunteer to his work, training him for it as necessary and giving him continuing support'. The 'crash' programmes to recruit volunteers seem in danger of neglecting the findings of the Government's own research indicating the sensitive and skilled operation that is required to engage volunteers at all satisfactorily.

5.18 Volunteers are a distinct group within the whole voluntary sector in that they can offer help through the aegis of a voluntary organisation or statutory agency. They can therefore both reinforce the informal networks and provide additional strength to the statutory services. The interlocking of all these parts is very clearly illustrated by Abrams and others (1981) in the review of Good Neighbour schemes in England. They found that some schemes which recruited good neighbour volunteers had a problem of shortage of clients. What emerged was that the informal carers were operating very effectively, leaving only psychiatric or other complex cases to be helped. The volunteers, lacking the training and skills of the social workers which they saw as needed, felt unable to tackle these. For this and other reasons, some schemes were not therefore able to use the volunteers recruited. We mention this because it would seem damaging in the extreme for schemes currently aimed at the unemployed then to have to face the latter with the news that there were not even opportunities as a volunteer.

5.19 We do of course acknowledge that the volunteer cannot be stereotyped as untrained, inexperienced and unreliable. On the contrary, with unemployment so high and retirement occurring earlier in people's lives, volunteers could be highly trained and experienced. Sometimes, therefore, volunteers will be able to deal with more complex situations than a particular social worker. However to date the evidence from such bodies as the Volunteer Centre (153) clearly suggests that professional services have not been renowned for their skilled use of volunteers. The role of social workers in relation to volunteers does therefore require some comment.

5.20 Again the role of the social worker is very much focussed on co-ordinating, assessing, supporting and other familiar features of indirect service work. Nothing essentially new would be required of social workers but as the Volunteer Centre (153) argues, 'what may be "new" is what is required from the agency which is the legitimacy and time for this work'. The organisation and management of an agency, perhaps in this instance the statutory agencies in particular, require some new approaches if consistently good use of volunteers is to be achieved. Holme and Maizels (1978) argued that a major reason for social workers' failure to use volunteers was not an over-professional attitude but rather a problem in defining their own roles and developing acceptable notions of accountability. To do that management has to be at one with the field social workers.

5.21 Nowhere would the need for clear definition of accountability be greater than in the use of clients as volunteers. We do not feel that clients should be seen simply as recipients of a service, therapy or care. It is important that they are all regarded as potential 'volunteers'. We note with interest and enthusiasm the attempts of organisations like Community Service Volunteers to find openings for the service of those who have been treated for most of their lives as if they had nothing to give. In this connection, we feel that segregation of clients into age-groups or categories may emphasise their frailties or needs and mask their potential contribution to other groups of people. An elderly person may have plenty of time to give to younger people, for example, but this will be difficult to achieve in a residential home for the elderly. Teenagers may have energy and ideas that could enliven the lives of some of the elderly, but segregation will prevent their enthusiasm being directed appropriately.

5.22 It is vital of course to see volunteers within their own context and system of networks in order to support them in tasks they can do there. Too often volunteers are taken out of familiar situations and groups in order to be used by a social worker somewhere else. This may be beneficial to many, but it may also weaken the original networks. Instead of recruiting volunteers haphazardly, social workers need to look for them where they are wanted in order to supplement existing networks and systems of care.

Formal voluntary organisations

5.23 We received a considerable amount of evidence from this part of the voluntary sector. It is these organisations which are concerned with the roles and tasks of social workers as employees.

5.24 There is a temptation – which we believe should be avoided – for the larger, formal voluntary organisations to model themselves on the lines of the statutory organisations. Rather, one virtue to which they can realistically aspire is avoidance of the negative features of local authority bureaucracy. But Hadley and Hatch (1981) are being practical and realistic when they question 'whether the unreliability and unevenness of the presently fragmented and marginal voluntary sector in this country can be overcome without it assuming the negative bureaucratic features of the statutory system'.

5.25 A social worker in a voluntary organisation experiences different opportunities and constraints from one operating in a local authority setting. However, there is little in the evidence to suggest that the roles and tasks of the social worker in voluntary organisations are essentially different from those in the statutory sector. The National Council for Voluntary Organisations in their evidence (123) list six types of activity common to both settings, 'problem management, advocacy, information-giving, therapy, tending, development'. These are very similar to the tasks we outlined in Chapter 3. There will, however, be differences between the two sectors in the emphasis given to particular activities, and perhaps in the way in which they are carried out. Again it is the context or setting in which the social worker operates that is the crucial factor. Some of the evidence (320) from clients showed that they could distinguish between voluntary and statutory settings and did not necessarily attribute resultant differences in work to the quality of individual workers.

The watchdog or independent role

5.26 Voluntary organisation social workers, like the organisation itself, will often, quite properly, be observing 'critically, both central and local government and pressing for change through creative conflict' (258). They will frequently find themselves engaged in debate or conflict with a number of departments or organisations responsible for particular services which affect their clients (e.g. social services, housing, the Department of Health and Social Security, health authorities, schools). The extent to which a family's life is determined by local authority and statutory services is often underestimated. In a run-down inner city area for example, the school, careers service, job centre, social services department, council housing department, and borough engineer will impinge on a family's life far more than on a family in an affluent suburb. Local authority social workers can be seen by clients as part of the 'system' which has produced a hostile and unresponsive environment, especially if they have to justify unpopular policies. In such a situation the attraction of a non-local authority social worker becomes clear. It does also raise the question of how critical an organisation can be when its main source of funding is the local authority and we return to this issue when we look later at the importance of partnership between voluntary organisations and local authorities.

The specialist role

5.27 Many voluntary organisations are set up to work with a particular client group, and social workers employed by these organisations will acquire special knowledge and skill in working with such clients.

5.28 Within social services departments there is a degree of specialisation in particular age groups, in residential or field services, and in clients with special needs; but we frequently had it brought to our attention in the evidence that clients expected social services department social workers, most of whom carry out generalist as well as specialist tasks, to have more specialist knowledge than they possessed or were every likely to possess. Even a walking compendium would have been hard-pressed to provide information on every subject mentioned to us. While there are clear limits to the degree of specialisation which workers in a social services department can undertake, voluntary organisations are often set up for the specific purpose of responding to the special needs of a particular minority group.

5.29 A good example of this need to specialise was given to us by the Muscular Dystrophy Group of Great Britain (179). This group had found local authority social workers 'ineffective' in helping the parents of boys suffering from Duchenne muscular dystrophy in that the cases were 'closed' after practical help had been provided and at best they had had a series of one-off visits by different social workers. The group are therefore 'in the process of expanding their own programme of family care and employing more workers to specialise in helping these families'.

5.30 The specialist's role is not related only to client groups however, it relates to the method and style of work also. Self-help groups may choose a social worker, if they need one, primarily because he has experienced the problem for himself. They may want someone who has himself been an alcoholic, divorced, blind, handicapped, or epileptic (for example), and this element of choice on the group's part as well as their identification with the social worker will affect the way in which he works.

The preventive role

5.31 Social work is often said to be too preoccupied with helping people through crises which need never have occurred if suitable assistance (maybe by social security or housing) had been available earlier. It is important therefore that thought should be given to the role of social work in preventing crisis, damage or disaster. Voluntary organisations, without statutory responsibilities, and able, in many instances, to concentrate with specialised knowledge on one minority group, are better placed than most social services departments to concern themselves with the preventive role (112, 120, 209, 239). Much social work in any setting is concerned to prevent further deterioration or difficulties but here we are referring to primary prevention: activity before there is a distress signal. Family Service Units (120) for example outlined the work of 'one unit working specifically on an estate to create supportive networks and greater inter-dependence which has to date resulted in a reduced referral rate from the estate to the local area social services team'.

Innovative role

5.32 While much innovation comes from the voluntary sector, there is also clear evidence that innovation is increasingly common in local authority social services departments, though interestingly it was rarely cited in their evidence to us. In stressing the innovatory role of social workers in voluntary organisations, we are not suggesting it is their sole preserve, but that they may be encouraged (for some it may be their *raison d'être*) to explore situations and to test out new ideas.

5.33 The evidence from the National Council for Voluntary Organisations in reference to voluntary organisations, spelt this out to us unequivocally: 'They can take risks which statutory authorities with their public accountability would often find impossible' (123). For example, Mill Grove, a residential establishment which some members of the Working Party visited, was originally set up to care for motherless children. It now provides support to the families of children, provides day care for local families, is experimenting with elderly and children in the same residential setting, is actively involved in field work in the locality, is helping to develop the local community and has helped a local association to undertake research to assist the statutory services in assessing the needs and resources of the locality. The sheer variety of the innovatory work undertaken by Mill Grove is possible largely because it is in the voluntary sector. It has been able to assess needs in new ways and pioneer new methods of care largely because it is not publicly accountable to a local authority and is prepared to concentrate unashamedly on certain people and a certain area, while leaving local authorities to support others.

5.34 Voluntary organisations have been able to make use of housing associations to provide, in the case of the Peter Bedford Trust for example, ways of enabling very handicapped and chronically institutionalised people to take greater control over their own lives. Other organisations with housing associations have deliberately mixed different needs – the elderly, unmarried mothers, ex-prisoners – and provided support and accommodation for them. Much of this work, as in the development of alcoholism hostels by voluntary organisations, has been done without the need to have residential staff.

5.35 Holman's work (Holman, 1981) on the Edgetown estate aiming to prevent children going into care and to help delinquents is a good example of social work in a preventive and innovative role, that would not easily be undertaken initially from a local authority base. Indeed accounts (e.g. Harlesden Community Project, 1979) of parallel innovative and experimental work within a social services department show how much more management and accountability have to be taken into consideration. The problems that the local authorities have in adjusting easily or quickly to new sets of circumstances may be one reason why voluntary organisations have been able to meet the requirements and criteria of urban aid circulars and programmes (Department of the Environment, 1980) and why 82% of good neighbour schemes were initiated by the voluntary sector (Abrams and others, 1981).

Overview

5.36 While there is much that the voluntary sector can do, no amount of rhetoric can disguise the fact that there are things that the voluntary sector cannot and should not be expected to do. Equally we feel there are things that it can do better than the statutory sector or which it can add to the statutory sector's range. Of these, we specially note the five that follow:

● The voluntary sector provides ordinary people with the opportunity to give their time or their money to help others. It allows an opening for the need we all have to be needed.

● The voluntary sector provides clients and the public as a whole with some elements of choice between alternative services. This is particularly important for social services clients who are often deprived of the choices other people take for granted. Some of the evidence we received made this point clearly (81, 120, 123, 321). The religious or moral preferences of a client or family may be better met by a voluntary than a statutory agency; or it may be possible for a client to seek alternative or independent advice from a social worker outside the local authority.

● The voluntary sector is, or should be, more flexible than statutory services. Whereas the statutory services are bound by the powers conferred by legislation and can be bureaucratic and ponderous in their operation, the voluntary sector may do anything within the scope of each organisation's charitable purposes (and the purposes for which it receives grants or raises money from the public), can take risks, break with precedent, and concentrate on one area or group without taking into account all the repercussions of such discrimination. There is a real sense in which the strength of the voluntary sector lies, as Westland (1981) has pointed out, 'in not being like central or local government'. This is not to claim that it is better, but that it is distinctive.

● Some parts of the voluntary sector may be better placed than statutory services to assist a family as a whole; most volunteers and informal carers and non-specialist voluntary organisations are not constrained by the functional and geographical demarcations which may sometimes inhibit social services departments.

● For some people, though not for all, there is less shame attached to being a client of a voluntary organisation than of a social services department. For those who prefer the voluntary alternative for this reason, it is obviously important for their self-esteem.

5.37 But however strong the voluntary sector is, we do not believe it is realistic to assume that it ever can or indeed should replace the statutory sector. We feel this is important because some had assumed that our Working Party was set up to endorse a view that statutory provision should be cut back and the work done in the voluntary sector expanded. We do not feel there is any 'proper' proportional division of work between the two sectors, but it has become clear to us that the two sectors need each other if any comprehensive social caring is to be developed or maintained. It is the potential complementarity of the two sectors that is so striking to us.

Ethnic minorities

5.38 We shall refer later in the report (Chapter 9) to the particular issues now facing social workers and their agencies in working in a multi-racial society. The Association of Directors of Social Services itself has concluded (1981) that their response to multi-racial communities has been 'patchy, piecemeal and lacking in strategy'. The voluntary organisations have on the evidence available to us not been significantly more responsive on this issue. We know very little about the informal caring systems within ethnic minorities but we do wonder whether at times they may be expected to bear too heavy a burden operating as they are within a different culture. Mutual aid groups and self-help groups seem to be a very strong feature of some of the ethnic communities though we were not able in the time available to learn as much as we would have liked about their style and strength. Such evidence as we have received on volunteers is marked by a singular absence of any reference to volunteer schemes within ethnic communities or schemes that attempt to cross cultures. We cannot generalise from our meeting on one visit two enthusiastic and committed volunteers working with elderly people of their own community.

5.39 Voluntary organisations are potentially in a strong position, in view of the roles outlined above (5.26–35), to pioneer and develop social work with ethnic minorities. However it seems likely that new voluntary organisations may need to be established in order to achieve this. To date the well-established voluntary organisations have not, with a few exceptions, been major contributors to social work with ethnic minorities. Some more recent community-based voluntary projects have been successful. Cheetham (1982) describes the Tooting Project which 'combines educational advocacy, support and recreational activities for young people, most of whom are black, who do not use other established services'. Significantly the author goes on to say that 'it is a sad characteristic of these projects that they are often, for various reasons, cut off from mainstream social services when their approach has much to offer the staff of statutory agencies'.

Partnership between the statutory and voluntary sectors

5.40 The final comment above is yet another reminder of why in this report we are arguing for a genuine partnership between the two sectors based on a realistic appraisal of the strengths, possibilities and disadvantages of each. Our discussion of the roles possible for social workers in some voluntary agencies has suggested that some of these roles may be less easily assumed by local authority social workers and this provides another reason for our insistence upon the need for partnership.

5.41 The evidence was in varying degrees critical of both the statutory and voluntary agencies. When we compared these criticisms they suggested strongly that the characteristic deficiencies of one sector could to a considerable extent be compensated by the characteristic strengths of the other – but only if each sees the other as a complementary service, and if both work together to plan a partnership which is mutually reinforcing. But it is important to underline here the fact that how social services departments see their roles and tasks, and how they operate, will have repercussions on the voluntary sector in their areas. A rigidly defensive social services department will restrict the innovative and critical voluntary organisations; a highly innovative department may well take over some of the traditionally defined voluntary sector work. Because, to some extent, social services departments control the budgets of voluntary organisations and can withhold clients and tasks from voluntary organisations, they will either help to support and develop that sector or tend, by omission or by policy, to undermine it.

The nature of the partnership

5.42 As a Working Party we are urging a movement towards community social work and we are in no doubt that this has significant implications for the relationship between the statutory and voluntary sectors. The voluntary sector is potentially an equal partner with the statutory in the planning and provision of services, but, in our view, the relationship to date between the two sectors could seldom be described as a genuine partnership. It sometimes resembles rather that between statutory master and voluntary servant.

5.43 We do however wish to be both positive and realistic about the voluntary sector. We have noted for example the recent work of

Knight and Hayes (1981) which indicates something of the limits to the potential of self-help in the lives of inner cities. We recognise, as Westland (1981) has done, that 'it does voluntary organisations and voluntary effort no good to attribute to them characteristics which they do not and cannot possess'.

5.44 Most documents concerned with partnership between the statutory and voluntary sectors concentrate on the formal part of the voluntary sector at the expense of the informal caring networks. (This is true, for example, of the report *Working Together* by the Association of County Councils, the Association of Metropolitan Authorities and the National Council for Voluntary Organisations [1981].) In examining the issues we see as vital in any discussion of partnership we attempt to bear in mind the whole of the voluntary spectrum. This reflects our view that the client or clients of social workers must be seen within their total environmental and social context as far as possible and that many of the most significant resources will be outside the formal social services.

5.45 There are, of course, examples of extremely productive co-operation between the voluntary and statutory sector. The evidence from the Restormel Council for Voluntary Service (94) listed a number of combined projects in the provision of social care by statutory and voluntary effort jointly. Unfortunately, evidence suggests that such full-blooded partnership is not as common as we would like to see. It is therefore important to try and examine some of the issues that seem to evoke concern or anxiety on either side.

Joint planning

5.46 Like other local government departments, social services departments often tend to plan things internally before involving the voluntary sector. The evidence from the Volunteer Centre (153) put the point in a nutshell when it insisted that community involvement should be part of the whole planning process, not an afterthought. We recognise that there are real difficulties in this even where a social services department is seeking to involve the voluntary sector, but we remain convinced that no partnership can develop without it. In some local authorities this may call for a philosophical revolution – for to consult the voluntary sector before making planning decisions may seem like, and in fact may involve, a change in the nature of the control traditionally exercised. It may equally call for changes of thinking in the voluntary sector: it is not a unified body and different interests within it may be resistant to partnerships either with each other or with the social services department.

5.47 The report *Working Together* gives some indication of what is entailed: 'Most fundamentally, there is the need to take a broad view of all statutory and voluntary services which impinge on the social services area. There needs to be machinery for ensuring that services can be looked at as a whole, whether across the personal social services field, or client group by client group or both. Through this joint activity the best use may be made of existing resources, and mutual agreement may be reached about priorities for future activities. Consultation arrangements which facilitate an effective form of joint planning are still relatively rare. We consider such arrangements to be essential to effective liaison.'

Distribution of roles and tasks

5.48 Often, because of its statutory obligations, a social services department has the responsibility for deciding who should perform certain roles or tasks. If a child needs residential care, for example, the department must decide whether foster parents, a voluntary child care organisation or a residential unit run by the authority should be used. This distribution is an art in itself and requires planning and openness. If a voluntary organisation is 'starved' of clients it may eventually close down and will probably never be reopened. The result of a local authority policy always to fill its own units first may be to deprive children of the best form of care for them.

5.49 We received evidence that social services departments were ready to hand over to voluntary agencies some kinds of work and not others and that such decisions were not necessarily made in consultation with the voluntary sector. For example, Age Concern (239) told us that they took over 'the social support of the elderly and handicapped in one area because the social services department said they could not undertake the work'.

5.50 Clearly, a rationale for the distribution of roles and tasks is essential but it must be drawn up by all the people involved. At present, social services departments often keep their own counsel and the voluntary sector is often confused about what the division of labour is and why.

5.51 Some departments do have agency agreements with voluntary bodies whereby there is a written contract stating clearly what the grant aid is given for, and the type of service that is to be provided in return for the grant aid. For example, one local authority requires one Family Service Unit to work with 100 families in any one year. There are arguments about how far such agreements fetter voluntary bodies but experience suggests that the explicit nature of the contracts does much to remove uncertainty and potential conflict from the voluntary/statutory relationship.

5.52 If a social services department is reluctant to enter into agreements with a voluntary organisation because of concern about the quality of care or level of staffing it should say so, rather than simply divert clients elsewhere. This applies equally to the largest voluntary organisation and the smallest family or local group.

5.53 We feel that some clarification of the roles and tasks most appropriate to either sector is necessary. In our view, the local authority will usually concentrate on assessment of needs and resources in a particular case or area, and also be involved in standard setting, inspection and the preservation of minimal levels of care. It has a duty to consider the needs of everyone in its area, which is at once its greatest strength and greatest source of potential weakness. The voluntary sector will tend to provide services for particular groups of people once assessment is complete. We would however stress the importance of such assessments using all available local information rather than relying solely on local authority sources of information.

5.54 This distinction is brief to the point of caricature, but it does show that there are (at least theoretically) quite distinct roles and tasks that may be more appropriate for one sector or the other. It seems to us that one of the greatest sources of confusion between the two sectors has been a lack of clarity about their respective roles and tasks. The distinction we have made is however offered only as an example. It is for each local authority to work out with the voluntary sector how roles and tasks are to be shared.

Accountability

5.55 A common reason given for not allowing voluntary organisations a greater say or share in planning and providing social services is that they are not accountable in the same way as the local authority social services department. This is true, but it may be useful to explore a little further the nature of accountability.

5.56 Accountability here has two aspects. One is financial and the other is concerned with democratic or public control. As regards financial accountability voluntary agencies are probably scrutinised at least as closely as are local authority departments as to how they spend the money they have.

5.57 Being accountable to the public is held to be a valuable check to abuse of power, since those responsible for services can be questioned and ultimately dismissed by elected representatives. Those employed in voluntary agencies are accountable only to their managing committees, who may be out of touch with the needs of ordinary people.

5.58 The issue, however, is more complex. If the touchstone is accountability to clients, then mutual aid groups can claim to be more accountable than social services departments. If, on the other hand, general public opinion is being made the criterion of accountability, then social services departments are likely to be more closely in touch than a voluntary organisation particularly dedicated to one client group, and partnership must recognise this.

Equitable distribution of resources

5.59 One of the most intractable problems for social services is to find an equitable way of allocating resources to respond to need. It is compounded in relation to the voluntary sector because it does not necessarily concentrate its efforts in areas of most social need. Voluntary organisations are unevenly distributed for several reasons: they do not see the even distribution of services as a primary objective; in some areas they are not encouraged by the statutory sector; they cannot get supporters or resources in others; they may even be committed to discriminate in favour of their area or client group.

5.60 It is, in our view, important to note that this characteristic is not totally unrelated to the attitude of the statutory sector to voluntary organisations. Organisations like Age Concern, Citizens Advice Bureaux and the National Society for Prevention of Cruelty to Children, which have been encouraged to expand and take on responsibilities, have been willing to aim for a greater evenness of distribution.

5.61 Unfortunately, it is in the areas where the social need is greatest that the statutory services are often most stretched. Despite the Resource Allocation Working Party, Educational Priority Areas and Urban Aid, the distribution of statutory services still does not relate directly to observed need. Indeed as a society we seem remarkably unable to match needs and resources.

Not like with like

5.62 Partnership can imply that both partners broadly resemble each other. As we have seen, this is by no means the case in statutory/ voluntary partnerships despite the fact that the aims of each side may be identical. Organisation in the voluntary sector is sometimes non-hierarchical, boundaries may not coincide with those of local authorities and areas of concern may only partly replicate those of a social services department. Social workers may make a conscious choice that they will work in a voluntary agency and this will affect their attitude to the statutory department. This difference can be a strength in the partnership or can serve to undermine it.

5.63 A good example of the strengths to be found in differences is provided by foster care. Foster parents are not usually seen as employees of the local authority although they may receive financial support over and above that actually needed to provide for the physical care of the foster child. They can be regarded as part of the voluntary sector (though, as in some 'good neighbour' schemes, the concept of 'paid volunteer' comes in). As a result of open sharing and experimenting the potential of fostering has been seen to be far greater than had been realised earlier. A number of schemes – such as the Kent Family Placement Project – are under way. This will never be a straightforward or easy undertaking but the contribution to social caring in Britain is already significant.

The future for partnership

5.64 In this section we list briefly some practical issues which need to be addressed if a partnership of the kind we envisage is to evolve. Behind all of them lies the assumption that both sectors need each other and that neither is automatically the main sector in any particular situation. Local authorities must accept that the services they provide are a drop in the bucket compared to the social caring that goes on day and night, week-ends and year by year everywhere, and we focus below on ways in which they might reorient and reorganise themselves in relation to this vast army of carers.

5.65 Partnership must start with joint planning and joint analysis of the needs which the services and networks are required to meet.

5.66 Consultative and collaborative machinery is required which will allow decision making to be at the very least fully informed by (and consideration given to how it might in some circumstances be shared by), not only formal voluntary organisations but also local self-help groups and other parts of the caring networks.

5.67 The grant-making process of local authorities is by no means always open or clear enough for it to be readily understood by the voluntary sector. This can pose particular problems for new organisations, who may be challenging old methods of working or exploring new needs, and who may be quite reliant in their early years on local authority grants.

5.68 The secondment of staff from local authority to voluntary organisations and vice versa may provide a means of promoting partnership. Where we saw this in practice it clearly had much to commend it.

5.69 Joint research endeavours should be more actively considered particularly in relation to matters concerning informal networks and volunteers where we still know comparatively little.

5.70 Some of the informal voluntary organisations might well be in a position to offer more training opportunities to the statutory services because of their specialist work or their particular methods of working.

5.71 Active consideration needs to be given to the appropriate use of volunteers in a particular area or with a particular type of problem. Joint work needs to be undertaken if volunteers are to be fully used and properly trained and supported.

5.72 A partnership is most critically needed in social work with ethnic minorities and we can only lend our voice to the growing number of reports that highlight that need.

5.73 Written agreements exist between some local authorities and some voluntary agencies and serve to clarify questions of accountability. More use could be made of this method of making the partnership explicit.

5.74 Mr W.B. Utting, in discussion with the Working Party, took this last point further in suggesting that social services departments might wish to consider a system of contracting out services used in the United States and known as 'purchase of service contracting'. The essential difference from the usual arrangement of grant-aided or fee-paid services is the contractual arrangement for the non-statutory agency to supply a specified quantity of service to a pre-scribed standard at a certain price over a period. In Mr Utting's words, 'one of [its] more exciting possibilities lies in reaching beyond the institutionalised voluntary sector to release the service-providing potential of local community groups'. We recommend that this matter be further explored. What is perhaps important to note is Mr Utting's view that ' "purchase of service contracting" would not threaten the public sector in England, but would certainly require a shift in the orientation of the social services department'.

5.75 Clearly the issue of contracting out has implications for the use of the private sector also. We recognise the need for a full discussion and evaluation of this sector in this country but have not, during the course of our work, been able to devote enough time to it to make detailed comments or recommendations. Some members of the Working Party would like to see the Department of Health and Social Security commission research into the private sector to find out more precisely just what its contribution is to social care.

Implications of partnership for the role and tasks of social workers

5.76 The type of partnership we envisage between statutory services and all parts of the voluntary sector has implications for the role and tasks of all social workers, whether they are employed by local authorities or voluntary agencies. This partnership is one aspect of community social work which we describe in Chapter 13. It is only necessary for us to list here some aspects of the role and tasks of social workers which may require re-examination:

● Social workers must have a working knowledge of the extent and resources of the statutory and voluntary sectors in the area or specialist group with whom they work.

● Social workers will need to be skilful in working alongside existing networks in such a way as to strengthen rather than undermine them.

● Social workers will need to be involved as advocates and negotiators in obtaining the resources needed by the more informal parts of the voluntary sector.

● In some areas social workers will need to develop, encourage and support a weak voluntary sector until it can establish itself in its own right.

5.77 If social workers are to carry out these roles and tasks, management in both statutory and voluntary agencies must find ways of freeing their social work staff from what has been called the 'tyranny of the case'. Only if their workload is calculated in other ways, as some of the social services departments have now begun to do, can they promote the partnership we wish to see developed.

Final word

5.78 The voluntary sector is heterogeneous, but that heterogeneity reflects the diversity of the social conditions with which it is engaged. It is an essential part of the fabric of social services and has a distinctive contribution to make. It has its shortcomings. It is also in a good position to comment upon and improve the shortcomings of other services. But as we see the need for a new community emphasis in local authority departments, it seems more and more evident that the voluntary sector (formal and informal) should not be anything less than fully engaged with the statutory services in meeting the needs that each, until now, has tended to tackle in a separate compartment.

SUMMARY OF CONCLUSIONS

1. Without informal caring the social services would barely be viable: but it cannot be limitlessly increased (5.10–11).

2. Social workers need particular skills in developing relationships with informal carers (5.12).

3. The variety of mutual aid groups demonstrates the need felt for mutual support; we would encourage social workers to continue to be active in establishing and supporting such groups (5.13–16).

4. Engaging and using volunteers satisfactorily and within their familiar situations is a sensitive and skilled task; acceptable principles of accountability have to be agreed by social workers and management (5.17–22).

5. Clients are potential volunteers: segregation of client groups may mask their potential (5.21).

6. The role of social workers in formal voluntary organisations differs from that of their colleagues in statutory agencies in emphasis rather than activities: their independence enables them to adopt a watchdog role; they often specialise, sometimes in a narrow field, and have scope for preventive work; they should be encouraged to test out new ideas (5.25–35).

7. The voluntary sector provides an alternative to statutory agencies and is better placed to carry out certain functions, but cannot, and should not, replace them (5.36–37).

8. It is likely that new organisations are needed to develop voluntary sector social work with ethnic minorities; social services departments should establish appropriate links with such projects (5.38–39).

9. Statutory and voluntary services should be seen as complementory and a partnership should be developed between them allowing joint planning and agreed distribution of tasks (5.40–54, 62–78).

10. We recognise that accountability and equity are complex issues (5.55–61).

11. The grant-making process of local authorities should be open; mutual secondment of staff, joint research, and collaboration in developing use of volunteers are commended (5.67–72).

12. More use should be made of written agreements: 'purchase of service contracting' should be further explored (5.73–75).

PART TWO

THE CONTEXT OF SOCIAL WORK

Chapter 6

The economic context

6.1 The terms of reference of the Working Party clearly did not envisage a detailed analysis of the economics of social work, nor an evaluation of its cost-effectiveness. At the same time we recognise that social work cannot be discussed in isolation from current economic realities and priorities. Broadly speaking, we accept the fact that there is no endless pool of financial resources for the personal social services, so that priority setting both outside and within social work is as vital as cost benefit analyses of existing services.

6.2 We have many indications in our evidence that the pressure on social work from those in need is increasing. We argue that social work must hold fast to its commitment to the under-privileged and needy of our society and, therefore, that it must be involved both in securing a level of resources which relates rationally to the provision of a basic minimum standard of service throughout the country and in the determination of priorities between one service and another. But resources which do exist (both in terms of finance and manpower) can, we believe, and should, be used more effectively.

6.3 From 1969 to 1979 expenditure on the personal social services increased from £171 million (an exceedingly low base) to £1,641 million on revenue account, and from £28 million to £86 million on capital account. In real terms the revenue expenditure increased by more than two and a half times; annual capital expenditure in real terms fell in the same period by about 15%. These may seem to be large figures but as Sir Charles Carter was able to point out, in the 1981 Eileen Younghusband lecture, the total spent in the last year of this period was less than half the amount by which annual spending in this country on alcohol *increased* over the same ten years. If the personal social services are satisfactorily to complement housing, health and education it must be recognised that the social services contribution is seriously underfinanced and requires a programme of planned growth until a plateau of basic provision has been reached.

6.4 But the present situation is one in which the struggle is to maintain the existing levels of expenditure rather than to consider the possibility of increase. It follows that increases in future will have to be tenaciously argued and fought for not only by proving unmet needs but also by demonstrating that additional financial resources are the most appropriate means for meeting those needs.

6.5 There are, however, other factors which are relevant to any consideration of future levels of personal social services budgets. First, levels of expenditure on other services, and in particular on housing, health, education, employment and social security, may affect the demands made of the social services – hence the virtues of a coherent strategy for investment and expenditure on all these services are apparent. Secondly, because of the social services' relatively small expenditure now compared with expenditure on other services, a marginal adjustment made to the budgeting of other services without altering the total overall could represent a big difference in that of the social services.

6.6 Claims for maintained or increased expenditure on personal social services have generally been based on arguments from demography and social change, from alleged 'unmet need' and from the policy of successive governments to substitute, particularly for people who are mentally handicapped or mentally ill, care 'in the community' for care in hospitals. In examining these arguments we cannot, at this stage, separate expenditure on social workers, who are the subject of our enquiry, from expenditure on social services generally. Nor can we take into account explicitly the expenditure of voluntary organisations (except to the extent that it is met by local authority grants or fees). We estimate, and will return to the point later, that the staff costs of social workers and assistants and those, whatever their title, carrying out in fact or potentially the role and tasks of social workers in residential establishments and day centres amount to about one-third of the gross expenditure of social services departments. The cost of field social workers and assistants alone is only about one-tenth of the total.

6.7 The number of very elderly people is expected to continue to increase for some years, but after 1990 the total number over 65 is expected to decline. It is of course very elderly people who place the greatest strain on services. In the population at large there has been an offsetting decrease in the number of children, the second main group of social services clients.

6.8 But the real pressure on the personal social services, apart from the very old, comes from social rather than demographic causes. The number of one-parent families is expected to exceed one million by the mid-1980s compared with 570,000 in 1971. Divorces have increased from 27,000 in 1961 to 148,000 in 1980. The number of children in care has increased by 40% since the 1960s. We are only just beginning to assess some of the effects of the present high rate of long-term unemployment and the extent to which it is associated with ill health, family stress and other social problems. The Scarman report has highlighted some of the deep-seated problems of the inner cities.

6.9 Medical progress has made possible a substantial increase in the expectation of life of mentally and physically handicapped people. These and other factors, all having obvious implications on children and family life, have been strongly brought to our attention in the evidence submitted to us. Lastly, the degree to which the very elderly can be kept in the community and the mentally ill and mentally handicapped transferred to the community from long-stay hospitals is governed to a large extent by the resources available and by suitable measures for the transfer of resources from health to local authority budgets. All these factors indicate areas of increasing need and deprivation and it is in this context that a lack of resources dominates much of the daily round of social workers in the field.

6.10 The variation in provision of local authority social services is wide. The figures for gross expenditure planned in 1981/82 work out at just under £46 for each member of the population. But this average conceals a range from £27 a head to £142 a head, made up as follows:

Non-Metropolitan counties	£27 to £48
Metropolitan districts	£28 to £95
Outer London Boroughs	£41 to £91
Inner London Boroughs	£90 to £142

Expenditure is influenced by local social conditions and policies and by variations in the provision of relevant services by health authorities and non-metropolitan district councils, by other departments of the same authority, and by voluntary bodies from their charitable funds. We lack a clear picture of what practical effect the variations attributable to policy differences have. There are opportunities for research here, but we recognise that the variations in social and economic conditions which have to be taken into account are neither unchanging nor readily measured.

6.11 It is not our function to offer any judgement on the level of provision of social services which in present circumstances can or ought to be the aim. But we owe it to those whom we visited and those who gave us evidence to say that nowhere did we get the impression that services were being provided irresponsibly and that everywhere there is evidence of unmet need, some of it we believe urgent. It is also clear that throughout the country local authority social services departments are conscious as never before of the need to keep to budgets and to control all areas of expenditure. Thought and experiment is widespread in seeking ways to deploy limited resources more effectively. We have no doubt that additional resources could be used to the immediate benefit of many disadvantaged and weak members of society. Many of us, as individuals, feel that additional resources would be better so deployed than on alternative uses. But we believe, and we think most local authorities would agree, that there is continuing scope for improvement of services within existing resources.

6.12 Moreover, there is, we believe, scope to bring new resources into play and make existing resources go further through imaginative strategies already pioneered by many local authorities and voluntary bodies to extend, for example, the scope and use of foster homes (not solely for children), group homes, Intermediate Treatment, warden schemes and community groups of all kinds.

6.13 The National Council for Voluntary Organisations suggested to us (123) that wider use of voluntary organisations, supported by grants or other payments from public funds, and of voluntary workers would help existing resources to go further. We have discussed the role of the voluntary sector and the development of partnership between voluntary and statutory services in Chapter 5. We believe there are some things which voluntary organisations can do better then statutory agencies – and some things which they can do which the latter cannot. And they do in practice provide some services more cheaply. There is scope for greater use to be made of voluntary agencies but there is, we believe, a delicate balance here and it cannot be assumed that the voluntary sector can undertake more than a limited part of the total burden.

6.14 Many of the financial resources in the social services have to be converted into people and expertise or into bricks and mortar before needs are met. For this reason, we stress in our report the importance of bringing into play the full potential of individuals, families, groups and neighbourhoods in the caring process. We see the use of volunteers as one aspect of this, particularly in residential and day services. But we do not see volunteers and neighbours as the panacea for all the problems brought to the social services. That they have a vital part to play we do not doubt, but we believe that to be fully effective there must also be good assessment, planning, preparation and support. In stressing the potential of ordinary people and communities, therefore, we are not talking about care 'on the cheap'. (We refer to the use of staff other than social workers to carry out tasks more usually performed by social workers in Chapter 3.)

6.15 We are recommending changes in the direction of social work and it is only right that the economic implications of these changes should be explored. In those parts of the country in which a community orientated organisation of social services departments has to a greater or lesser extent been adopted the resource implications have not yet been fully measured. To do so is an extremely complex task. It may be that initially local authorities who switch to the more preventive strategy which we recommend in Chapter 13 will meet an immediate increase in resource requirements to enable increased attention to be given to indirect work while the existing burden of crisis intervention and statutory activity is, as it must be, borne. But even in the short term new resources brought into play as a result of a redirected strategy and expenses saved by avoiding an extra burden of institutional care have to be brought into the calculation. Furthermore we are convinced that our strategy must be adopted in the medium term simply to help to cope with mounting needs. Thus we believe that it is possible to follow our recommendations without a large injection of extra resources provided that change is carefully planned by the reorganisation of existing manpower and increased delegation of responsibility by senior management to local areas and sub-areas, providing consequential savings in head office overheads.

6.16 In addition we would make the following points:

● In believing that the existing resources can be used more effectively, we point to the fact that social work experiments since the Seebohm Report and particularly in the last few years have yielded alternative strategies and methods.

● Second, in recognising the links between social work practice and political, economic and structural decisions, we realise that some economic interventions may be better made in services like housing. We cannot simply endorse increased aid for social work if it is at the expense of other services, deficiencies in which may impose further burdens on social workers.

● Third, we do not believe that the use of community networks can replace formal social work. These networks are not alternatives but partners in the caring process.

● Fourth, we do not see social services simply accepting the way the current financial cake is cut. In dealing with the poor and the deprived, social workers and their organisations will always be engaged in a struggle for more resources for their clients.

● Fifth, any additional resources may need to be allocated in a new proportion between the statutory and voluntary sector.

6.17 It is in the overall economic context sketched in this chapter that our recommendations made in this report are partly to be judged.

SUMMARY OF CONCLUSIONS

1. Personal social services are not adequately financed satisfactorily to complement other services (6.3).

2. A coherent strategy for investment and expenditure on social services generally is needed (6.5).

3. Social, even more than demographic, changes are exerting pressure on the personal social services (6.8); medical and health policy developments add to them (6.9).

4. There are opportunities for research into the effects of variations in levels of local authority expenditure (6.10).

5. There is scope for more effective deployment of existing resources and for constructive use by the personal social services of additional resources (6.11); social workers, by reason of their commitment to the disadvantaged, will always struggle for more resources for them (6.16).

6. Some wider use of voluntary organisations is possible but they can undertake only a limited part of the total burden (6.13).

7. Bringing into play the full potential of ordinary people and communities is not a means of providing care 'on the cheap' (6.14).

8. A community-oriented service may initially demand increased resources but will bring new resources into play and make savings in some categories of expenditure. It is the only way in which we think it possible for the personal social services to cope with mounting need. If changes are carefully planned a large injection of extra resources will not be needed (6.15).

Chapter 7

Social policy and the development of social work

Introduction

7.1 Having set the economic scene, we attempt now to say something about the social policy which has provided the immediate context for social work and lay out the broad policy approaches that may determine its role. We do not go into great detail because this was not our brief, but we could not ignore social policy because social work cannot be defined, understood or performed without reference to it.

Social work in industrial societies

7.2 The provision by statutory bodies, or by voluntary organisations under agency arrangements, of social work and of social services is a feature of all complex industrial societies. These services, discharging everywhere very similar functions, have emerged over time in response to a variety of human needs which were judged not to be met adequately for all people by self-help or informal mutual aid, by charitable organisations, by purchase within the powers of those affected, or by other established public services.

7.3 The provision of personal social services in any society will reflect particular views about what ought to be the relationship between collective provision and individual forms of self-help; what ought to be the scope and policies of other services; and who ought to qualify to receive these services. These issues of balance and degree arise in all industrial societies. No such society denies the need to make collective provision. Nowhere is individual self-help entirely disregarded. In between the two extremes there is a range of different policy options, and what happens in England and Wales at present is a reflection of political and public priorities which are not inevitable or immutable.

Three approaches to social policy

7.4 In examining social policy as a background to our consideration of the role and tasks of social workers, we made a distinction between three broad sets of assumptions about the relationship that should hold between the state and those of its citizens with social and personal needs which they cannot meet from their own (or their families') resources.

7.5 We called the first the **safety-net approach**. This holds that individuals, families and local communities are (and ought to be) the primary source of social care. State provision should be kept to the minimum, complementary to what informal networks in the community provide, lest it undermine both their capacity and their moral resolution to 'care for their own'. Indeed, the less the state interferes in any aspect of its citizens' lives, the more likely it will be that the 'free market' economy will create sufficient wealth to enable most people to make provision for their own welfare.

7.6 Public services to the needy will therefore be limited to the rescue of casualties who fall through the net of family and community self-help and whatever charitable bodies supply. Since needs are assumed to be caused by personal rather than structural deficiencies, any provision made will be spartan, to deter people from resorting to it save as a last resort. 'Social work' will be a matter of separating the deserving from the undeserving and rationing provision of services, with no scope for social planning or advocacy of policy changes. Some such set of assumptions, historically, underlay the Poor Law.

7.7 The second approach we termed the **welfare state approach**. Its fundamental assumption is that the state has an obligation to provide comprehensive services to respond to the problems of poverty, old age and disability whatever their cause. All citizens have a right to these services – and should not be left to depend on informal, voluntary or private provision, which might operate unevenly and inequitably. There may be insurance schemes giving individuals some personal responsibility for such provision, but state-sponsored collective action is essential to tackle the root causes of problems, and make adequate provision for those in need. Self-help is not necessarily spurned, but is seen as supplementary to state-provided services.

7.8 There are many possible variants of a policy based on these assumptions. We outline two of the most obvious. The first prescribes that the state should be the provider; resources are firmly channelled in the direction of the public services, with voluntary organisations and informal community networks left little part to play. People would have a right to expect their needs to be supplied but would have little say (save through the electoral system) in how services should be run. Income-maintenance services would be maintained at a generous level. Social workers would be free to specialise in intensive counselling and would tend to be highly professional and specialist. In practice, such a policy has never been systematically pursued nationally in England and Wales, although it has not lacked advocates.

7.9 The second variant, while committed to comprehensive personal social services, available to any citizen on proof of need, favours a partnership between state provision, the services of voluntary organisations, and the self-help initiatives of local communities. The state is in the lead and controls most of the resources, but other providers and clients are to be consulted about the way services are run, and involved to some extent in decision-making. Community self-help is to be encouraged, and some resources devoted to its development. Stress is laid on public accountability, and public servants take the blame for failures or defects.

7.10 Under this policy variant social workers are expected to identify and respond to a wide range of needs. They have both generalist and specialist roles to perform, but may have little influence over the policies and organisational structures of their employing agencies. Some such variant of the welfare state approach has been the predominant policy adopted by successive governments broadly since 1948, and more particularly, in its application to the personal social services, since the Local Authority Social Services Act of 1970.

7.11 The third approach to social policy might be termed the **community approach**. This assumes that lay people have more potential, ability and commitment to care for each other than is assumed by the welfare state approach. Power and decision-making in social services ought to be devolved as far as possible to local communities. Skilled social work would continue to be necessary, but policy would aim, first and foremost, to give informal local networks resources and support where they existed and develop them where they were weak or non-existent.

7.12 The second policy variant of the welfare state approach is in sympathy (as the Seebohm Committee certainly was), with the view that local communities should share in decision-making about social services provision. But a thoroughgoing community approach would entail a greater decentralisation of social services and of control of resources than was contemplated by the legislation following the Seebohm Report. Social workers would need to be closely in touch with, and have detailed knowledge of, the local communities they serve. Their primary task would be to motivate others to care, and to enable them to take part in the caring process, rather than to take on themselves the responsibility for action and intervention. They would be accountable, through mechanisms devised at neighbourhood level, to the people they served and only secondarily to any representative organ of government. Specialist services and personnel would continue to be needed but as resources to the front-line social workers (rather as hospitals provide specialist back-up to general practitioners in the health service).

The development of personal social services 1948–68

7.13 From 1948 provision by local authorities in England and Wales of services under the legislation which superseded the Poor Law (the National Health Service Act 1946, the National Assistance Act 1948 and the Children Act 1948) was the responsibility of separate committees and departments – the children's department, the health department and the welfare department (or a combined health and welfare department). Social work functions developed quickly in children's departments where, from the first, assessment – the sizing up of sensitive situations and relationships – was essential to the department's work, much more slowly in the other departments. But from the early sixties onwards, the thinking of those concerned with social policy locally and centrally was increasingly influenced by the conviction that services should be designed to enable people in all age groups to continue, wherever possible, to live in the community rather than in residential care. The services needed by adults living in the community were predominantly practical services – home help, meals on wheels and aids and adaptations for the physically handicapped. But it was realised that skilled assessment and, for some, counselling, were required also and this was where formal social work was seen to be needed. Although social workers constituted a minority of the staff, even in children's departments, they were seen as the key workers in implementing community care policies.

7.14 With services organised in separate departments, there were difficulties about the distribution of resources; the departmental divisions led to over-narrow assessment of problems and definition of responses. Different officials operating incompatible policies might visit the same family, ignorant of the involvement and plans of others. Individual people were not seen sufficiently as part of their family and social context. Clients and families found the organisation a source of confusion, and those referring people for help were often unsure whom they should be approaching. There were gaps and also duplication in the services provided.

The Seebohm Report and the developments that followed

7.15 It was against this background that the report of the *Committee on Local Authority and Allied Personal Social Services*, under the chairmanship of Mr Frederic (now Lord) Seebohm, was published in 1968. Among the committee's recommendations were the following proposals:

● 'A new local authority department, providing a community-based and family-oriented service, which will be available to all.'

● 'In general the social service departments should be administered through area offices, serving populations of between 50,000 and 100,000. Each area office should be controlled by a senior professionally trained social worker with a grasp of administrative issues and wide powers of decision.'

● 'As far as possible a family or individual in need should be served by a single social worker. Decisions on whether to involve other social workers . . . should be taken by the social worker primarily responsible . . .'

● 'A unified department will provide better services for those in need . . . it will ensure a more co-ordinated and comprehensive approach and . . . should be more effective in detecting need . . . we can and should encourage those who need help to seek it.'

● 'The maximum participation of individuals and groups in the community . . . is essential . . . It may be fruitful to experiment with new forms of bodies advisory to the area office . . . including as members local councillors, direct consumers of the services, and voluntary workers.'

● 'The social service departments and the voluntary organisations should ensure genuine consumer participation, and help the spontaneous development of neighbourhood interests and activities in meeting need . . . the . . . department should be involved in social planning and . . . must become a focal point to which volunteers can offer their services.'

7.16 Despite the scale and cost of residential provision by the local authority welfare services (then, as now, far outweighing field and domiciliary provision both in financial outlay and in numbers of workers employed), the report, reflecting the thinking of the time, has relatively little to say about residential care, and only the briefest of references to the contributions social work has to make in the residential setting. The report takes it for granted that the most important aspect of the personal social services is social care in the community, and that 'field' social work is the key instrument for ensuring its provision. As we note in Chapter 4, this view of the respective importance of fieldwork and residential social work is still prevalent.

7.17 The organisational recommendations of the Seebohm Committee were broadly given effect by the Local Authority Social Services Act 1970. The new, large departments, under statutory committees and with the appointment of directors of social services required by law, were able to attract resources both to identify needs and to respond to them. There was a rapid increase in local authority expenditure on the personal social services – an average of 10% or more per year in real terms for the first few years. Managers were initially preoccupied with the reorganisation and structure of departments and priorities for allocation of resources rather than matters of social work practice. The upheaval caused by the structural changes and the rapid expansion of services affected the morale and pattern of work of social workers. Many of them were subject to abrupt change, almost overnight, in their workloads, as departments interpreted the Seebohm Committee's view that, as far as possible, an individual or family in need should be served by a single social worker as requiring early abandonment of former specialisms. The notion of a generalist social worker was seized upon and put into practice, rather than a notion of a generalist team.

7.18 In 1974 both local government outside London and the health service were reorganised. Health service social workers were transferred to the employment of local authority social services departments. During all this time, the volume of work that fell to departments increased markedly. This was partly a result of increasing public expectations, partly because the new departments sought to explore unmet needs, and partly because new legislation laid additional duties on local authorities.

7.19 Apart from the obvious direct effects of these factors, certain other processes were set in train that have left their mark on the services and their organisation today. The new recruits for the expanding number of social worker vacancies were young by comparison with many of their clients and of their colleagues in other professions: this has left an impression of youth and inexperience that still persists despite the changes we note in Chapter 2. The expansion of departments meant that many social workers were rapidly promoted to positions of supervision or management: the management training and experience available to departments was limited. These promotions meant that social workers in immediate contact with clients tended to be the less experienced or the less able. The range of clients' needs and situations these social workers encountered was daunting. Many had specialised in working with children but were now expected to cope with elderly, mentally ill, and mentally or physically handicapped people. Some of the new tasks they were expected to perform, like arranging provision of a stair-lift in the home of a handicapped person, hardly seemed to be formal social work, but often required specialist knowledge they did not possess. All in all, it is no wonder that social workers, clients and the public have been puzzled at times about the roles and tasks of social workers and questioned their ability to perform them all adequately when they were described.

7.20 From the middle of the 1970s, the economic climate within which the social services operated began to change. There were cut-backs in planned programmes of expenditure in many central and local government services. With rising inflation, the voluntary sector felt the pinch too. It became clear that the vision of a generously funded service continuing to expand (actually built into the local authority ten-year plans in 1972) would not be realised in the near future, if at all. In his inaugural lecture as Professor of Social Work Studies at the London School of Economics and Political Science, Professor Pinker (1981) summed up the drastic change in attitudes and practice this was to cause: 'The coverage of the personal social services is profoundly affected by fluctuations in the coverage and funding of every other major service. As times have grown harder . . . the personal social services, once envisaged by the Seebohm Report as the last major addition to a generously funded system of social welfare, have been transformed from a first resort to the last ditch.' Not only has the expansion of the personal social services slowed down, inflation and tougher-minded policies by other public services have led to an increase in the number of people with financial problems coming to social services departments.

7.21 The combined pressures of an unfavourable economic climate and growing demands have rendered local authority social workers sometimes incapable of meeting the authority's statutory obligations, let alone pursuing discretionary powers. (*The Study of the*

Boarding Out of Children, DHSS 1982, showed, among other things, that minimum statutory requirements were not always being met.) This has had a damaging effect on the image and morale of social workers. They have come to be, and be seen, more as withholders of resources, than as distributors; nor have they any clear criteria for making decisions about who should receive and who be refused service. Is a child at risk of physical or emotional harm, for example, to have priority over an elderly person needing full-time care? The decisions made often have to be based on subjective and arbitrary criteria. The fact that they have to be made at all is at odds with the social policy endorsed by the Seebohm Committee that social services should be available to all.

7.22 More recently, the general increase in unemployment threatens to bring additional complex problems to social workers. In times of full employment social workers are in touch with a high proportion of the unemployed – the very reasons which make it difficult for them to find work, acute mental illness perhaps or multiple family problems, bring them to social workers. But when unemployment rises, many with less acute handicaps or social problems face the same difficulty and cease to be able to manage for themselves. It is not in social workers' power to restore the morale of neighbourhoods where unemployment is particularly high, but they must expect to be called on to play an increasing role in the support both of individuals and families and of local communities.

Social policies and the 'political' role of social workers

7.23 Some of the confusion now felt about the role and tasks of social workers stems from a lack of clarity and certainty in our national social policy. We have slowed down the expansion of social services without necessarily accepting some of the implications. We may have as our aim a service available to all in need, but we expect it to be quietly rationed. We may wish to think that we have left the Poor Law behind us but fail to see the stigma and selectivity which for many are the practical realities of social services and social work. We talk in terms of client groups and thus disguise the relative poverty that unites almost all who seek social work assistance.

7.24 Social workers are operating under a social policy which is in theory a variant of the welfare state approach we outlined earlier in this chapter. In practice, as we have seen, they often feel that they are operating much more like a safety net. This is bound to cause confusion and resentment both inside and outside formal social work.

7.25 The confusion is compounded by uncertainty, and dispute, about what we hold to be an integral part of the role of social workers, a 'political' role. It is sometimes argued that social workers employed by local authorities can, as social workers, have no such role: they are to take existing political, economic and social structures and policies as given, and carry out the tasks for which they are employed, counselling those in need so as to help them to adapt to the situations in which they find themselves. It is assumed that political issues are for elected members, campaigning for policy changes should be left to pressure groups and political parties, and there is no place for such campaigning by social workers or their departments.

7.26 Many social workers see, however, links between social policies and the problems clients bring, and are inclined to question underlying structures, not because they see every problem as structurally caused but because there seems very often to be an intertwining of personal and structural causes. Since one of the things social workers are employed to do is to help their clients, they see it as their duty, if they find that institutions or policies are working to their clients' detriment, to seek to change them and, in particular, if their employing authority is pursuing policies which seem harmful to their clients, to make this clear. Their relationship with their clients depends on trust and this will be dissipated if they are seen by clients as unquestioning servants of what is regarded as a hostile authority.

7.27 It is not the role of social workers, or of social services departments and voluntary agencies, simply to accept things as they are and work silently with individuals and families. Social workers are working with the poor and disadvantaged; they are uniquely placed to assess the effects of social policy on the lives of such people; what is more, they are one of the few voices such people have with access to any corridor of power. Social workers would be failing in their duty if they did not speak out in the light of their personal knowledge and the evidence amassed from contact with such people, challenging, when in the light of this evidence they need to be challenged, policy decisions or the way resources are allocated. This 'political' element of their work is, therefore, an integral part of the whole. Likewise, departments and organisations would be failing if they did not provide, and seek out, channels through which the knowledge and experience of social workers could be brought to the attention of those who take decisions. Certainly it is for social workers to implement organisational policies, but they need also to be influencing them if consistent patterns of social care planning for the benefit of clients and communities are to be developed.

7.28 We would urge elected members to recognise this 'political' element of social work and to ensure that social workers have channels open to them within the departmental organisation, or through the voluntary agencies in which they work, to bring their assessments of the effects of policies forward. We would urge them to arrange also that social workers are given an understanding of the reasoning behind policy decisions, and the way their assessments have been taken into account. They are often in the place of brokers between their employing authority and their clients. They cannot fulfil this role without an appreciation of the factors influencing what may seem to their clients damaging decisions. We recognise that, in the last resort, social workers, like other local authority employees, have to accept the decisions the authority takes or, if they see an unsupportable conflict between their clients' interests and the authority's policy, move to other jobs.

The importance of residential care and of ordinary people

7.29 The lack of attention paid to residential care both before and after the Seebohm Committee reported, should, in our view, be balanced now by a greater realisation of its importance and potential. There are good historical reasons why residential care has been regarded as a last resort. The workhouses are still part of the living memory of many elderly people. The potential which residential services possess ought now to be examined in detail. They need to be poised ready to assume wider responsibilities and ranges of work as policies relating to care 'in the community' (as opposed to hospitals) for yet more elderly, mentally handicapped and mentally ill people gather momentum.

7.30 It has sometimes been assumed that the services social workers provide to clients all require specialist skills and knowledge if they are to be delivered accurately and effectively. This has militated against recognition of the valuable resources in ordinary people and in community networks. Clients themselves may be resources. If every client, family and social problem is seen as a need requiring formal social work help or intervention, social workers will always be expected and expecting to do too much. If, however, social workers see and draw out the potential in others, their ability, in conjunction with others, to respond to need will be enlarged.

SUMMARY OF CONCLUSIONS

1. Policies for the provision of personal social services and the role of social workers reflect wider social policy assumptions (7.1–3).

2. Three broad approaches to social policy can be distinguished – a **safety net approach**, a **welfare state approach** and a **community approach** (7.4–12).

3. The organisational changes following the Seebohm Committee's report and subsequent developments led to social workers' being faced by a daunting range of tasks (7.15–19).

4. While in principle current social policy follows a **welfare state approach**, resource constraints and growing demands have made social workers feel they are operating much more like a **safety net** (7.23–24).

5. The resulting confusion is compounded by uncertainty about the 'political' role of social work (7.25–27).

6. Elected members should recognise the 'political' element in social work, providing channels for social workers to make known their assessments of the effects of policy decisions on their clients and to be informed of the reasoning behind decisions taken (7.28).

7. Social workers would do well to realise more fully the importance of residential care and the value of ordinary people, including clients, as resources (7.29–30).

Chapter 8

Interactions with other services

Introduction

8.1 Some clients, perhaps one in three, approach social workers directly, on their own initiative or at the suggestion of relatives or friends. The majority are referred to social workers by others to whom they have turned for advice or who have become aware of problems which they believe call for a social worker's help or intervention. Referrals may thus be made – and this list makes no pretence to be comprehensive – by doctors, health visitors, housing officers, teachers, officials of the Department of Health and Social Security, police officers, local councillors, clergy, officials of fuel boards or business firms in connection with unpaid debts, or by the courts.

8.2 In their turn, social workers need to work closely with other services, and to make frequent calls on their resources, if their clients' problems are to be resolved. Such collaboration often takes place with the original referring individual or organisation, but (except in the simplest cases) can seldom stop at this. Social work is characterised both by the vulnerability of clients and by the complexity of their problems. Dealing with a vulnerable person with a complex problem often entails the development of a network of collaborative relationships between social worker, client, family, local community, others who may be concerned and one or more of the public or voluntary agencies which have relevant interests or resources.

8.3 In this chapter, our theme is the nature of the interactions between social workers and members of other professions and services. We begin by examining some of the factors that influence the way in which the services relate to each other. We then trace the effect of these influences on the current interactions between social work managers and practitioners and their counterparts in other services, and go on to ask how collaborative efforts are affected by the expectations that other services have of social workers.

Factors influencing interactions with other public services

8.4 Most public services – in particular health, education, housing services and the police – cater for general needs that all of us share in common: freedom from illness, sufficient knowledge to cope with the worlds of work and leisure, shelter and personal security. The supplementary benefit service and the personal social services (including social work) are concerned with particular needs which most of us have either intermittently or not at all: but between these services there is a difference equally fundamental – the supplementary benefit service must observe defined conditions of eligibility for specific benefits, the personal social services are able to look more widely at each individual's problems and what can and should be done about them. These differences raise two difficulties in collaboration between other services and the personal social services. First, the work of other services is geared to deal with the majority, or at least with those who fit defined conditions: their systems cannot, or can only with difficulty, cope with the problems of what are sometimes seen as troublesome exceptions. On some occasions, and it seems at times as a result of internal policy decisions, people in the 'troublesome' category are referred to social workers, not so much for a specific purpose as in the hope that they will somehow cope with the problem. The fact that another service has difficulty in dealing with a problem does not necessarily make it a social problem to which a social worker is the right person to respond. Secondly, whereas the nature of the work to be done in other services is usually clear and intelligible to the public at large, it is much more difficult for either the public or those working in the other services to grasp precisely in what the activities of social workers consist. Referrals to social workers are sometimes made, therefore, with only the haziest notion of what they can or should be able to do to help resolve the problem in hand.

8.5 The various public services developed separately from one another. Some, for example the medical and educational services, have roots reaching deep into the past and have developed a high degree of professional self-confidence, while others are relatively recent creations. Social work is one of the newcomers and social workers remain uncertain about the extent to which it is or ought to be considered as a profession. There is no generally established tradition of collaborative effort between social work and other services, and their interactions may be characterised by mutual wariness, consciousness of differences in prestige and defence by each of its own territory, as much as by concern for the clients they share.

8.6 These difficulties are often compounded by the differences in organisational structure between the services. Doctors, for example, including those employed by health authorities, have a well recognised autonomy and powers to make independent decisions, whereas social workers, if employed by local authorities, are much more subject to control. Because different services have different systems of internal accountability and work allocation, social workers frequently find that their 'opposite numbers' in the other services are at higher or lower levels of seniority than themselves (we illustrate below some of the constraints on effective collaboration that stem from this). The different ways in which the public services are distributed and organised geographically often mean that their boundaries differ – with the consequence that those working in a particular service in one area may have to develop working relationships with two or more groups of workers in another service.

8.7 Collaboration may be further complicated by differences of opinion about the nature of a client's problem. Social workers may differ from a referring agency in their view of it – and the client himself may not agree with either. Such disagreements may give rise to tensions which will spill over into the general relationship between the services if they are not alive to the need both to explain to each other the premises on which their work is based and the constraints upon them, and to understand what each other is and is not able to do.

8.8 Despite the above factors, we have heartening evidence, both from written submissions and from our own visits, of effective, sensitive, and well-planned collaboration between social workers and representatives of other services. There are, however, indications that point in the opposite direction – to instances in which the reciprocity, mutual trust and sense of partnership between equals, that are essential for effective collaboration, are either scanty or absent. We do not intend to imply that this is always the fault of other services or that it is for them to come into line with social workers. Social workers equally may fail in their understanding of the role of other services or in their readiness to trust them as partners. All concerned need to develop awareness and understanding of the factors that influence interactions between them.

Examples of interactions between social workers and other services

8.9 Interactions that are vitally important for collaborative work between social workers and others at front-line level take place between senior managements of their respective organisations. In the corporate management of local authorities, for example, the director of social services and his headquarters colleagues, relying on the knowledge and experience of the department's social workers and other staff, have the task of making the case for resources for their work and for policies throughout the authority which will provide a consistent approach. Staff at various management levels will be engaged in joint care planning and taking decisions on the use of joint finance with their NHS colleagues; in the planning of collaboration between statutory and voluntary agencies; in discussions with other local authorities, with central government departments, with public utilities, to reach agreement on policies and methods of communication which will develop mutual understanding, ease as far as possible the day-to-day working of front-line staff, and contribute to the welfare of clients.

8.10 A social worker may approach others either because a problem has been brought to him which he cannot do anything himself to resolve or because a response could only be provided by the joint action of his own and at least one other service. Similarly, he may be approached, or people may be sent to him, by a member of another service or profession for either of these reasons. Time is saved and misunderstandings avoided if, in making a referral, the referrer is at pains to be as precise as possible about the reason for it.

8.11 In some instances the approach will be for information. A court or a health care team may ask for a report on the social background of someone with whom they are concerned. A social worker may seek a teacher's views on the progress of a child under supervision or in care, or the help of the police in checking the suitability of those who have applied to adopt a child.

8.12 More often the request will be for a service. A doctor may ask for a place in a residential home or the provision of home help for an elderly patient. An official in one of the public utilities may refer someone who is having difficulty in paying his bills for help in budgeting. A social worker may approach a housing officer about someone whose difficulties seem to stem from living arrangements which are in some way unsatisfactory; or a local office of the Department of Health and Social Security to get staff to look into the eligibility for benefit of someone who is having difficulty in making ends meet.

8.13 All the examples given above relate to public services. But there will be approaches to, and by, voluntary organisations and individuals (Members of Parliament, clergy, solicitors). And social workers in voluntary organisations will themselves have much the same range of contacts as those in social services departments.

8.14 For some social workers work is not simply referred between them and other agencies; they are part of a multi-disciplinary team in which work may actually be shared between members of different professions. This occurs most frequently in medical settings where social workers are appointed to work in hospitals, both general and psychiatric, or in child guidance clinics or (in some authorities) are attached to general practices. There are, however, other forms of multi-disciplinary or multi-agency teams which are created when, for example, social workers are attached to voluntary groups, or teams are created of doctors, nurses, psychologists and social workers to provide services for the mentally handicapped. Social workers also make links as a team with other services. The staff of a residential home may have a collective link with the local general practitioner and nursing services and those working in a children's home will relate to schools and youth clubs in a similar way.

8.15 Where social workers are members of a multi-disciplinary team, the relationship with other team members may properly be described as partnership. Our evidence suggested that social workers in psychiatric hospitals and child guidance clinics were considered to be equal partners by the members of other disciplines with whom they worked. We are not sure that these social workers would always agree. But partnership and mutual respect should, we believe, be the basis for relationships between social workers and other services generally.

8.16 There are special circumstances affecting social workers' relationship with the courts. Judges and magistrates have no doubt that there is a role for social workers in providing a service to the courts, submitting objective and impartial social enquiry reports (but not acting as advocates), and giving effect to care and supervision orders with reference back to the courts when and as necessary.

8.17 The relationship between doctors and social workers in general hospitals or attached to general practices is often a good deal less one of equals than that which we are told obtains in psychiatric settings. Historical antecedents are influential here, for much of the work social workers perform has its origin in activities essentially supplementary to the established profession of medicine. Some of the evidence we received from the medical field argued that social workers should in principle carry out all their work under the supervision of doctors. Other evidence from the same source, however, notably that of the British Medical Association (39), looked to social workers to act outside the range of the health professions in co-ordinating provision of services to patients facing difficulties of other kinds, in addition to sharing with members of the health professions in the education of the public to understand the needs of, for example, mentally handicapped or mentally ill people.

8.18 A different kind of imbalance in relationships is illustrated by the interactions between social workers and the education and housing services. The imbalance here arises not from history and professional standing but from the structure of the services. Co-operation between a school and a field social worker who has responsibility for one of its pupils is likely to be in the child's interest; but the head teacher may expect the social worker to approach him rather than (or at least before) consulting the child's own teacher. The head is likely to be a relatively senior officer of his employing authority, the social worker relatively junior. There are awkwardnesses here which cannot always be overcome by goodwill; they stand in the way of easy, straightforward co-operation.

8.19 A paper from the Institute of Housing argued that 'at present liaison between social services departments and housing departments is too often incorrectly balanced, with junior social workers having to consult more senior housing managers'. Housing officers are concerned to apply objective standards of priorities for allocation of houses, and to practise techniques of management which they believe will develop independence in their tenants. Typically a social worker's emphasis on the individual problems of his client may strike the housing officer as over-protective, while the social worker thinks the latter's attachment to objective factors inflexible and bureau-cratic. Misunderstandings are easy, particularly perhaps in non-metropolitan counties where they serve different authorities. Many clients of social workers have housing problems; with the reduction in recent years of housing investment programmes, housing departments are likely to have growing difficulty in resolving them. Many whom they are able to help have other problems, in relation to which housing officers look to social workers for assistance – which they in turn are not always able to supply. But these are resource and organisational issues which individual social workers cannot themselves resolve.

8.20 A similar imbalance of relationships is seen in the interactions between social workers and local offices of the Department of Health and Social Security – though here it is the social worker who may feel that he is dealing with a relatively junior member of staff. The complexity of the social security system adds to the difficulties of these interactions. Many of those who gave evidence to us were very critical of the standard of welfare rights advice given by social workers. We think the expectations of some respondents unrealistic, while agreeing that social workers need to have a broad general understanding of what benefits are available and to know where more detailed advice about an individual client's position may be obtained. We see this detailed advisory role as a specialist task which some social workers may undertake but which may often be undertaken by others, including, increasingly we hope, members of the staff of the Department of Health and Social Security.

8.21 This discussion of the nature of relationships between social workers and various other social agencies may serve to show how complex co-operation and collaboration are. As social workers have particular responsibilities – to act in accordance with the requirements of the law, their employers' policies and principles of fairness and good practice – they are unlikely to, and in our opinion should not, simply provide what the referrer requests. It is, for example, appropriate for them, rather than an elderly citizen's doctor, to decide whether he should be offered a place in a residential home, since the decision rests upon social rather than solely medical factors, though these must be given proper weight; if there is a difference of opinion it is important that it should be discussed with full understanding of the policies and constraints that apply.

8.22 The complexity of inter-agency and inter-professional relationships has often been obscured by the rather simplistic view that all that is required to ensure co-operation on behalf of the client is goodwill. We certainly recognise the value of goodwill, but suggest that it should be seen as only one of many factors where the costs and benefits of co-operation are not necessarily equally divided between the agencies and staff involved.

Comments from other agencies and professional groups

8.23 The evidence from judges and magistrates compares social workers unfavourably with their colleagues in the probation and after-care services, seeing them as less familiar with the law, with the courts' preference for objective and jargon-free reports, with court procedures and with the dress and behaviour they expect from an official witness. It was suggested to us that the appointment of a court liaison officer has proven value in supporting social workers, who may well view court appearances with some apprehension (as they are likely to be involved only occasionally), and in helping the court to reach an understanding of the social services, the place of the social worker and the constraints under which he may be operating. Magistrates have been encouraged by the Lord Chancellor to arrange periodic meetings with social workers at which general issues may be discussed. This provides a means of helping social workers to appreciate the needs of the courts and gives them an opportunity to explain to magistrates the policies their authority follows in dealing with those committed by the courts to its care or supervision. Magistrates also suggested that probation officers and local authority social workers should have some experience of work in each other's setting either during or after their qualifying training.

8.24 Probation officers, themselves social workers, showed in their evidence a keen understanding of the pressures under which their local authority colleagues labour. The Conference of Chief Probation Officers (180) appealed for an end to the division of responsibilities between the two services for children appearing before the courts and the welfare of children of divorced parents. While we recognise the untidiness of the present arrangements, we consider that there may be advantages to both services and to clients from the flexibility that they allow.

8.25 We received a considerable amount of evidence from the medical profession. Some, as we have noted, of our medical respondents consider that social workers should in effect be medical auxiliaries, carrying out treatment prescribed by doctors. This, however, was not the prevailing view. More common was the concern expressed that social workers should more fully meet the conditions which doctors take as the hallmarks of a true profession – full training, an ethical code, a regulatory body, provision for senior practitioners to remain in practice, wider opportunities for clients to choose to whom they should go. They see such developments as the key to fuller partnership, reducing the difficulties of communication of confidential information and enabling social workers to act with greater confidence and independence of bureaucratic or political constraints. We comment in Chapter 12 on the central issue here.

8.26 Medical evidence also suggested that social workers' functions under the Mental Health Act 1959 should be carried out only by specialist workers with experience of this field. This arrangement appears likely to be embodied in law by the Mental Health Amendment Bill which is before Parliament as we write.

8.27 We found the evidence from nurses and health visitors of great interest. Hospital nurses valued particularly the informality with which a social worker could approach a patient and the time he could spare him. Health visitors had a clear view of their role and its priorities and how it differed from a social worker's. Their prime duty, as they see it, is to maintain regular contact with all children under five and their mothers – a preventive duty which would be gravely disrupted if they undertook intensive support of families in exceptional difficulties. Hence their Association's firm policy (116) that under no circumstances should health visitors ever accept appointment by case conferences as 'key workers'. They further guarded their freedom from any responsibility for 'social policing' by their equally firm policy that health visitors should not give evidence in court unless subpoenaed.

8.28 While we understand why the Health Visitors Association takes this stand, we are also aware that many individual health visitors do take on what, in effect if not always in name, are key worker roles in relation to families where children may be at risk of non-accidental injury. This may be greatly to the benefit of the families involved, and in some circumstances essential for the protection of a child; we are concerned that health visitors in such circumstances should be adequately protected and supported.

8.29 The Association of Chief Education Social Workers suggested to us (295) that the existence side by side of two social work services for children was anomalous and inefficient, and that these services should be concentrated within education departments or in independent education social work departments. This proposal echoes a debate that goes back to the time of the Curtis Committee. It was then concluded that responsibility for the emotive task of protecting children at risk – a minority – sat ill with the general responsibility for the education of children. The issue is not within our remit: but we note that either change would be a direct reversal of the notion of a family service on which social services departments were, and in our view should continue to be, based. The National Union of Teachers (228) proposed joint liaison committees between education and social services as one means by which joint planning of collaboration might be achieved.

8.30 Our evidence from the police attributed any difficulties that arose between them and social workers rather to the bureaucratic systems of the two organisations than to the relations between operational police officers and social workers. Their evidence (269) quoted the recommendation of the Royal Commission on Criminal Procedure that 'consideration should be given to placing some obligation on local authorities to make provision for social workers to be available out of ordinary working hours'. We believe that the police themselves, who are always available, often deal with considerable skill with the crises and emergencies to which they are called, but we support their view that some at least of these emergencies would be more satisfactorily dealt with if a social worker were involved. Medical evidence also stressed the need for a twenty-four hour cover by social work staff experienced in dealing with personal and family crises. We know that some authorities have concluded that the occasions are so few that it is uneconomic to provide a stand-by service. A study of the effects should take place. In the light of the comments we have received our opinion is that twenty-four hour cover is essential: crises which demand social work attention inevitably are not confined to office hours.

8.31 Several points were made repeatedly in evidence from those whose work brings them into close and regular touch with social workers. Without exception they argued for specialisation by social workers in a particular range of work. A few, but only a few, wanted the Seebohm unification reversed; most accepted the advantages of the single department but asked for specialisation to be more widely developed within it. Many of those who wrote to us or talked to us made it clear that they set a very high value on a social worker's experience, and regretted the frequent moves of experienced social workers to management duties.

8.32 Of all those who gave us evidence explicitly from the viewpoint of other services and professions only in one submission (149) was doubt expressed that there was a valuable role for social workers. Many of our respondents had criticisms of the way social workers carry out their tasks; they were, it was said, woolly in thinking, diffident and indecisive in action, slow to respond to referrals, prone to disappoint people who came with a practical request by providing 'talk', and to fob off those who explicitly sought counselling with some practical substitute. But we noted that those who were working in the closest relationship with social workers took it for granted not merely that social workers had a particular contribution to make but that this contribution was valuable in its own right and, as submissions said again and again, essential to the success of their own activities.

The impact on social work of expectations by other services

8.33 The evidence has directed our attention to two features of formal social work. The first is a tendency for the staff of other services, when they are faced with problems which do not fall neatly into one of the categories with which they are accustomed to deal, to refer them to a social worker. Sometimes a social worker can do something to help. Sometimes he can pass the problem on to another agency which has powers. Sometimes, for whatever reason, the problem is intractable. But it is clear from what social workers told us that their morale and sense of purpose is gravely affected by the role in which they are thus cast of being the last resort, or as some of them put it 'the dustbin'. The conclusions we reach in Chapter 2 lead us to believe that there is a strong case for other services to have a welfare role in relation to their public and to employ staff – housing welfare officers, for example, and fuel debt liaison officers – to carry it out. They would then pass to social workers those problems only that are particularly complex or require statutory action by social services authorities.

8.34 Secondly, it seems that social workers are very generally expected to take responsibility for the co-ordination of the efforts of all the services concerned when a problem has to be faced which calls for a joint response. Perhaps the most difficult problems of this kind, and certainly those which receive most publicity are those which concern child abuse.

8.35 Decisions about children at risk are now taken in multi-disciplinary case conferences. We consider that such conferences require extremely skilled chairing if the difficulties created by differences of training, rank and legal requirements are to be submerged in the interest of the child. Experience has shown the problems of communication between different professionals and our evidence drew attention to the reluctance in some areas of general practitioners to attend case conferences (we were also told that in some areas such conferences are habitually timed at hours which clash with regular surgeries), and of a tendency in some agencies to seek to shift all responsibility to social services departments.

8.36 It should be clear from the foregoing that the expectations of social workers by those who work in other services are high – in some cases formidable. Whether or not these expectations are realistic, social workers commonly attract more or less severe censure when they are adjudged to have failed. But if the social workers currently in post were to vanish overnight, other services would certainly feel their absence acutely and, indeed, would have to find means of replacing or re-inventing them.

8.37 Evidence to support this conclusion comes from the industrial action in which some field social workers were involved in 1978. Although it was suggested at the time that their absence would not be noticed, this was not the view expressed to us by the staff of services who felt the effects at first hand – hospital and district nurses (57, 246), health visitors (116) and police (269).

8.38 Ward sisters found themselves distracted from their nursing functions by having to carry the burden of arrangements normally made by social workers for the discharge of their patients and the support they needed after discharge – home helps, for example, and meals on wheels. Health visitors became deeply involved in support and surveillance of the minority of families in which children were felt to be at special risk: despite the help of the National Society for the Prevention of Cruelty of Children and police juvenile bureaux, they had to put aside their own basic preventive work. They found particular difficulties, because the facilities at their disposal for the purpose were limited, in coping with the mass of letter-writing and telephone calls this unaccustomed work demanded. District nurses, on the other hand, found their direct liaison with the staff of homes for elderly people helpful and had some regrets about the restoration of the filter through area teams when the strike ended (particularly where social worker posts were unfilled and remained unfilled for some time).

8.39 The police were not the only observers to find it difficult to reconcile social workers' industrial action with their claim to be a caring profession. They were concerned that social workers were not available to act under the Mental Health Act when compulsory admission to hospital seemed desirable, and at the addition to the general flow of social problems which come their way even when social workers are not on strike.

8.40 Voluntary organisations certainly felt additional pressures. Some clients of social workers said that they were disillusioned. Some were glad to have them off their backs. Some social workers felt guilty, but argued that they had struck for conditions which would enable them to maintain the standard of service to clients. Some claimed that having the confidence to take industrial action marked the coming of age of social workers as a profession. Some saw it – despite the lead already given by some hospital doctors, members of a much older discipline – as marking the rejection of professional standing in favour of a trade union structure. It is impossible to reconcile all these attitudes. The differences between them illustrate the uncertainties social workers and others feel about their role and their relationships with their employing authorities, their managers and their clients.

8.41 It seems to us that the social worker's role, whatever the setting in which he works, is one that is essential – essential both to his employing agency to enable it to carry out its obligations, and to his clients to provide them with help, support or control to which they have a claim. The strikes proved that it is possible to get by with substitutes for a period, but only at severe cost to those services with whom social workers collaborate most closely.

SUMMARY OF CONCLUSIONS

1. Social workers and employees of the public services with whom they collaborate should take steps to inform themselves accurately about the scope and limits of each other's work, and develop greater awareness of the factors that influence the interactions between them (8.4, 8).

2. When problems are referred to or by social workers, the referrers should be as precise as possible about the reason for the referral (8.10); there is a case for other services to have a welfare role (8.33).

3. Collaboration between social workers and other services generally should be on a basis of mutual respect; as regards the courts social workers' relationship is that of providing a service (8.15, 16).

4. Goodwill is not enough to guarantee adequate collaboration between social workers and other services. Arrangements for collaboration need to be planned, and factors which affect relationships to be understood and not allowed to give rise to tensions, by both senior managers and practitioners in the relevant agencies (8.9, 22).

5. A study of the effects of not providing a stand-by service should be mounted (8.30).

6. Other services set a high value on specialisation by social workers; those respondents working most closely with social workers regard them as essential to the success of their own activities (8.31–32).

7. If social workers disappeared overnight other services would need a substitute for them (8.36).

Chapter 9

Issues of organisation and management

Introduction

9.1 The nature of the organisation in which social workers work and the way in which they are managed may directly assist or impede the effectiveness of their activities. The shape of organisations needs to be decided according to local circumstances and be capable of adapting as circumstances change, but we wish in this chapter to underline some important general principles. Most of our comments relate to matters which have direct bearing on organisation and management issues affecting social work rather than the whole range of social services.

9.2 Almost all the concern expressed by our respondents about issues of organisation and management came from social workers within the statutory sector. This is not surprising in view of the size and complexity of tasks of social services departments, but it may also suggest that there may be some scope for statutory services to learn from or adapt the management models of some voluntary organisations in the social work field. We are, however, aware of concern in the voluntary field to pay attention to improving the effectiveness of their organisations. The Handy Working Party Report (National Council for Voluntary Organisations, 1981) is an important step in this direction, drawing attention to the need to provide better arrangements for helping voluntary organisations to tackle various levels of problems which can reduce their effectiveness. This becomes particularly important in the light of our argument in Chapter 5 advocating a greater degree of partnership between the statutory and voluntary sectors. If this is to succeed, then voluntary bodies may well have to consider in more detail some of the management issues facing them. Some of the strengths of the voluntary sector that are often cited, such as innovation and flexibility, will only flourish if voluntary bodies have effective organisational structures.

The organisation of social services departments

9.3 We concentrate, however, in this chapter on matters relating to the organisation and management of local authority social services. Social services departments are big business. Collectively they employ over 200,000 people and spend more than £2,000 million per year. The bulk of their activity is directed towards the organisation and delivery of large-scale services and it is not, therefore, surprising that they have adopted hierarchical structures similar to those found in large companies or in other big departments in local government.

9.4 As we noted in Chapter 7, social services departments grew out of the former health, welfare and children's departments of local authorities.

Typically they were organised in divisions each embracing one or more of the main functions they undertook (day services, residential services, domiciliary services, fieldwork, administration, training and research). Fieldwork services generally were divided on a geographical basis, with area offices serving populations of 20,000 or more. But most day and residential establishments continued to serve a single client group. Some fieldworkers continued to work mainly with a single client group and many authorities appointed specialist advisers for their front-line and often inexperienced social workers to consult.

9.5 The structure of departments, as seen by the front-line field social workers and their colleagues in day and residential services, was complex and the lines of authority long. Three themes emerged from the evidence we received and the discussions we had about organisational influences:

● confusion and ambiguity among social workers as to how far they were expected to act on their own judgement, and how far they were simply expected to carry out the orders of their departments;

● a degree of frustration at the complexity of the structure of social services departments, and at the difficulty of getting decisions made or resources allocated;

● a feeling among social workers that their managers neither understood them nor supported them.

9.6 Social workers' feelings of confusion and of frustration arise, we think, in part from a conflict between the expectations which clients and the public have of them and what they find they have the resources of time, and the access to facilities and services, to provide; but also – and this is the issue to be considered in this chapter – from a divergence between the degree of authority, discretion and responsibility they often find themselves perforce carrying in practice and that which is formally delegated to them at the base of a pyramid of authority.

Delegation and decision-taking

9.7 We note that the conditions of service negotiated in 1979 lay down what is required by local authorities of social workers appointed to each of the three levels then defined. And we note that in relation to particular duties, especially dealing with children at risk of non-accidental injury, authorities have prescribed detailed procedures. But, in practice, the circumstances of many clients and the events that bring them to a social services department are not of a kind that can be neatly covered by a job description or a rule book, however lengthy. Judgement has to come into play, and a response fitted to individual circumstances. That is the task for which social workers are employed. They must, moreover, frequently cope with unforeseen emergencies or changes of circumstances of clients which disrupt plans and require immediate action. Many clients feel that agreements and arrangements for services are made as much with the social worker personally as with his employer. This expectation of personal involvement and authority from the social worker results in his bearing a considerable degree of responsibility for his actions, even though it lies formally with the authority itself or with the senior management of the department.

9.8 Policy rulings, however, may require many issues to be referred to higher levels. We note in *Social Work in Conflict* (Glastonbury and others, 1980) a (perhaps extreme) example of a department in which 70% of major decisions in child care cases involve at least four levels in the hierarchy. In some authorities, we understand the chairman and members of the social services committee are involved in such decisions. It is for each local authority to decide whether there are any decisions affecting individual cases which requre the involvement of elected members but we consider that it should be exceptional for them to make the decisions. That is not to say that difficult matters concerning clients should not be brought to their attention.

9.9 The longer the line-management chains, the greater is likely to be the delay in obtaining decisions on issues which may directly affect the welfare of clients. And the higher up the chain an issue is referred the less knowledge there is of the client and the client's circumstances. We recognise that departments have worked hard to improve their lines of communication, but, as a general principle, we believe that decisions about individual clients should be taken by the person best equipped by skill, experience and knowledge of the circumstances. This would suggest that such decisions should not normally be referred above team leader level. We advocate, in other words, the greatest practicable degree of formal delegation to front-line social workers and their immediate managers (in day and residential services as well as in fieldwork) to plan and carry out their work. This is not to suggest that their accountability to senior management and employers should be weakened. Formal delegation of authority will need to be accompanied by measures to ensure that they have a close understanding of the constraints that surround their work; by the development of some form of budgetary guidelines; and by a formal system to enable senior management to monitor what goes on, and by which they can ensure that clients with similar needs are treated with reasonable consistency, that resources are fairly allocated and that staff overstep neither the boundaries of the law nor generally agreed standards of conduct.

Lines of communication, consultation and support

9.10 Greater formal delegation of responsibility and formal systems of monitoring afford a means of shortening lines of communication by reducing the number of levels of decision-making in the departmental hierarchy. They make possible also more immediate consultation between senior management and front-line staff, with greater scope for the latter both to bring their experience to bear on policy-making and to understand the reasoning behind policy decisions which they have to implement and to explain to their clients. It is for senior management to make the policy-making machinery less remote for front-line staff in day, residential and fieldwork settings.

9.11 We believe that there will always be a degree of tension between practising social workers and the organisation which employs them and the public at large. In dealing with some of society's intractable problems social workers are standing between the disadvantaged and delinquent and a society which has mixed or hostile feelings towards them. In befriending delinquents, helping understanding of mental illness, begging for more resources for the elderly, explaining to clients why they cannot receive a service, social workers have, inherently, an unenviable job. The resulting tension needs to be recognised and catered for within the organisational structure. This we believe requires more than the formal recognition of the responsibility social workers carry, and of their claim to bring an influence to bear on policy-making. They need to be confident that they have the trust, support and protection of senior management and employers to operate properly in the emotionally-charged and uncertain situations with which they are called on to deal.

9.12 As we see it, the challenge for local authorities is to find ways to reconcile controls with a substantial and consistent degree of delegation to social workers. Much of the present tension seems to arise from the fact that social workers have a great deal of *de facto* discretion and that they need to have it in order to help people properly, yet they work in a structure in which, in theory, they have little or none.

9.13 Some tension will persist. The broad perspective of elected representatives and that of social workers dealing with the problems of troubled individuals or groups will inevitably differ. But skilled management will enable the causes to be identified and understood in such a way as to be a source of constructive dialogue within the organisation rather than simply a cause of frustration and cross purpose. The challenge for social workers is to use their delegated authority and discretion in the best interests of their clients and work with each other and with other disciplines according to an explicit understanding of respective roles and responsibilities.

9.14 This may appear trite, but we are aware, for instance, that professionalism in residential and day settings is increasing and social workers in these settings will be assuming degrees of authority and responsibility hitherto only held by the field social workers and their line managers. Provided that staff in the different settings have a consistent minimum level of competence, matters such as who decides when a child goes home or to a foster home or who assesses suitability for admission to a day centre will not necessarily be for the field social worker. The decisions may be better taken by the residential social worker who knows the child best or the day centre manager who best understands what the centre has to offer and what its limitations are, but the crucial point here is that all concerned need to know who carries the authority and responsibility and why. These matters should not be left unclear or they will cause tension between the social workers to the detriment of the client.

Risks and safeguards

9.15 In calling for greater delegation to social workers, we do recognise that there are reasonable limits which should be set to this process, for the protection both of the public and of the social workers themselves. Some decisions (for instance in child abuse cases) are so critical that we think that they must always be shared, except in dire emergency; and we would draw a very clear distinction between the independence to be accorded to a very experienced practitioner and the close supervision needed by a social worker newly-qualified. (Some of our evidence indeed, suggested that too much freedom is given to inexperienced social workers rather than too little.) The first safeguard is, we believe, the check and scrutiny that is provided by the team organisation within which social workers operate and the opportunities of consultation which are afforded to them. We return to this point in paragraphs 9.23–25 below.

9.16 The granting to social workers of more formal discretion would seem to carry with it the inevitability of increased risk both to management and to the authority as a whole. Regrettably, the nature of the work of social services departments is such that things are bound to go wrong from time to time and this needs to be accepted by management, elected members, and the general public. We are not convinced that the imposition of rigid hierarchical controls can actually prevent accidents and tragedies: on the contrary, if such controls inhibit good practice or undermine individual responsibility, as we believe they may, it is more, not less, likely that disasters will occur.

9.17 We repeat what we have said earlier, that discretion already exists *de facto* in the hands of front-line social workers. The formalisation of this discretion, if it brings about an improvement in the working partnership of management and practice, should actually improve the quality of practice and hence reduce the risks. It should also reduce the time spent on, and the cost of, procedures to check and control actions.

Social work in the statutory sector

9.18 The problems conveyed to us in the evidence or in discussion are not in our judgement so intractable as to suggest that the solution lies in the removal, which one or two respondents suggested, of responsibility for social work from local government or the abolition of social services departments as such. Indeed, a review of the options theoretically available indicates that there is no more desirable alternative at the present time which provides for access to substantial public funds, democratic control at local level, public accountability, opportunity for joint planning with other services within and without the local authority and a framework for adjudicating the competing claims of agencies, localities and client groups. This still leaves a very wide range of options as to how departments might best be organised to provide effective services to clients.

9.19 Bearing in mind this background we wish to recommend that a review by employers and managers of the organisation and management of social services departments be carried out to ensure that there is a degree of formal delegation, matching the responsibility in practice devolving on social workers and a definition of the accountability which goes with it. The objectives of such a review would be to establish:

● a clear organisational structure with a minimum number of layers of decision-making and maximum possible delegation to front-line social workers and team leaders;

● systems of formal and informal consultation to ensure that the practical problems of operating in the field, the priorities dictated by the clients and the degree of urgency implied by clients' problems are properly understood by management and by those responsible for the social services at the political level and taken into account in policy-making;

● systems of communication to ensure that the fluctuating and sometimes conflicting constraints and demands which exist in the environment which surrounds social work are properly understood by social workers in the front-line; and that they have assurance of management's understanding and support;

● systems for monitoring and maintaining standards, reasonable consistency and fairness, and regard to clients' interests.

Teams and team leaders

9.20 That many social workers do not at present feel adequately supported or protected by their departments, despite existing formal lines of supervision and accountability, was a persistent theme in the evidence we received. We were conscious, both from the evidence and from our discussions that the first-line manager was a particularly crucial figure in the provision of support.

9.21 The role of team leaders and of officers in charge of day or residential units contains a number of different elements. They are responsible for organising and allocating work and for maintaining systems of workload management; providing a link between each team and other teams and agencies (and, in outposted settings, other professional groups); allocating resources and taking decisions, or helping social workers to reach decisions, on difficult issues; they may be practising social workers themselves whilst acting as formal line-managers, ensuring that departmental policies and procedures are implemented. The team leader is thus required to be both a competent administrator and a more competent practitioner than most members of the team.

9.22 We have been told that many team leaders find particular difficulty in combining these two roles and some advocate the splitting or limiting of the role in various ways. In particular it is suggested that the consultation and counselling aspects of the role cannot be combined with 'line management'. While emphasising the high degree of skill and experience required, others would argue that analogous activities and responsibilities are typically combined in other fields of administrative and professional activity and that it would be confusing and ineffective to separate them.

9.23 We referred in paragraph 9.15 to the team organisation in which social workers operate and the opportunities of consultation they are afforded. We would emphasise the importance of teams – working in all settings. A well-organised team, whose members represent a wide range of generalist and specialist skills and knowledge, is far better placed than any individual social worker could be to assess the levels of social need, reach decisions on priorities, and provide any appropriate service – whether to one single client or to a client group. But team work of this kind requires highly skilled and sensitive management if it is to be effective. Work must be distributed among team members, for example, in such a way that the collective resources of the group are available, when needed, to all clients: a considerably more difficult operation than simply allocating one worker to one client.

9.24 In addition to this, the team leader needs to build up in his team a sense of corporate identity, secure agreement on desirable policy changes to recommend to senior management, and ensure that all members of the team are in touch with, and know how to use, other available services and informal helping networks in their local community or otherwise available to individual clients or residents, or to groups among them. There will inevitably be occasional conflicts of opinion both within the team, and between the team and outside people whose collaboration is essential to the team's work; attempts to reach a helpful resolution of such conflicts will be an important part of the team leader's duties.

9.25 The notion of consultation is an important one in social work and involves the provision of expert advice and guidance without necessarily removing the accountability for the decisions made from the social worker concerned. It is, therefore, possible for the consultant role to be carried out by someone outside line management. There is no assumption that the team leader is the source of all knowledge and authority and that other members of the team are merely aides and supporters. Nor is there any suggestion that a team leader should act in some standard, uniform, routine way.

9.26 On the contrary, a central skill of the team leader must be to adjust his role and actions to suit the circumstances. A particular member of the team, or of a multi-disciplinary team in which a social worker operates, may have greater skills or more experience in relation to certain tasks than the social work team leader, who should allow the team to benefit from such assets and encourage flexibility within the broad remit of good management principles. Indeed, it is true all the way up the hierarchy that the greatest social work practice skills will be found nearer the base of the pyramid.

9.27 Some of the evidence suggested that there is an uncomfortable gap between team leaders and higher management and a feeling of 'them' and 'us' which can exist, also, between leaders and their teams. We believe that such negative and in some cases destructive attitudes can be minimised by enabling staff at all levels to participate in, and be properly informed about, key decisions, policies, opportunities and constraints. This will certainly involve regular discussion by managers at each level with those who answer to them, but this is time profitably spent.

Senior management

9.28 We say something in our discussion of social care planning in Chapter 3 about the role of senior managers. Here we must, having regard to our recommendations about delegation, make clear certain implications. First, if social workers in area teams and the staff teams of residential and day units are to operate with increased autonomy, it will be impossible for senior management to continue to hold all the reins of departmental resource allocation. This is, we recognise, a difficult issue, since at all times the management does have a great responsibility to ensure that resources are distributed fairly and equitably. Even if it is not possible to allow social workers to make direct calls upon all resources, it is possible, by such devices as area budgets, to bring more decisions about the allocation of resources down to a level at which social workers can exert a direct influence and carry some of the responsibility.

9.29 Secondly, delegation may be found to give rise to differences in standards of practice and levels of provision. It is necessary for senior managers to retain clear and unequivocal responsibilities for co-ordinating policies and practices and monitoring standards of provision and to be knowledgeable about the range of services throughout the whole local authority area, and beyond, for the client group or function for which each is responsible.

9.30 This is not to say, however, that such a senior manager has to carry line management responsibility for the staff concerned. Nor does he have to be centrally based. It would be possible to allocate the co-ordinating and monitoring function to principal officers throughout the organisation so that, for instance, a manager in charge of all residential and day services for the mentally ill is given a broader departmental responsibility also for this area of work. An area manager may undertake overall departmental responsibility for services to physically handicapped people, leading project teams, keeping abreast of new thinking and developments and initiating improvements in services. In this way expert advice is available to both generalist and specialist social workers and the agency as a whole, without the creation of a large group of consultants or advisers at head office.

A career structure for social workers

9.31 An issue presented to us in the evidence and in discussion was how to recognise and use the skills of those social workers of great experience, skill and expertise who have no interest in (and perhaps no potential for) progressing up the management ladder. There can be no point in turning an excellent practitioner into a bad or irrelevant manager or of losing the more competent practitioners from the field.

9.32 We were informed that at the present time people usually have to leave direct practice and go into management if they are to improve their position and increase their salary. This is clearly undesirable from the standpoint of the individual and the organisation and above all the clients. We consider it is essential to retain mature, experienced people in direct practice. It is entirely credible that some people should spend much or all of their working life as practising social workers and salary scales should appropriately reward outstanding competence in social work.

9.33 It is difficult to conceive of direct practitioners of the kind envisaged solely engaged in their own individual practice although this might be justified in certain cases or situations. Most of them would be involved also in such activities as supervision, practice teaching, research, work in specialist settings, advisory work and contributing to the development planning of the department. Such activities are clearly vital to the quality of service to clients and should attract the same status as equivalent indirect practice and management activities.

9.34 We envisage that such a career structure would enable social workers who met the demanding criteria set to progress in salary and status beyond the current scales. We believe that this is appropriate if more recognition is given to the delegated power and authority highly experienced and qualified social workers should carry and the advantages, to the service, of breaking away from the domination of the traditional hierarchical structures which give so much more status to management responsibilities than to social work practice ones. We hope employers and the Trade Unions affected will find means to move in the direction we indicate here.

9.35 The implications of a career grade for social workers on the structure and organisation of social services departments and voluntary agencies are considerable. The career grade practitioners would obviously need to be accountable to a designated manager but the manager would not need to be on site in the area office, residential or day care establishment, or the detached multi-disciplinary team. The manager or supervisor who is on site could be paid at the same level as, or a lower level than, the career grade practitioner and still be involved in work which directly affects the work of the latter, for example, the overall allocation of work and resources.

9.36 We recognise that the development of such a career structure for social workers may have resource implications. The cost of employing a suitable practitioner will be greater than that currently spent on a social worker. On the other hand, this and other of our proposals (about delegation and minimising the number of levels of authority) would reduce the number of management posts necessary, while the career grade practitioners would be relatively few in number, holding posts only to be filled by candidates who met strictly defined standards of qualification and experience and competence. While, in general, we take the view that first line supervisors or managers are needed for each group of social workers and ancillary staff up to about five of six in number in order to ensure proper supervision and support, career grade practitioners would not need the same ratio of managing staff.

Levels of work

9.37 In large organisations distinctions are inevitably made between the jobs which people do. In social services agencies work of a kind that requires face-to-face contact with clients, or otherwise directly affects clients, is divided according to a number of factors. The volume of work, the requirement for expert or technical knowledge, the type of work and the efficient combination of functions are among the relevant considerations, together with the level of responsibility carried and the degree of difficulty or the routine nature of the tasks to be performed.

9.38 Work coming into an agency may be dealt with by allocation among a group of staff with the same status and designation, for example social workers. Work is likely, however, to be of such a volume and varied nature as to make it appropriate to differentiate between the tasks according to the knowledge, skill, training and experience required to carry them out.

9.39 Different levels and types of work may be identified within different settings and between settings. For example, the nature of the social work coming to social workers in a child guidance setting may require social workers only to deal with it. They will not be doing the most skilled formal social work all of the time, however. By contrast, the volume and range of work coming into a local area office or undertaken in a day or residential unit will be such as to employ different grades and types of staff. These differences are often denoted by such designations as social work assistant, welfare assistant, home help, care assistant, social worker, senior social work practitioner and so on. Some of these designations imply concentrations on lower or higher levels of tasks.

9.40 Differences in levels of work reflect both the degree of difficulty and the degree of personal responsibility carried and the amount of discretion exercised. A care assistant in a home for elderly people might repeatedly undertake, day by day, specific, basic tasks of a fairly routine nature in providing physical care for the residents. That is her primary role but, during the course of it, she may develop a close, personal relationship with the residents and be their confidante. Similarly, the social worker working with a family with multiple problems of child care and living on the poverty line may spend time each day taking the children to school or preparing a meal with the parents. If, however, these tasks have to be repeated over a considerable period of time they might appropriately be handed over to a family aide or home help. In this way the social worker's time may be conserved for specifically social work activities, for example counselling for these and other clients for whom it is appropriate.

9.41 Distinctions between levels of responsibility are not at all clear-cut, however, nor are arguments about allocating work according to degrees of difficulty and complexity. There is a strong tradition of 'one worker, one case' and not all social workers feel that all the less interesting work ought to be put onto others. There is also a limit to the amount of intensive counselling a social worker can do without some relief. Nevertheless, some distinction in work levels is possible and necessary in our view, and this is most practicable where there is close teamwork and an emphasis on 'team responsibility' for cases.

9.42 The National Scheme of Conditions of Service of the National Joint Council for certain local authorities staff contains salary scales which identify three levels of work for the purpose of determining the rate of pay of social workers. The levels are as follows:

● **Level 1** social workers under close and regular supervision are expected to manage a caseload which may include all client groups and all but the more vulnerable individuals or those with complex problems. Such social workers are not expected to make decisions affecting the liberty of clients or in relation to place of safety orders.

● **Level 2** with supervision and advice are expected to manage a caseload which may include the more vulnerable clients or those with complex problems and may be expected to accept responsibility for action in relation to the liberty or safety of clients in emergency situations. They may be expected to concentrate on specific areas of work where such concentration arises primarily from organisational needs and to supervise trainees or staff other than social workers.

● **Level 3** with access to advice and within normal arrangements for professional accountability are expected to accept full responsibility for managing a caseload which will include the more vulnerable clients or those with particularly complex problems in situations where personal liberty or safety is at stake. Such officers are expected to contribute to the development of other social workers. They may be expected to concentrate on specific areas of work requiring more developed skills. They may be expected to contribute to the development of new forms of work or service.

9.43 We are aware of much criticism of the way in which these levels are described and applied but they do suggest an acceptance of differentiation of roles and tasks. Interpreted according to local discretion there are different designations for posts apparently covering a similar range and type of work. The designation 'social worker' will no doubt remain in common usage to cover the general professional role with special designations or additions being used to denote specialist roles such as Intermediate Treatment officer, residential social worker, community worker. (This is not to suggest that all

Intermediate Treatment workers and all community workers are or need to be social workers.)

9.44 We see the logic in confining, as some employing agencies do, the title 'social worker' to holders of the Certificate of Qualification in Social Work. Some of us feel that this may encourage the more careful deployment of limited numbers of trained personnel and would prefer this usage to be followed everywhere. We see, however, that many holders of the Certificate in Social Service, and many members of staff who have neither qualification, in practice undertake jobs which include a high proportion of formal social work. We have not therefore found it possible to recommend that the title 'social worker' should be restricted only to holders of the Certificate of Qualification in Social work.

9.45 Some of us would like holders of the Certificate in Social Service to be able to do a special course or module to convert their qualification into a Certificate of Qualification in Social Work if they wish to pursue a career in which formal social work is to be the dominant role. But the relationship between, and the training for, these qualifications are matters for the Central Council for Education and Training in Social Work. We welcome the review of the issues that arise which the Council is undertaking with the interests concerned.

Clerical and support services

9.46 A problem which was mentioned several times in the evidence, is the tradition, still prevalent in most authorities, that social workers should operate with very little direct clerical or secretarial support. We can understand, given that the grading of social workers was until recently little higher than that of clerical staff, that directors may have great difficulty in persuading elected members and other chief officers that social workers should have the sort of clerical support normally provided only for middle and senior management.

9.47 It is our strong impression, however, that many field social workers and team leaders (and even more so residential social workers) spend far too much time dealing with routine paperwork and that their available time is often not deployed to the best advantage. Given that they are, as a group, not selected for their clerical skills, we think that there is a strong case for giving them more direct clerical support than their status in the authority might otherwise warrant. We recognise also, that the development of computers and other modern technology will assist in record keeping and other operations to support social work practice.

9.48 Staff in residential and day centres would be free to spend more time on their professional work if they were adequately supported by staff from other disciplines. We have in mind visiting occupational therapists, doctors, dentists, psychologists, psychiatrists and so on. They should be adequately supported also by domestic staff, handymen and gardeners where it is possible and necessary to split the tasks and functions in this way. The size of the establishment may be relevant and also the purpose, in that clients themselves may appropriately be involved and indeed assume responsibility for domestic tasks in some staffed, as they must in unstaffed, homes or hostels.

Structures

9.49 Public accountability and legal powers and constraints affect the way in which local authorities devise their organisational structures for social services. Also, the resources devoted to, say, a decentralised structure of area teams and other outposts will depend on the view the local authorities have of the desirability and cost effectiveness of this kind of decentralisation as compared with centralised services. We must here sound a note of caution. We are aware that some authorities are responding to resource constraints by closing local offices and bringing their staff into centralised accommodation. There may be local reasons for this of which we are not aware. We are however concerned at such moves which may, we believe, be damaging to social work as we would like to see it developing.

9.50 Factors influencing organisational structures include the size of the authority's area, lines of communication, in particular of public transport, within it, the amount and complexity of work coming from a particular geographical area or from a client group, the minimum number of staff needed to make a viable working unit. Thus social work, with, for example, the relatively small number of mentally handicapped people and their families in the area of one authority might be concentrated on a large hostel for the mentally handicapped plus the multidisciplinary community mental handicap team, whereas young offenders might present such a large volume of work in a particular geographical district that it requires several workers in a local office devoting time exclusively to them. By contrast a group of social workers outposted in a small rural town or a particular housing estate might be capable of dealing with the complete range of work from compulsory admission to psychiatric hospitals to arranging meals on wheels or the selection of foster homes and the placement of children.

Special needs

9.51 The structure and staff deployment in a social services agency may be influenced at particular times and in particular places by special needs that arise and require special measures to deal with them. We consider one such issue in the following paragraphs – that arising from the multi-cultural nature of society.

Work with members of ethnic minorities

9.52 Our evidence suggested that social services departments and voluntary agencies should develop organisational and manpower arrangements which take the needs of ethnic minorities explicitly into account. Only then would social services departments be able to make use of what the 1978 report of a joint working party of the Association of Directors of Social Services and the Commission for Racial Equality describes as their 'particularly good position to take the lead in demonstrating what a service that is responsive and sensitive to different needs can achieve . . .'

9.53 Legislation, in the form of section 11 of the 1966 Local Government Act, recognises that some minority groups may face difficulties for which special provision ought to be made. (We note that the working party just mentioned felt that some local authority social services departments had made less use than they might of grants under this section, but that its provisions by no means covered, as they stood, all that was needed.)

9.54 It is, we believe, essential for social workers, managers and members of social services committees to keep an open mind about the precise way in which the cases of members of ethnic minorities are dealt with. The standard criteria for fostering and foster parents may, for example, be found inappropriate. Ellis (1978) has drawn attention to the particular fostering needs of West African children of whom there are some 6,000 in British foster homes. The private fostering favoured by West Africans is not yet adequately supported and protected by legislation and a clearly defined role for social workers in this area of cross-cultural fostering is urgently needed. Others have argued in relation to West Indian children in care that 'child-care co-operatives' might need to be considered to prevent family break-up and reduce the number of black children in care; successful single parents in the black community might prove valuable as adopters if adequate financial support were provided.

9.55 Similarly, the criteria for admission to residential homes or for domiciliary support may need to be reappraised by social work managers. New programmes of Intermediate Treatment, perhaps involving the ethnic minority itself, may need to be evolved and novel procedures devised for accounting by self-help groups for grants they receive. What we are suggesting here is not specially favoured treatment – it is treatment which takes into account in an informed way individual characteristics and circumstances.

9.56 Social services departments and voluntary agencies also need to consider the question of staffing for work with ethnic minorities. First, there is the question of language. The report of the working party of the Association of Directors of Social Services and the Commission for Racial Equality drew attention to the importance of interpreters wherever the social worker, or other official, is unfamiliar with the language used by the client or potential client.

9.57 Interpretation, whoever does it, causes problems. This is particularly so if complex personal issues need to be explored. It is not a matter of translating the literal meaning of words but of conveying in both directions the underlying feelings and implications. This itself requires a professional expertise which is unlikely to be possessed by the well-meaning relative or friend or volunteer, still less by the school-age children of the clients.

9.58 Asian workers told us that they found themselves all too often being pressed to act as interpreters. This cannot be a satisfactory practice. We recognise the difficulties of deployment if professional interpreters are employed, but this must be the best arrangement. The difficulties can, we believe, be reduced if the social worker, though unfamiliar with the language, has at least a good grounding in knowledge of the traditional way of life and customs which the client takes for granted.

9.59 Such cultural knowledge is required with other ethnic groups even when they and the social worker share a common language. At times this may only serve to mask the differences in culture between them. The need for this knowledge of the culture is, we think, a conclusive argument for specialist workers to be employed at least for the initial contact with a member of a minority group. We recognise that this is only practicable for particular minorities where there is a significant concentration of them in an area, though it might still be the best course even if the area covers more than one local authority and a joint appointment is needed.

9.60 We recognise too, that there are some minorities for whom even on this basis it will be impracticable. But, as regards the main minority groupings this judgement of ours is reinforced by our belief that help or intervention is likely to be more acceptable to such clients if it is distanced from outward marks of authority – if the social workers are accessible in an informal setting and are to some degree known personally in the minority community, and certainly in touch with any acknowledged leaders it may have and with any self-help groups within it.

9.61 This is not necessarily to say that the social workers must, or can, always come from the ethnic minority affected. We would give every encouragement to the recruitment of social workers from ethnic minorities and to the continuation and, where possible, the expansion of provision of 'foundation' courses to enable candidates who have missed other opportunities to reach the required level of general education. But the range and nature of the cultural and language differences within the main ethnic minority groupings means that matching social worker to client will, in any event, often be impracticable.

9.62 How then do we think such specialist workers should be fitted into the organisation of a social services department? One way which was suggested to us, is that a group of specialist workers might operate as a resource unit taking a major share of statutory work affecting members of minority groups, screening other referrals and advising other members of staff to whom some of them will, no doubt, be passed or who find themselves dealing with emergencies. Such a unit is bound to need high level management support and well-developed methods of professional consultation and supervision.

Resource implications

9.63 In so far as these recommendations may have resource implications we recognise that they can only be implemented as resources are released by other changes. The motivation for change, as it is for the recommendations, will be the wish to secure 'value for money' by ensuring fuller use of the skills and energies of experienced staff and more efficient organisational arrangements.

SUMMARY OF CONCLUSIONS

1. Involvement of several levels of management, or of elected members, in decisions affecting individual clients should be exceptional (9.8).

2. There should be the greatest possible delegation of decision-making to front-line social workers and their immediate managers (9.9).

3. This should be accompanied by clear information about constraints affecting their work and budgetary guidelines (9.9).

4. Senior managers should make the policy-making machinery less remote for social workers in day, residential, field or other settings (9.10).

5. Attempts to impose rigid controls will inhibit good practice of social work; they will not prevent things from going wrong; it must be accepted that from time to time they will (9.16).

6. As regards social workers' contribution to statutory services, there is no better alternative to their employment by local authorities, and no case for disbanding social services departments. (9.18).

7. Local authorities should review the organisation of social services departments as it affects delegation to social workers, monitoring, and maintaining standards, fairness and regard to clients' interests (9.19).

8. Team leaders should retain both administrative and social work responsibilities (9.21–25).

9. Employers and unions should seek the development of career grade posts (9.31–36).

10 We welcome the decision of the Central Council for Education and Training in Social Work to review with the interests concerned the relationship between the Certificate of Qualification in Social Work and the Certificate in Social Service (9.45).

11. There is a strong case for increasing clerical and other support available to social workers (9.46–48).

12. Local factors inevitably influence organisational structures (9.49).

13. Special provisions may be required to provide equal services to members of ethnic minorities (9.52–62).

Chapter 10

The influence of values, methods, skills and knowledge

10.1 Many of our respondents believed that at the heart of formal social work were certain values either unique to it or more influential in it than in other occupations. These values were spelled out in one piece of evidence we received as 'values of respect for all persons, of compassion, of understanding, of sympathy, of justice, of equality and of fairness'.

10.2 We are clear that there is nothing unique to social work about such values. They are shared explicitly or by implication by workers in many other fields and – though we may attach a variety of interpretations to words like 'equality' – by most of us in our private dealings. We cannot therefore agree with one of our respondents (148) who told us that 'social work should be defined in terms of the values it espouses rather than in terms of specific roles and tasks'.

10.3 But we agree that these values have a particular significance for social workers – for two reasons. First, the legislation which gives to local authorities powers and duties in exercise of which they employ social workers itself recognises values of this kind (as also do the declared purposes of voluntary organisations). The law provides, for example, for the protection and care of people who are vulnerable because of their age or youth or handicap; for the standards of care to be monitored and inadequacies remedied; for powers of control to be exercised over those who are a risk to themselves or to others; for help, support and advice, aiming where practicable at change and rehabilitation, to be given to those in difficulties; and for preventive action to be taken where the risk of difficulties is foreseen.

10.4 Secondly, among the people with whom social workers are mainly in touch are people in need, people in distress, vulnerable people, people who find it difficult to fit in; among them are some whom, with the best will in the world, it is not easy to like or to treat with respect.

10.5 Members of certain other occupations work within comparable frameworks of legislation. But perhaps only other social services staff and those in the probation and after-care or prison services or dealing with recipients of supplementary benefit are, as consistently as social workers, in touch with human inadequacy, or distress.

10.6 But if these values are of particular significance for social workers, what are the practical consequences? First, they impose on social workers a need to understand their own personalities, prejudices and attitudes and the ways in which these will, unless they are aware of them, unconsciously influence their reactions to clients. And they impose equally an obligation to try to see each client in the light of his individual characteristics and circumstances, uninfluenced by stereotypes.

10.7 But secondly, social workers must have the courage to find answers to dilemmas that face them where interests of child and parent, client and relatives, one client and another, conflict; or where lack of resources (lack, it may be, of their own time), or priorities laid down by a local authority or voluntary body conflict with what are seen as the best interests of a client; or where a client's problems are literally insoluble. Comparable dilemmas however, are commonplace enough in the experience of other occupations, and the difference between the position of social workers and of others lies, we believe, not in their values but in the relative powerlessness and vulnerability of many of their clients, in the very 'messy human complexity', to quote one of our respondents (49), of the issues affecting them, and in the directness of the relationships social workers will often have. The tension felt by social workers is the greater because the dilemmas have to be resolved by the individual concerned, with what advice is available to him, without the authoritative backing of a binding code of conduct such as some at least of the other occupations enjoy.

10.8 A third logical consequence of the significance for social workers of these values is a concern for clients' rights of confidentiality, and, within the law, to self-determination. In neither can there be any absolutes. Discretion and the social worker's judgement have to come into play. Some information social workers receive in confidence they must pass on, whether the clients concerned wish them to or not, in the clients' own interests or for the protection of others or if disclosure is ordered by a court. And although a social worker may want to treat such information as the clients' property, only, normally, to be passed on with the clients' consent, some clients will for one reason or another not be able themselves to appreciate the implications of a decision one way or the other. Local authority social workers may feel an added awkwardness knowing that their records are not their personal property, but the authority's, that elected members may in some circumstances have access to them, and that the authority may wish to use the information in relation to issues outside the concern of the social services department. We believe that elected members should so order the authority's affairs as to enable social workers to guarantee to clients that information they receive in confidence will, except where it has to be passed on for the protection of the client or of others, or because of the court's ruling, be treated in confidence by all who have access to it, and used, save with the client's consent, only for the purposes of the client's dealings with the social services department. This has practical implications for the preparation and custody of written, or computer-held, records. We note that there are additional complications about the interchange of confidential information with members of other professons or services who have their own established standards of confidentiality.

10.9 Somewhat similarly, there are limits to the degree, even within the law, to which clients' self-determination can be honoured. Facilities may simply not be available to allow a client to live where he would like to live or spend his time where he would like to spend it. His choice may need to be over-ridden for his own protection (or someone else's – maybe his child's), or he may be incapable of making a choice. Where the law, in the form of an order of a court, applies, the choice will be restricted. Respect for a right to self-determination here leads into a duty to explain as fully as is practicable the whys and the wherefores.

10.10 The duty to explain extends more widely if respect for people is taken seriously. Clients will need to be a party, where they are able, to plans that are made for them and to the review of such plans. It may be argued that this would mean their attending case conferences: we are aware that practice varies and that many social workers believe attendance in some circumstances is not in a client's interests. In so far as this must be a matter of judgement, we would not, as a Working Party, seek to lay down a rule, but clearly clients' views should, wherever they are able to give them, be ascertained and considered and explanations given of decisions taken. We are well aware that, however careful a social worker may be, a client may be convinced that he has never been told something he was unwilling to hear. Where the issue is a major one, the importance of an adequate record of the information given is obvious.

10.11 The values referred to at the beginning of this chapter may seem to some social workers, and to some readers who are not social workers, to be incompatible with social workers' involvement either in tasks which are directed at control or modification of individuals' behaviour for the protection of society rather than straightforwardly at the well-being of their clients or in actions, such as strikes, which may clearly be to their clients' detriment. As regards control, 'social policing' as some of our respondents called it, a few pieces of evidence argued that social workers should be relieved of such tasks, which were seen as a source of fear, suspicion and resentment which reduced social workers' ability to carry out their 'proper' function of helping and supporting the weak and disadvantaged.

10.12 This, we believe, is to ignore the element of control which is always actually or potentially part of helping and supporting. Where someone is in danger of doing physical harm to himself or others, measures of restraint and control are clearly in his best interests. Where a young offender is ordered by a court to be subject to care or supervision, his social worker will certainly be a representative of 'authority' in his eyes. As the Morison Committee said of the probation officer, the social worker's task is to help him to see that, in the sense that he 'cannot realise his potential for contented living while he is at odds with society . . . his interests and those of society are identical'. Constructive use of the authority a social worker derives from an order of a court is thus one of the skills of formal social work. We accept that there may be circumstances in which the social policing role and the care and protection role in respect of one client may require division of responsibilities between two social workers both of whom may be fieldworkers or one a residential social worker and one a fieldworker.

10.13 All social workers are faced with a difficult and contentious task in holding the line between a commitment to their clients' self-determination and upholding recognised norms of behaviour. Social workers have often been criticised for applying what are described as 'middle-class' standards in dealing with clients whose experience has been with 'working-class' ways. They have also often been accused, as Juliet Cheetham (1981) points out, of having 'supported or implicitly sanctioned behaviour regarded as problematic or deplorable by the majority'. Nowhere is the difficulty greater than in work with members of ethnic minorities whose different values and norms it may not be easy to understand, much less confidently to accept.

10.14 We note elsewhere some of the effects experienced by other professions and services of strikes by social workers. We recognise that many striking social workers felt that their main motive was to contribute to the maintenance of standards of service. Few outsiders found it possible to take this claim seriously, any more than they found it easy to regard as undervalued an occupation of which the functions and purposes were so little understood, or the cause of local negotiating rights sufficient justification for such drastic action. Some members of the Working Party would argue that social workers should never strike. Others accept that there may be exceptional circumstances in which a strike or some partial limitation of their service may be justified. All would urge any Trade Union calling social workers out to agree to provision of emergency services in the field and in hospitals and generous cover in day and residential work.

10.15 The recent instances of strike action taken by staff of children's residential homes has shown there exists an urgent need for discussions between those who share responsibility for what happens on the ground in the event of an industrial dispute. As local authorities carry responsibility for the provision of social services we suggest the local authority associations initiate such discussions involving the relevant Trade Unions, the professional associations and Government Departments with the aim of agreeing a set of guidelines to be followed if residential social workers should decide that there is a need to take industrial action, so as to ensure adequate protection of those in local authority care.

10.16 But however fully social workers themselves may live up to values such as those we have quoted, the image the public has is one which, though it may be tinged with compassion for their clients, is not one of respect for them. It was clear to us in our meetings with them that clients often felt a sense of shame about their involvement with social workers. It was clearer still from comments made by other people with whom we talked and, for example, from many of the responses to the survey of public opinion which the Gallup Organisation undertook, that the public very generally feel that social workers are for 'people of a certain kind', people who cannot fend for themselves, people often who are unpopular with their neighbours. This is what social workers mean when they say that stigma attaches to the service they provide.

10.17 This stigma will not readily be removed. Parliament in enacting the Children and Young Persons Act 1969 sought by changes both in the judicial process and in their subsequent treatment to reduce the particular stigma attached to young offenders; but it was suggested to us that the effect has been to extend this stigma to children who are not offenders but find themselves in community homes. Be that as it may, stigma will remain unless the public (and, because of their influence on the public, the media) can be convinced that it is unjustified or unjust. We believe a greater openness about the work of social workers, finding language to talk about it which does not strike other people as jargon-laden mumbo-jumbo, would help. Employing authorities and organisations have a public relations responsibility and should use their public relations resources to this end, not only defensively when something is said to have gone wrong, but to paint the picture of what is done constructively for many people for whom the natural human feeling will be one of compassion rather than contempt.

10.18 One element in this picture will be an explanation of the methods social workers use and the skills and knowledge they bring into play. The following paragraphs make a few points which seem to us important in this connection.

Methods of formal social work

10.19 Social workers are usually said to employ three methods of work – 'social casework', group work and community work. 'Social casework', meaning originally nothing more mystifying than 'dealing with particular cases', later acquired a specialised use puzzling to outsiders and owing something to the pattern of work of psychotherapists with their patients. In this sense it meant what a social worker did in establishing and making use of a relationship with a client in which he sought through counselling to change the client's attitudes or feelings. Many social workers now feel somewhat embarrassed or ambivalent about the term and prefer to use the terms 'work with individuals or families', and 'counselling'.

10.20 Group work extends in range from work done with small therapeutic groups whose members share a common problem (e.g. delinquent youngsters, adults recovering from mental illness) through the formation and guidance of groups for mutual support (e.g. single parents, parents of handicapped children) to acting as consultant for groups in a particular locality wishing, for example, to secure some resource, such as adequate play space for children.

10.21 Community work, in which social workers carry out

activities overlapping, but not co-extensive, with those of community workers includes direct work with local community groups who want (as above) to gain resources, to have a greater say in the development of local authority policies, or to offer services themselves; and the indirect work of contributing to the planning and organisation of services as a whole.

Social work activities

10.22 We do not find, however, the distinctions made between casework, group work and community work as methods of social work particularly helpful. These terms identify the client, without telling us anything clearly about social workers' activities or the settings in which they are undertaken. It seems to us that social workers, whether working with individuals, groups or communities, will, save in very specialised circumstances, be undertaking in some measure both of the activities we distinguished in Chapter 3 – social planning and counselling. Either, or both, may be at a superficial, or at a much deeper, level. There are differences, but also overlaps, in the demands they make. But it is by concentrating on these activities that we think the skills and knowledge that will be helpful to social workers can most readily be identified.

Social work skills and knowledge

10.23 Three sorts of skill are needed – skills in human relationships; skills in analysis (assessing people, analysing situations and evaluating the effects of action taken); and skills in effectiveness (carrying out action planned).

   10.24 The first includes an ability to listen, an ability to respect the other person on his or her own terms, an ability to stand firm where issues of personal integrity are concerned. The second includes gathering information, interpreting its significance, weighing the pros and cons of alternative courses of action, selecting one of those courses and recording its progress and processes, estimating its effectiveness, and modifying the plan or programme in accordance with that estimate. The third includes: collaboration with social services colleagues, administrators and managers, negotiation with employees of other occupations and organisations for services and resources, advocacy on behalf of clients with a range of public service agencies, crisis and risk managment, supporting volunteers or members of the family, or of a community, in direct contact with clients, and putting clients in touch with helping networks in local communities, acting indeed as 'brokers', as one of our respondents (122) put it, between the range, wide or narrow, of 'interested parties to a relationship'.

10.25 Social workers' involvement with people and the nature of the organisations and settings in which they are employed call for the use of other skills – skills in communicating, skills in managing, skills – at least for those working in day or residential services – in tending, skill in reaching decisions in conflicting and uncertain circumstances.

10.26 We should explain the reference here to skill in managing. We are writing primarily of front-line social workers. They are responsible to team leaders and other managers but, however good the management and supervision they receive, we see a management responsibility resting with them – for their use of their own time and effort, for any ancillary staff or volunteers formally attached to them, perhaps for a team of street wardens, home helps, domestic or clerical staff.

10.27 Skills such as we see to be demanded of social workers presuppose possession of knowledge of two kinds: practical information for immediate use, and knowledge that provides insight into the behaviour of people, organisations and societies, and into how that behaviour is likely to change under the influence of alternative courses of action.

10.28 The practical information includes: knowledge of the neighbourhood or area and agency in which the social worker works, and of the resources (people, organisations, services and materials) available; a working knowledge of the relevant legislation, with detailed knowledge of those Acts of Parliament and related regulations most central to a particular social worker's sphere of concern; knowledge of local government structures and procedures, and how these link with the work of voluntary bodies and of other providers of social services, such as health and income-maintenance services; knowledge of the policies of the worker's employing agency; a broad understanding of the services and benefits available to different client groups and of where more detailed information can quickly be obtained.

10.29 Knowledge that provides insight into behaviour includes: an understanding of one's own effect on other people and of ways of behaving which engender trust on the one hand and evasion on the other; understanding of social policy and administration, of how societies, cultures and organisations function, with particular reference to structures of social control, the forces generating social change, and the ways in which control and change are affected by different political creeds; understanding of the way people's minds work, of mental development from childhood and into old age, of family and community relationships and how they differ in different cultures; understanding that all such knowledge rests on evidence that can be differently interpreted from different perspectives, that moral and philosophical or political assumptions underlie all formulations of theory, however 'objectively' they are presented, and that social workers have both to make choices among courses of action and learn to accept that no one course of action can be guaranteed as infallibly right.

Specialisation in social work

10.30 So far in this chapter we have avoided discussion of specialisation in social work. We recognise its importance but are also acutely aware that as a Working Party we have not given this subject all the attention it requires. Others, however, have done so. The social work press has given considerable space to what is sometimes called 'the patch versus specialist debate' and Professor Stevenson (1981) in her book *Specialisation in Social Service Teams* makes a major contribution to the discussion.

10.31 As she points out, there are many possible forms which specialisation might take in the personal social services. Our evidence – notably from voluntary organisations – however, suggests that when people claim that social workers should specialise they are usually referring to the need they see for some social workers to have special knowledge about, and skills in dealing with, problems facing a particular client group. The group may be a large one as, for example, deaf people or families with a mentally handicapped member. Similar comments have been made to us by smaller groups whose members have to deal with a relatively rare problem such as childhood autism.

10.32 The second type of specialisation to which reference was made in some evidence was in relation to the organisation of work. We were told of the value of dividing work between intake and long-term teams and between teams serving the elderly and disabled and those serving children and families.

10.33 Most members of the Working Party believe that social workers should be equipped to undertake social planning and counselling for any client group in a competent but basic way. They recognise that this implies acquiring either a wide range of knowledge and skills, or an ability to transfer knowledge and skills acquired in work with one client group to others. But they also regard the development of specialist skills in some fields as essential.

10.34 Thus we agree with the conclusion of the Seebohm Committee that 'as a general rule, and as far as possible, a family or individual in need of social care should be served by a single social worker'. The work of each social worker tends, however, to develop a particular bias or emphasis. This may be the result of organisational factors, such as the kind of team to which a social worker is appointed, or of the social worker's interests and opportunities. We consider such an emphasis is desirable and that specialisation in the sense of greater expertise may grow from it if opportunities for further training and development are available. Since it is clear that only a part of the range of relevant knowledge and skills to which we have referred in this chapter can be acquired in the two years which are the usual period of initial training, we believe it is vitally important that the continuing and widening provision of post-qualifying training for social workers be given attention by local and national government.

10.35 Administrative structures may so relate the work and social workers together as to allocate most work of a particular kind to specially designated staff. The division of work may be broadly based, as perhaps all work connected with children in care or at risk of coming into care, or narrowly, for example, the boarding-out of elderly people.

10.36 Over-narrow specialisation has the danger of distorting the social worker's view. Where work is defined in a narrow or very specific way, therefore, it should as far as practicable, be so organised as to ensure that each specialist social worker is linked with a more general team. Thus workers in a unit specialising in adoption and fostering of children would benefit by being also part of a wider team and participating in its work. They may liaise with, or be posted for part or all of their time to area teams. Similarly, social workers in a multi-disciplinary community mental handicap team should be closely associated with an area team as well as with the specialist resources of a hospital or residential home, and should deal with problems arising in their clients' families not directly associated with the mentally handicapped member, bringing in another social worker for advice or action when necessary.

10.37 The volume of work is a relevant factor. It may be small enough to require a small specialist team, centrally based rather than divided up on an area basis, in order to allow sufficient technical knowledge and experience to be built up and devoted to the particular field of work. Social work with blind people may be an example.

Another may be innovative or project work that requires the attention of a specialist team for a limited time.

10.38 In Chapter 13 we argue that social services departments should develop a community approach. If they do so a new balance will be called for between the skills we have considered in this chapter, if social workers are to work in close partnership with other social services staff and with social networks, be these within local communities or within communities of interest which cross over geographical boundaries. There is nothing inconsistent between this approach and our support for specialisation. Whether or not an individual social worker is a specialist, we argue that the 'community dimension' of his practice must always be taken into account and applied by him in carrying out his work. This merely reflects the need for a general change in attitude to which we refer in our last chapter.

SUMMARY OF CONCLUSIONS

1. Employers' affairs should be so ordered as to enable social workers to guarantee confidentiality, to be broken only for the protection of the client or others or under court order (10.8).

2. Clients, where they are able, should share in the plans made for them and be given explanations of decisions taken (10.9–10).

3. Social control should be regarded as an essential element in formal social work (10.11).

4. If industrial action by social workers is contemplated (some Working Party members hold that it can never be justified), then Trade Unions should agree to provision of emergency fieldwork services with generous cover in day and residential units; the local authority associations should initiate discussions on guidelines to be followed as regards action by residential workers (10.14–15).

5. Employers should accept a continuing responsibility to give the public and the media a clear picture of social workers' work (10.17).

6. Social work and community work should be regarded as overlapping but not co-extensive activities (10.21); community social work will require a new balance of skills (10.38).

7. Social workers should be equipped to undertake social planning and counselling activities at a basic level for any client group but development of specialist skills is natural and in some fields essential (10.33–34).

8. Wherever possible specialist workers should be linked to more general teams and take part in their work (10.36).

9. Central and local government should ensure provision of widening opportunities for post-qualifying specialist training (10.34).

PART THREE

CLIENTS, COMMUNITY AND SOCIAL WORK

Chapter 11

Views of
social work

Introduction

11.1 In this chapter we summarise what we were able to find out about clients' own views of social work. We were aware from the start of our enquiry of the difficulties which lie in the way of those who want to discover what the clients of any social service think of it. Some of these difficulties arise from the very nature of clients since they are seldom organised into the kinds of formal grouping which make it possible to obtain representative views; others are difficulties of interpretation, since questions may be framed by reference to ideas which are alien to clients' thinking and what clients say may be discounted as special pleading of one kind or another. We were also aware that a failure to obtain clients' views would seriously weaken our report. The chapter concludes with a discussion of the meaning of all the information and evidence we were able to assemble about the effectiveness of social work.

Getting the views of clients

11.2 We were anxious to have as full as possible a picture of clients' views and, in addition to seeking evidence from 'user' groups, we did our best to ensure the widest possible circulation of the general invitation we issued to all who had an interest to write to us.

11.3 We did not expect this general invitation to be acted upon by many clients, so we considered early in our work the possibility of commissioning a major survey. All the advice we had was that to design a survey which would carry general credibility and to gain the consent of the authorities and voluntary bodies affected, of the individual social workers whose clients would be interviewed and of the clients themselves, would take too long, even if the technical problems could be resolved. Some members of the Working Party believed that despite this advice we ought to have insisted on provision of funds by the Secretary of State to enable us to commission such a survey; most of us concluded that we ought rather to suggest that a survey of this kind should be considered either by the Department of Health and Social Security or by individual local authorities on a local scale.

11.4 Professor Harry Specht and Mr Gordon Craig collected together for us the existing research studies of clients' views. (The resulting report is available as a separate paper from the National Institute for Social Work.)

11.5 We were able to add to this picture in a number of ways. Family Service Units commissioned for us a survey of a sample of their clients (320, Phillimore, 1981). Remploy undertook, and reported to us the outcome of, a survey of their employees' views (125). The Family Fund similarly made available to us the replies to a questionnaire they sent to a number of families receiving grants. We gathered more information through the Gallup survey of public opinion which we commissioned jointly with the journal, *New Society*. (*New Society* published an analysis of this survey on 8th May, 1981; we say more about it later in this chapter.) And we received a number of submissions reporting studies, unpublished, of clients' views.

11.6 Letters inviting evidence were sent to national and local organisations representing the interests of groups from which social workers' clients come. Many of them sent us comments. We also made arrangements, whenever we could, for members of the Working Party and its secretariat to meet individual clients or groups of clients for less formal exchanges. We met in this way in London, and during our visits in other parts of England and Wales, elderly people, people with various physical handicaps, mentally handicapped people, people who were suffering mental illness, children in care and parents of children in care or regarded as at risk. Some of them were in residential homes or hospitals, some in day centres and some came to meet us from their own homes. Some of them were members of ethnic minorities.

11.7 We recognise that the evidence we have received is in no sense a balanced, scientific sampling of clients' views. We could only note consistency, or lack of it, and pick out for consideration such novel issues or emphases as we came upon. The same is true of the initiative we took in asking directors of social services to place in waiting rooms or other appropriate places slips specifically inviting anyone who wished to write to us. We received a number of criticisms of this initiative both because it was, as we recognised, wholly unstructured and unscientific, and because it was thought (mistakenly, as it turned out) that we should receive responses only from those with oversized chips on their shoulders. We comment later in this chapter on the letters which we received prompted by these leaflets or by the mention of the Working Party in the press and on radio and television.

11.8 A sub-group of the Working Party gave particular attention to clients' views and reached a number of tentative conclusions:

● The same client is often both critical and satisfied.

● People in general have only a vague idea about social workers and what to expect of them. Those who are clients are likely to share in this. They may have no reason to distinguish, as we must, social work from social services. Their comments are thus likely to relate to the availability and appropriateness of resources and facilities and to the performance of the social services department or voluntary organisation generally rather than to the role and activities of a social worker or his actual performance.

● Some clients would find greater clarity, definiteness and simplicity about the purposes, roles and powers of agencies and their staff helpful and would understand better a more purposeful approach.

● Our comparative ignorance of the views of social work is paralleled by similar ignorance of the views of users about other services such as teaching and medicine.

Views of a range of different clients

11.9 Our various attempts to get clients to write in to us resulted in over eighty replies. These included a few which were, so far as we could tell, not from clients but from members of the general public and another few from foster parents – some with enclosures from foster children and from foster parents' own children – or members of other professions working with social workers. A very few letters were from people who had (anyway at the time they wrote) no time for social workers. Rather more were tributes of praise to individual social workers.. But most contained carefully thought out comments often on the difficulties of a social worker's task and on the part social workers could play in relation to particular problems; sometimes on the inadequacy of the knowledge and experience of social workers they had encountered; sometimes on the slowness and complexity of the system in which social workers operate.

11.10 We think it worth giving a few quotations from these letters which either seem to us representative of widely felt responses (including minority responses) or raise an issue in a particularly vivid form:

> 'Most social workers think they are God.'
> 'They are speaking so sarcastic to clients.'
> 'They tend to make promises, then they don't keep them.'
> 'It is against natural justice for a person not to be represented when some very important decision is being made.'
> 'Clients should be able to contact their social workers. It is very difficult to talk to a duty officer who doesn't know your case.'
> 'Social workers do a good job.'
> 'They should have more power.'
> 'No one should be ashamed to get in touch with a social worker.'
> 'I don't know what our family would have done without her.'

And, from a verse tribute from a client suffering mental illness:

> 'You gently took my child's hand and led me through the jungle of despair into hope . . .'

11.11 In the next few paragraphs we give some account of issues raised with us in discussion by individual clients or groups of clients whom we met or by organisations speaking for clients.

11.12 We were particularly concerned not to overlook the reactions of clients who were critical of social workers. They were, we felt, a better guide to what was important to clients than the more general statements of those (the majority) who expressed satisfaction or praise. (Typically the more quotable comments tended to be critical.) We found such reactions among four groups – the parents of children in care under court orders; young people in care or recently out of care; physically handicapped people, including deaf people and blind people, and parents of mentally handicapped children; and members of ethnic minorities.

11.13 There is no doubt that relationships between social workers and families whose children are in care, or are seen as being at risk of being received into care, against their parents' wishes, is coloured by fear and suspicion. Typical comments were:

> 'You don't trust social workers.'
> 'All they do is attempt to take you over.'
> 'You can't talk to them.'

'They don't think deeply about what going into care means to the child or
to the parents.'
'Training leaves their feelings behind.'

Local authority field workers' 'lack of time to listen' and 'secretiveness' was contrasted with the friendliness and openness of staff of
family day centres (which clearly match the attitude of the Family
Service Units mentioned later). Some parents told us they wished
they had some means of raising complaints about the way they or
their children were being dealt with to a body independent of the
local authority.

11.14 Some argued that the remoteness of the social worker
based in an area office was part of the problem. It would be better to
have a 'beat' social worker who was known to everyone, involved in
the activities of the neighbourhood and who visited everyone, not
just those 'of a certain sort'. He needed to be able to look beyond the
interests of his own clients to those of the neighbourhood, for example when it came to finding a flat for a disruptive family. Yet those
who volunteered these suggestions wanted the social worker to have
specialist knowledge relevant in particular to the practical needs of
his clients – housing, for example, income maintenance, day care for
children. But they emphasised too the value of self-help groups –
some of them rating the help such groups can give way above
anything social workers provided.

11.15 Young people in care had mixed feelings about field social
workers. They confessed to having felt frightened on their first contact with a social worker. They often disliked their social worker (or at
least their present social worker) and yet wished to see him more
often, and wished they had not had so many changes of social
worker. They often found it hard to understand what social workers
were saying, they felt social workers too often took action behind
their backs and that they should be allowed to attend reviews (with
independent panels to decide whether a child was old enough to do
so and to be available to consider complaints). They, like the evidence
(278) from the Voice for the Child in Care, set the personality of the
social worker before knowledge and skills. They rated maturity,
self-awareness, consistency and commitment highly. They suggested
that there should be provision for regular review by the court of the
local authority's performance as 'parent'. They were critical in particular of unimaginative procedures in care: for example, use of order
books for clothing; over-rigid, as they felt, but not uniform, rules and
regulations in community homes; and in dealing with eighteen-
year-olds leaving care (where they suggested specialist after-care

workers were needed who would know all of the options open).

11.16 We have already referred to the plea by physically handicapped people that they should have social workers with specialist knowledge and skills. The British Deaf Association, for example, made very clear to us the dependence of deaf people on interpretation between English and the different language of signing in which they are accustomed to express themselves. A means of communicating is clearly a prerequisite to any social worker's helping a deaf person either in relation to practical problems or to emotional difficulties, which may be his lot no less than a hearing person's. But, whatever their disabilities, all the handicapped people who gave us evidence emphasised that they had had little contact with social workers, and that when they had, while they had when in hospital generally found social workers there helpful, their experience of social workers in the community was that they too rarely had knowledge of the range of services and benefits available or where to get the knowledge.

11.17 The emphasis by physically handicapped people was very much on material help. But they recognised the need for support and help in coming to terms with handicap and for families in coping with the emotional stresses and tensions within marriages to which dependence or handicap may give rise.

11.18 Much of what physically handicapped people said was echoed by parents of mentally handicapped children, with the difference of emphasis that they would perhaps place first support and help in accepting their child's handicap when it is recognised and only second knowledge of and guidance in securing services and benefits. The latter, however, is still important and not always available. For example, a survey undertaken by the Harlow Council Community Services Department (124) showed that many mentally handicapped people attending a training centre 'had not been advised properly about what benefits to claim'.

Views of members of ethnic minorities

11.19 Our evidence contained some statements from people who identified themselves as belonging to an ethnic minority and also comments by others about the way social work is viewed by minority groups. Some members of the committee and the secretariat had meetings with minority group members.

11.20 Once again, it was not easy to disentangle views about the provision of personal social services from views about social work. It was clear, however, that language differences, cultural attitudes and cultural practices mean that some members of ethnic minority groups do not know about or understand the social services which are available. For access to these services, they are peculiarly dependent upon the sensitivity, skill and competence of social workers.

11.21 It seemed to us that many members of ethnic minorities viewed social workers as representatives of authority, an authority with which they preferred to have as few dealings as possible or which they actively mistrusted. Black people to whom we talked regarded social workers as 'nosey' interferers; they recognised that they did sometimes provide practical help but did not think of them as people with whom they would want to discuss problems. Social workers with particular experience of minorities told us that their members were unlikely to come to a social services office of their own accord to seek help.

11.22 It is not just that social workers represent authority but that the authority is seen as alien and lacking in understanding of the cultural practices of particular groups. One West Indian group stated: 'Your wonderful child care institutions have evolved out of your own experience. That is good for you. One man's meat may be another man's poison, and the West Indian experience is somewhat different from yours.' Similarly, we were told, failure to understand cultural factors may lead to mistaken attribution of the behaviour of members of non-European minorities to personality traits defined in terms of European experience and European psychological theory.

11.23 We were told that social workers are liable to adopt one or other of two easy ways out when confronted by problems which do not fit their accustomed terms of reference: dismissing the problem as merely a manifestation of cultural differences to be tolerated in the name of respect for ethnic minority traditions; or evading responsibility by emphasising the self-help traditions of other cultures and assuming that the minority will 'consume its own smoke'. One of our respondents (324) illustrated the over-facile adoption of 'cultural conflict' as the explanation with the following example:

'A 14 year old Asian girl was referred with a history of running away from home, temper outbursts, refusal to speak to her father and siblings. When questioned the girl spoke of her unhappiness at home, having to do housework and wash clothes in cold water. This case was quickly seen as a case of cultural clash and it was said that the girl was showing identification with English girls and their way of life. A record of emotional disturbance and a history of depression and instability was present but the usual range of explanations were not identified as major kinds of target problems. Later investigations revealed many complications and a history of sexual advances by her father.'

We came upon one example of admirable voluntary work being done by volunteers from ethnic minorities in visiting, for example, elderly black people and organising clubs for them. But these volunteers were the first to stress their reliance on backing and support from statutory and formal voluntary organisations.

11.24 Another charge levelled at social workers by members of ethnic minorities was a lack of sensitivity to the subtleties of minority groupings, instanced by thinking in blanket terms of 'West Indians' or 'Asians' as members of single groups. Others, rightly or wrongly identified prejudice on the part of individual social workers; a lack of concern for the difficulties of members of minority groups generally or of particular categories of them – elderly black people, for example, or half-caste children; and a failure to challenge racial prejudices of other agencies. However well or ill-founded these charges, they undoubtedly influence the attitudes of minority groups and are a part of the context in which social workers operate.

11.25 Those who gave evidence to us all argued that special knowledge and experience was a prerequisite in social workers; all believed that special methods of working were called for; all saw a case for recruitment of more social workers from the minorities.

Views of advice column journalists

11.26 Much of the evidence from clients suggested that they were looking for practical help rather than counselling. We thought it might be useful to consult a number of those who are responsible for the advice columns in national journals. They, without exception, told us that they receive very large numbers of letters from people of all ages, men and women, with emotional problems. Most of these letters are dealt with by other means than published replies – by referring the writers to marriage guidance councils or other local advisory services, or by sending information leaflets or personal letters. Writers are rarely referred to social services departments because of an acute awareness that local authority social workers are already under great pressure and, in some cases, that readers will feel a sense of shame about taking their problem to a social services department.

11.27 One of those consulted told us:

'There is a terrible shortage of counselling services. In most areas there is simply nowhere to suggest that young people, say from their teens up to the age of 25, can go to talk over often acute emotional problems. The Samaritans provide an invaluable service but these youngsters need somewhere aimed at their age group, and less identified in the public mind with depression and suicide. The young people I am thinking of may be facing anything from incest to horrendous family rows, from pregnancy to a mix of unemployment and acute shyness.

While at present I recommend many readers to go to their local Marriage Guidance Council with problems, since they do claim to help with *any* relationship problem, I am very conscious that MGCs in most most areas are now overloaded . . . In any case, many of the problems are a complex mix of social factors and emotional ones . . . Many of the people, though not young, are not married or even co-habiting, so try as I might to say that MGCs help the unmarried, the MGC doesn't seem the place for a fraught mum to talk over stressed reactions to the children, for example.'

Views of the media

11.28 We have already referred (in paragraph 3.61) to the attitudes of the media and their coverage of social work. Because social workers deal with highly controversial issues, people in situations of stress and deprivation, and personal tragedies, it is only natural that the coverage is sometimes extensive and highly dramatised. Media interest in cases of non-accidental injury is the most obvious example.

11.29 It is right that the media should scrutinise social work: such scrutiny is one of the checks that exists in our society on the use of power by people or organisations whose decisions may have far-reaching consequences. We are bound to say, however, that some media coverage seems to us to have been unduly vindictive and sensational in its focus and conclusions. Reports have sometimes failed to recognise that difficult and agonising decisions have to be taken, that they are taken almost invariably after consultation between members of a number of different professions and services and with the advice of senior and experienced staff, and that social workers immediately concerned have been carrying out such joint decisions, not acting arbitrarily, relying on their own judgement.

11.30 We recognise on the other hand that some media treatment of social work is concerned and enquiring, ready to praise where praise is due but also to raise questions and to be careful to respect the wishes and the privacy of clients, anxious to broaden public knowledge. This is unreservedly to be welcomed.

11.31 We note that to one of the questions asked in the Gallup survey we mention in paragraph 11.5 two-thirds of those questioned replied that they had seen nothing recently in the media to make them feel either less or more favourable towards social workers. But three times as many said they had seen something that made them feel less favourable as said they had seen something which made them feel more favourable.

Research and survey findings

11.32 The survey of research found clients' stated satisfaction with their field social worker or agency consistent across studies, most figures falling close to 66% while those expressing dissatisfaction were about 20%, most of these finding the social worker unhelpful, his visits too irregular or infrequent, or the service wanted too long delayed. But fewer than 10% of clients responding in the studies failed to find their social workers understanding, easy to talk to and sympathetic.

11.33 Studies of children in care suggest they hold similar views about residential staff. When they are critical of staff they comment upon a lack of consultation and upon secretiveness in record keeping. They also complain that the staff who look after them change too often so that there is little continuity of care.

11.34 Studies of other groups unfold a more complicated story. The views of a substantial proportion of parents of children in care under a court order, of motherless families and of battered wives are much more critical of their social workers – with strong elements of suspicion, apprehension and resentment. Where parents of mentally or physically handicapped children are studied, a high proportion are found to have had no contact with a social worker, and some of those who have report only occasional contact and that no help was given when it was most needed during the first few years of the child's life. Parents are reported to complain of social workers' lack of knowledge about handicaps and inadequate provision of information about services and benefits available and voluntary organisations offering support. Such families are often unaware of services available from the social services department itself and of the functions of social workers. Similar findings come from studies of handicapped adults.

11.35 Our research staff drew our attention to certain limitations of many of the individual studies and to problems of interpreting what researchers, let alone clients, meant by satisfaction. We recognise that there are problems and that social researchers are properly cautious about studies of clients' views. None the less, what seems to us particularly significant is the consistency of the studies reported with each other and with all other indications of clients' attitudes which came our way. The following paragraphs, which summarise other material we received, will allow readers to decide for themselves the weight to attach to this evidence.

11.36 Family Service Units' survey depicts the reactions of families with chronic practical and emotional difficulties. They attach importance to swift practical assistance, to having someone they can talk to and, perhaps above all, to having someone to help them in their dealings with 'authority' in particular with social security, housing, schools, public utilities. The report also threw into clear relief the great difficulty many of the men of these families had in coming to terms with a social worker's involvement, but showed, perhaps even more starkly, the unacceptability, to these families, of any notion of reliance on informal networks of family, friends or neighbours, their vivid fear of being victims of gossip, and the importance they attach to confidentiality. It also highlighted the value these clients set on the informality and small scale of a Family Service Unit, compared with a social services department area office, on the readiness of access (and always someone ready to listen if the visitor's own social worker is not available), the time the social workers are able to give, the opportunities some Units provide for clients and staff to eat together at midday, the use of the premises for groups, clubs, facilities for simple things like 'washing your hair'.

11.37 The Remploy survey added to the evidence that many people with handicaps find that social workers lack specialised knowledge of their particular handicap and have a limited and stereotyped view of their problems and needs. Remploy employees felt that links needed to be developed between each Remploy factory and the statutory and voluntary social services agencies to make more information available. The survey showed that many handicapped people had little or no contact with the personal social services. We recognise that some people with handicaps are no more in need of the personal social services than are any other citizens, but we share the view contained in the Remploy evidence that contact would be desirable where, for example, elderly parents are caring without support for their adult mentally handicapped sons and daughters.

11.38 The clients of the Family Fund (who are the parents of severely handicapped children) reinforced this impression, making clear their view that one of the main tasks of social workers is to help people find the resources they need to solve their problems. One respondent described this to us as 'a kind of CAB role of a particularly flexible and useful kind'. These families had not generally found social workers very competent in this role. They commented: 'They can't seem to cope with your needs but pass you on . . . they can't make decisions without ringing another department first . . . should be given a chance to make a decision for themselves.' Yet a fair number of the respondents to this survey had been helped by social workers to get services or benefits of which they were ignorant, or just 'by listening'.

11.39 The Gallup survey, which we commissioned jointly with *New Society*, was designed to provide some idea of the general public's knowledge of what social workers do and of the image social workers have. Of those interviewed, 29% claimed to have had some personal contact with a social worker although by no means necessarily as a client. The question followed others which, while not in themselves leading questions, gave some indication of who was meant by the term 'social worker'. It was clear, however, from other comments recorded, that some respondents were referring to probation officers and others probably to home helps, health visitors or perhaps voluntary workers. A higher proportion of those who claimed contact, than of other respondents, showed, as might be expected, accurate knowledge of what social workers do. Some of these respondents also attached importance to social workers' helping people with emotional (as opposed to practical) problems. Of those claiming contact, 60% said they were satisfied with the help or information they received; 22% said they were dissatisfied. Individuals' comments ranged from:

'A load of rubbish.'
'Most are there for the money.'
'People who find it hard to keep in touch.'
through
'I didn't approve of his ideas in my case.'
'It was good but they were limited in their knowledge.'
and
'Reassuring in the main.'
to
'They all have a value in their way.'
'They were very good.'
'My view has become more favourable following a social worker's active participation in setting up a community organisation.'

11.40 The survey also listed ten different helping professionals (doctors, teachers, priests, social workers, etc) and asked respondents to say 'which of these people has the most value to the community?'. Social workers were ranked fourth from the top, after doctors, policemen, and Citizens Advice Bureau workers. Below them came teachers, health visitors, social security staff, clergymen, home helps and solicitors. Social workers obtained a slightly higher rating (although it did not change the ranking) from those who claimed to have had contact with them than from those who had had no contact.

11.41 If we were to sum up in a single sentence the message we take from the sources so far described, we would say that clients want to find in social workers knowledgeable people who can ensure an effective, speedy and comprehensive (and more often than not practical) response to problems without having to pass them on from one hand to another, to refer requests to 'higher authority' or other agencies or to disentangle knots of red tape. Such an expectation must often be unrealistic. But it is an expectation against which social workers will be judged.

Discussion and conclusions about the effectiveness of social workers

11.42 Social workers have been criticised for paying too little attention to assessing the usefulness of their work, and for failing to formulate objectives or describe what they are doing in a way that would allow evaluation. It is also argued that such evaluation as has taken place suggests that social work is ineffective or even harmful (Brewer and Lait, 1980, Fischer, 1976, Mullen and Dumpson, 1972, Wood, 1978, Wootton, 1960).

11.43 It is difficult to support or refute these criticisms, since they are very general and depend on a concept of effectiveness which is not always appropriate. Questions of effectiveness are most naturally raised in medical settings and, influenced perhaps by the medical tradition, researchers have enquired whether social work is effective against a particular social problem much as others have asked whether an antibiotic can cure a particular illness. Social workers, however, are not always attempting to cure social ills. For example, they are often involved in decisions analogous to those handled by judges or magistrates over whether a child should live with its mother or father or go into residential care. In such cases, it seems more natural to ask whether social workers are acting fairly and responsibly, or within the law, than whether they are effective. In many other cases, social workers are involved in advising clients or referring them to other agencies. It is reasonable to ask whether the advice is accurate, clear and courteously given, or the referral appropriate. However, the impact (and hence longer-term effectiveness) of the workers' actions will almost always depend on factors outside their control (for example, on the quality and resources of the agency to whom the client is referred).

11.44 In some cases, of course, the use of the term 'effectiveness' seems appropriate. For example, it is natural to ask whether casework by social workers can reduce delinquency. Even in such instances, however, three troublesome questions arise. First, from whose point of view is social work to be evaluated? Different outcomes may well be preferred by a delinquent, his family, his victim, his school, the local ratepayers and the community home in which he might be placed. Second, what standard of comparison is to be used? Is social work to be compared with the absence of any professional help, or with the activities of similar professionals, and how much weight should be given to the relative costs of social work and other forms of activity? Third, what is it that is being evaluated, and how should it be described? In particular, is the evaluation aimed at the role performance of people employed as social workers, or at their particular methods and activities? From the point of view of research, the more precisely an activity can be described the better, but this leads to problems in drawing general conclusions. The failure or success of a particular treatment in combating influenza says little about the efficacy or otherwise of general practice. Similarly, the success or failure of social workers in reducing truancy has a limited bearing on their overall usefulness.

11.45 In considering these questions of effectiveness, we reviewed the literature concerned with the subjective reactions of clients and the research studies which have used more objective measures. We received a helpful paper on studies of effectiveness from Professor Pritchard of Southampton University (114); other respondents made briefer comments. As we noted above (paragraph 11.4), Professor Specht prepared a paper on this topic for us, and Mr Craig provided additional material. One of our members organised two useful seminars in which researchers currently involved with social work discussed their ideas and results.

11.46 Our evidence highlighted the difficulties of research in an area which involves hard conceptual questions as well as questions of value and of research design. Not surprisingly, much of the research is inconclusive or conflicting: many researchers have failed to specify what they meant by terms such as 'casework' or 'group work', or have evaluated social work against aims which were over-ambitious or poorly defined. Despite these difficulties, we were able to reach certain conclusions, although in doing so we had to follow the conception of social work implicit or explicit in most of the research.

11.47 As implied by our earlier discussion, the way social work is described has implications for the criteria against which it is evaluated. For example, if social workers are described as monitoring clients, an evaluator would wish to know whether social workers are able to pick up danger signals, and if so whether they are willing to act. Different criteria would be used to evaluate the activity of 'counselling'. In practice, researchers seem to have concentrated on the following areas: **assessment; counselling** in the sense of providing advice, referral and emotional support; attempting to **change clients' behaviour** (e.g. delinquency); **career management** (e.g. deciding whether a client should be in care); and **residential work**. We have used these categories in our discussions, even though, as noted later, they do not include important areas of social work, or fully reflect our own views.

Assessment

11.48 Researchers have examined how far social workers identify the social and personal problems troubling their clients. It seems that the number of problems the workers discover depends on their setting, the time they have available, the client's perceptions of the worker's role, and possibly the worker's training (Goldberg and others, 1970, Geall, 1981, 328).

Counselling

11.49 Clients generally appreciate the moral and practical support they receive from field social workers. Field social work can also help clients resolve certain personal problems – for example, those connected with loneliness, difficult family relationships, depression, and poor morale (Cooper and others, 1975, Corney, 1981, Gibbon, 1981, Goldberg and others, 1970).

11.50 Social work is not invariably appreciated, and some researchers have suggested that the clients' appreciation in any case reflects low expectations or a reluctance to criticise, rather than the workers' good practice. Nevertheless, many of the criticisms (e.g. that social workers are unreliable, or lack expertise in a particular field) may simply reflect the workers' setting rather than their inefficiency or lack of concern. Thus the workers may find it difficult to be reliable because of the number of competing claims on their time, and difficult to acquire all the necessary expertise because of the variety of their work. In general, clients like what they get from social workers, and in one study they stated that they preferred a social work visit to a grant equivalent to the cost of providing one (Glendinning and Bradshaw, unpublished). The client's appreciation is surely one criterion of effective service.

Changing behaviour

11.51 A small number of studies have suggested that field social workers can reduce the incidence of delinquency (in some studies, by more intensive work and among certain groups) and difficult behaviour (Berntsen and Christiansen, 1975, Rose and Marshall, 1975, Shaw, 1974, Adams, Sinclair and others, 1974). It may also be the case that social workers using a structured approach influenced by behaviour therapy and aiming at small changes in behaviour can achieve results where social workers using traditional methods and aiming at larger changes have failed (Reid and Hanrahan, 1981). Nevertheless, the weight of the evidence relates to behaviour which others than the clients have defined as a problem (for example, truancy, delinquency or suicide attempts) (Brody, 1976, Berg and others, Gibbon, 1981). Field social workers are also unable to resolve problems connected with a shortage of resources which they do not control, for example, chronic poverty or, in many cases, lack of a suitable house in which to live (Fisher, 1976, Mullen and Dampon, 1972, Wood, 1978, Sinclair, 1981).

11.52 The fact that social workers may be unable to prevent these problems does not mean that they have no role with those who are troublesome or very poor. Thus social workers may be able to play a valuable part in monitoring the behaviour of clients to see if residential care may be needed, even if they are unable to modify the behaviour which may make residential care necessary. Similarly, social workers may help clients to solve particular debts even if they are unable to modify poverty. It should be remembered that social work clients often have chronic problems, and value social work not so much because they expect it to change their situation but because they appreciate someone who recognises their difficulties and stands with them (Glendinning and Bradshaw, 1981, Fisher and others, 1980).

Career management

11.53 In certain circumstances, field social workers can allocate resources in such a way that public money is saved and risk to clients minimised. For example, social workers given adequate resources could almost certainly prevent some admissions of elderly people to residential homes, with benefit both to the local authority and to the clients (Challis and Davies, 1982). Similarly, they may prevent children from remaining unnecessarily in care (Jones and others, 1976, Stein and Gambrill). It seems likely, although research evidence is lacking, that social workers also play a useful role in other instances where personal and social difficulties are costing the public money, for example, where the client is blocking a hospital bed for social rather than medical reasons, or where a depressed person is about to have the gas supply disconnected or to be evicted for non-payment of rent. Obviously, in many cases it is not possible to achieve a result which benefits all parties, and even in cases where this seems to be possible, social workers may not do so (Shaw and others, 1975, Rowe and Lambert, 1979). Nevertheless, it is clear that competent social workers with access to adequate resources can have an impact for good on the course of their clients' lives.

Residential work

11.54 As with fieldworkers, it is difficult to separate out the effects of a residential setting (e.g. the fact that the client has been removed from home) from those of the residential worker. Nevertheless, it is clear that residential social workers can have a major impact on the morale and behaviour of their clients while they are in residential establishments and on the length of time the clients remain there. It is probable that residential social workers do not have much impact on clients after they have left their care, and certain that their influence while clients are in care can be for ill as well as for good (Tizard and others, 1975).

General conclusion

11.55 These judgements are based on the current state of knowledge, and will no doubt be modified by the results of future research. They also highlight certain omissions. In the first place, it is striking how often the word 'can' appears. For example, it is certain that social workers 'can' make accurate assessments, but not that they always do so. The difficulty of generalising the results to cover all social work arises partly from the fact that the success of an experiment is not always repeated in ordinary conditions. Much research has also compared social workers with each other, rather than with other professionals. The fact that the effectiveness of social work varies depending on the setting and the social workers involved is, however, evidence for the importance of the social work task. Poor social work may apparently leave clients in institutions when they do not need to be there, or make clients in institutions much more unhappy than they need to be. Social work is not, therefore, ineffective in the sense of being irrelevant. Research on the awesome consequences of the decisions in which social workers take part (Tizard, 1981) shows just how important it is. A second omission is that some forms of social work have not been sufficiently studied for conclusions about their effectiveness to be drawn. It is clear, for example, that day care is appreciated by its users, and that staff in day care centres are very popular, but uncertain what part individual social workers play in achieving this result (Carter, 1981, Fennel and others, 1981). More importantly, from the point of view of our report, there has been very little study of indirect social work, and comparatively little thought has been given to how it should be described and evaluated.

11.56 There has been little research either into the accuracy of the advice and information given by social workers or the degree to which their allocation of resources corresponds to need. Their function in monitoring the frail elderly, or children at risk, has also remained unevaluated. Major parts of the fieldworker's role have therefore escaped assessment, and other areas of social work have received even less attention.

11.57 Finally, comparisons between social work and apparently comparable forms of professional activity (e.g. health visiting) have rarely been made. Despite Goldberg's pioneering work (1970), there is little research basis for arguing that any particular activity is best carried out by a trained social worker rather than by someone else. Again, this omission may matter less than might appear. Someone has to decide whether clients should be admitted to residential care, and look after them when they get there. In this sense it is not a question of whether social workers should exist (if they did not, they would presumably have to be invented), but rather how they should best be trained to carry out these important tasks. There is no other profession which is manifestly more popular than social work in a position to take over social work tasks or, on the research evidence, more effective at dealing with such intractable problems as delinquency (references in Brody, 1976). The area in which social work overlaps most directly with the activities of other professionals and volunteers is that of counselling. Here, it may well be that others could do much of the work now done by social workers at least as effectively. Evidence on this point is lacking, and clients who come into touch with social services over their personal difficulties are almost certainly different from those who are prepared to approach such agencies as the marriage guidance councils (Mattinson and others, 1979). As we note in paragraph 11.27, it has been suggested to us that the volume of counselling required by the community is not matched by the number of people available to provide it.

11.58 In these circumstances, we have thought it right to base our conclusions on the evidence and the opinions we received, as well as on the research brought to our notice. On this basis, we have concluded that social work is neither an ineffective nor an unnecessary profession. On the contrary, social workers are capable of doing a variety of useful and sometimes essential things. Our enquiry has led us to the conclusion that they cannot, with the resources now available, do them for all who might come, or might be expected to come, their way.

SUMMARY OF CONCLUSIONS

1. A structured survey of clients' views should be considered either by the Department of Health and Social Security or by local authorities (11.3).

2. The evidence we gathered was not a scientific sampling of clients' views. But we noted the consistency of all the indications which came our way (11.7, 35).

3. Clients look for a direct, and most often a practical response, to problems and expect social workers to have knowledge, including specialist knowledge, enabling them to provide it (11.41).

4. Evaluative research into social work has asked questions which are not always appropriate (11.43); of such research, much is inconclusive or conflicting (11.46).

5. There has been little research into a number of areas of social work, including indirect social work (11.55–57).

6. On the basis of our evidence and of the research brought to our notice, we conclude that social workers are capable of doing a variety of useful or essential things, albeit, with the resources now available, not for all who might come their way (11.58).

Chapter 12

Maintaining standards and protecting clients' rights

Introduction

12.1 In this chapter we consider how best clients may be protected from bad social work practice. We discuss first, ways of maintaining satisfactory levels of practice and conduct by social workers, and second, ways of protecting the interests of clients. We are in no doubt that these are two sides of the same coin, and do not see how either aspect can be properly considered except in relation to the other. Any discussion of standards not focussed on protecting the interests of the client is, in our view, particularly questionable. If it seems to the reader that we give too much importance to such protection and suggest too elaborate a range of measures to serve it, our justification lies in the powerlessness, inarticulateness and vulnerability of very many clients of social workers.

12.2 Some of the evidence sent to us, and most notably that submitted by the British Association of Social Workers (136) and the Residential Care Association (137), has urged us to recommend the setting up of a new body, with associated accreditation machinery, to maintain, develop and enforce standards of training and professional behaviour in social work. The case for setting up a General Social Work Council, or General Social Services Council, has been argued on both the grounds we have mentioned.

12.3 It is for this reason that we have decided to include a discussion of both these issues in one chapter. We consider first the maintainance of standards, the majority of us concluding after weighing the arguments on both sides, that it would be premature, at present, to recommend the setting up of a General Social Work

(Social Services) Council for this purpose. We go on to discuss how the interests of clients might best be protected, and put forward suggestions for safeguarding them that would, in the view of most of us, be more effective at this time than a General Council.

MAINTAINING STANDARDS OF PRACTICE AND CONDUCT

Professionalism

12.4 The establishment of such a body as a General Social Work Council is sometimes thought of as the outward mark of attainment of 'professional' standing. There have been many attempts to analyse the essential characteristics of a profession. Some say it is misguided to try to do so. 'Professions are simply those occupational groups who have been lucky or clever enough to negotiate themselves into a situation of high status or power' (Brunel Institute of Organisation and Social Studies, 1976). However that may be, the characteristics are generally agreed to include the possession of a commonly accepted central body of theoretical knowledge, the command of special skills and competence in the application of this knowledge, and professional conduct guided by a code of ethics, the focus of which is service to the client (Toren, 1972).

12.5 We have received directly contradictory evidence as to whether social work should now move towards full professional status (on a par with, say, medicine and law). Some are strongly in favour; others arguing no less strongly that this would be a move in the wrong direction. In considering the arguments on both sides and in reaching our conclusion we think it appropriate to state here, as we have been asked to do (213), that whatever view is taken about the professional status of social workers the fact is that social work has established itself as an essential component in an increasingly complex society. It is here to stay.

12.6 What is meant by 'full professional status' for social workers? It would, in the eyes of those who argue for it, involve the creation by statute of a General Social Work (Social Services) Council which would be responsible for the maintenance of a register of social workers. The Council would have power to remove from the register those who were found to be guilty of unprofessional conduct, and such removal would result in the individual being subsequently unable to practice either as a social worker in general or, if the powers were more limited, to carry out certain of the more responsible functions for which social workers are now employed. The Council, on one view, would take under its wing all matters to do with education and training (the Central Council for Education and Training in Social Work being thus incorporated in the new body) or on another view would have close links with the Central Council, while remaining separate from it (Malherbe, 1979).

12.7 The first professional social work register (since abandoned) was introduced in 1907 by the Association of Hospital Almoners and the Institute of Hospital Almoners, but whereas other activities in the welfare field (such as nursing) have always been reasonably clear, reasonably stable and well understood by the public, social work practice does not have such a clearly defined, coherent, or readily understood task or set of tasks. Thus although nurses had to wait forty-five years, from 1874 to 1919, before their register was established, social workers have already had to wait much longer.

12.8 Social work has, moreover, changed beyond recognition since 1907, and now covers a range of activities of which work in hospitals is a comparatively small part. Its boundaries are far from clear, opinions about it are deeply divided on many issues, and it is the subject of much public misunderstanding. The comparison with nursing reveals further distinctions which are relevant to professional status. Social work is concerned with social control as well as with caring for people, its knowledge base and skills are still being debated within the profession and, some would say, will be destined to remain in a state of flux. The fact that the knowledge base is not readily understood by the public at large is significant because like any profession it needs public acceptance and recognition before it can become established.

12.9 Social work is also the odd man out because its practice is not regulated by statute: 'All health and welfare professions which entail a practitioner/client relationship subject to a code of professional conduct and who carry responsibility for meeting the needs of individuals and serving the interests of communities (and not only for administrative purposes) are subject to statutory regulation of training *and* of practice, except social workers. They alone are subject to the statutory regulation only of education and training' (Malherbe, 1979).

12.10 In making any claim to professional status social workers have to contend with two more recent developments. First, the large bureaucracies which came into being following the creation of social services departments in the wake of the Seebohm Committee's report are one of the contributory factors responsible for the malaise which in part has given rise to this report. How can a social worker exercise professional discretion and independence where the demands of the organisation tend to run counter to them? Employers may pay lip-service to the need for social work to become more professional, so the argument runs, but will in practice resist the implication – namely that their control over social workers would become weaker. Bureaucratic development has also inevitably resulted in a division between management and worker which provides the basis for the influence of the Trade Unions. The move towards full professional status and the introduction of an intermediary in the shape of an independent professional body must constitute a threat to that influence. For lawyers and accountants in local government, their employer is their client. These professions have a long history of private independent practice. For social workers with no similar tradition there exists a much more difficult and confusing situation, the general implications of which we discuss in Chapter 9. Suffice it to say here that within the bureaucracy social workers may feel that they are constantly being pulled in different directions by the demands of their clients on the one hand, the requirements of their employers on the other and in between by the ethics and standards of their profession.

12.11 Secondly, the move towards self-help and community action is a recent development which also provides an unfavourable background to the development of professionalism. 'In a number of ways, community action and community involvement in services may be seen as part of a growing assault on professionalism itself. Among some community groups, particularly those with a strong radical orientation, there is a growing disrespect for professional authority, especially the authority of social workers and others involved in the welfare services. The professional traditionally interprets the client's needs through a filter of specialised knowledge, but community action often suggests that this professional filter must be put aside and the demands of clients met directly. Professional authority based on specialised knowledge and skill is under increasing attack' (Leonard, 1973).

12.12 Thus, without prejudging the issue, we have to accept that those who have pleaded the cause of full professional status for the social worker have had, in recent years, an increasingly uphill struggle to obtain general support for their views. Perhaps now that the upheaval following local government reorganisation in the first half of the 1970s has subsided, the going will become easier for them. This remains to be seen.

Accreditation

12.13 It is important to make clear what we mean by the expression 'accreditation'. It is sometimes used to describe the validation of social work educational courses. We use it in the sense of an acknowledgement, given to the individual practitioner that, after some form of objective assessment, he has achieved a certain level of competence. This is normally marked by an entry on a register. The register can merely be a document of record having no other effect. This is true of the registers kept by the Central Council for Education and Training in Social Work which include those who have been awarded the Certificate of Qualification in Social Work or Certificate in Social Service or have successfully completed approved advanced training. If, however, the register were operated by a professional body in conjunction with disciplinary powers of removal from the register, it would form the central weapon in the maintenance of good professional conduct and professional status.

12.14 A professional register as a means of ensuring professional competence, however, does not in itself achieve its object, contrary to the belief of several respondents in their submissions to our enquiry. Without machinery for regular re-registration on the basis of some arrangement for monitoring individual competence, and the encouragement of post-qualifying training from time to time, bad professional practice (as opposed to conduct) will continue. The register in such circumstances becomes merely 'a device to control access to practice' (Malherbe, 1979).

12.15 This distinction can be illustrated from the experience of the Law Society in its dealings with complaints against solicitors. Where the complaint arises from the professional *misconduct* of the solicitor (e.g. breach of professional confidentiality or dishonesty) then the Disciplinary Committee can act, but the vast majority of complaints arise from what is alleged to be professional *incompetence*. The complainant has to be told that his remedy, if any, is against the solicitor in negligence which in turn requires proof that the solicitor has not taken 'reasonable care' – reasonable in this context being judged against the standard of care generally regarded in the profession as being appropriate to the case in point. The position is precisely similar in the case of doctors and their General Medical Council. Neither profession has any regular test of competence (asssuming one could be devised) as a condition of re-registration.

12.16 The ultimate use of a register (which has not been pressed upon us in the evidence) is when it carries with it the exclusive right to a title (e.g. 'accredited social worker') with or without the right of those who are accredited to carry out certain professional duties. The situation at present in England and Wales is at the opposite extreme. The title 'social worker' is neither defined nor mentioned as such in any legal enactment, and there is no restriction on its use by any person who choses to consider himself a social worker. There are, at the time of writing, no restrictions on an unqualified social worker filling any post in the personal social services in England and Wales which are laid down by law.

The arguments in favour of a Council

12.17 The submission we received most strongly in favour of the establishment of a General Council came from the British Association of Social Workers. This association is: '. . . deeply committed to the view that no single proposal would have greater impact on the definition and actual performance of social work' (136).

12.18 The main object of a Council, in its view, would be the maintenance and development of standards of training and conduct. It would give reality to the concept of professional accountability (the consciousness in the mind of the practising social worker that not only has he a duty to his clients and to his employer but also, as a member of a profession, to the ethics and values laid down by that profession). Without an independent council which can give authority to the promotion and maintenance of professional standards the concept of professional duty lacks substance and morale and standards suffer.

12.19 Several other submissions support the need for a Council to raise standards of practice in order to enable 'both social workers and society to have a clearer perception, and greater confidence in, the social work role . . .' (79). It is also argued that the existence of a Council would strengthen social workers' credibility when arguing for policy changes.

12.20 The degree of power exercised by social workers, particularly in the case of children at risk has been a cause of concern in some of our evidence. Certain difficult decisions have to be taken by social workers, some affecting the liberty of their clients, and by their very nature they require the highest competence and integrity. A General Council has been suggested as a clear way of introducing both the guaranteed competence and the independence necessary in these cases.

12.21 It was argued that a General Council would help employers both by laying down uniform standards (although what this might include was not specified), and by clarifying the question of what constitutes unprofessional conduct and also by helping to define a reasonable standard of practice. Otherwise the disciplinary powers exercisable by the Council would be quite separate from employment law and would impinge on the relationship of employer and employee only if removal of a social worker from the register made it statutorily impossible for a local authority or voluntary organisation subsequently to engage him to carry out a specified range of duties. Consideration had only recently been given by the British Association of Social Workers, so far without any conclusion, to the question of how it would be proposed to link qualification and accreditation with the salary framework for social workers laid down in the national scheme of conditions of service negotiated in 1979.

12.22 We received strong evidence from the medical profession in favour of a more structured profession for social workers with a controlling body similar to the General Medical or General Nursing Council: 'Due to the failure to develop a properly structured profession, there also exist difficulties over the ethical accountability of social workers. This is a vital component of a successful profession, and is indispensable in its dealings with others who have such a structure. The exchange of confidential information between members of co-operating professions is perhaps the classic example of the need for confidence in each other that ethically suitable standards of practice are being followed. The very personal communication between the medical and social work professions which we have put forward in connection with the varying roles of the latter in different areas of care only serves to emphasise this' (39).

12.23 Finally, although private practice in social work is still relatively uncommon, it is likely to increase, and in the interests of protecting the public it should be controlled. It is argued that the Council is an appropriate vehicle for such control.

The arguments against a Council

12.24 The submission most clearly opposed to a Council was from the National and Local Government Officers' Association (in its supplementary evidence). While supporting the purpose of the Council it does not believe that the suggested mechanism is appropriate.

12.25 The attack is concentrated on the alleged absence of a 'generally recognised core of knowledge and practice necessary for, and appropriate to, social work'. The definition of a social worker is not clear in the public mind. While the older professions can be defined by reference to their qualification it is inappropriate to do so in the case of social workers because of the absence of core knowledge and the fact that the skills required have not been identified. How then do you choose the criteria against which to measure an individual's fitness to be admitted to a professional register? (92)

12.26 The need, when the register is opened, for 'blanketing in' those already practising, who would not be expected to have to pass any further examination, would, the Association suggest, mean that the register would fail in its object of creating public confidence. The status and careers of both field social workers and residential social workers who have no qualification at the time of blanketing in could be seriously disrupted because they would not rank for admission to the register. This would damage the interests of clients and employers alike. (We note however that precedents, e.g. at the registration of dentists, would suggest the blanketing in of all those in practice, holders of qualifications or not, and that this does not appear to have damaged public confidence or patients' interests.)

12.27 Misgivings are expressed about the proposed disciplinary procedures and the absence of objective criteria for deciding whether an individual should be removed from the register.

12.28 From the voluntary sector, the National Council for Voluntary Organisations (123) stated that what is required is less rather than more professionalisation. It argued that the primary skill of a social worker should be the ability to unlock the resources in the community and that the practice of social work is deficient in this area: 'In part this is due to a professionalisation of social work which shows every tendency to mimic other professions – the law or medicine, for example – professions that have increasingly resisted the involvement of the "non-professional". In all walks of life such moves tend to be detrimental to the recipients of services: social work is no exception.'

12.29 A professional structure would be likely to heighten the divide between registered social workers on the one hand and clients, voluntary workers and other social services staff on the other. This is the traditional anti-elitist argument pointing to the professional group acting in a self-protecting and distancing manner, often at the expense of, rather than for the benefit of, the client. The work of Ivan Illich (e.g. *Disabling Professions*) is perhaps the most thoroughgoing in its espousal of this argument.

12.30 On the argument that the need is to increase the accountability of social workers to their profession, it is said that creating a General Council would worsen rather than alleviate problems of divided loyalties. Social workers have enough to cope with in trying to reconcile their duty to their employers with the needs of their clients. They can well do without another structure of accountability.

12.31 The legislation which would be required is unlikely to find Parliamentary time in the near future and would in any event be likely to be politically controversial. To render the establishment of a Council a practical possibility public opinion must first be tested, and, if possible, won over. It must be convinced that a new professional body is in the public interest.

13.32 The final point against a General Council, and one that could not fail to influence our recommendations, is the fact that social workers themselves are not all agreed about its desirability. Only twenty or so of the 351 submissions we received mentioned the subject, and in our discussions throughout the country with social workers at all levels we did not find it to be a burning issue. Many feel that the subject matter of this chapter is wholly irrelevant to the true problems which surround the roles and tasks of social workers. It is significant that in mental health, child guidance and hospitals, where social workers are constantly in contact with other professions, the mood is different, but these constitute a minority of social workers.

Summary

12.33 We sympathise with the objectives of those who advocate a General Council. It is clear that they are motivated by a desire to increase standards, and improve conduct and competence, in practice. We are however divided as a Working Party as to the desirability of a Council in the light of the evidence received and arguments advanced for and against it. Some see the Council as ultimately the best way of dealing with the problems of professional autonomy and accountability, and believe that the achievement of full professional status by social workers is a legitimate and desirable long-term goal. They believe that it is not inconsistent with the community-oriented approach we advocate in our report, and that it is in the best interests of the client. Others see a Council as a step in the wrong direction. It, in their view, ignores the current requirement for a changed approach and would tend to harden barriers between the formal and informal aspects of social work at precisely the time when they need softening. It would thus be contrary to the best interests of clients.

12.34 Not only are we divided in our views of the desirability of a General Council; those of us who think it is desirable are divided on the timing of its introduction. Most of us feel it to be unrealistic to set up a Council (assuming, which seems improbable, that there are available resources to do so) at a time when it has limited support among social workers and there is no pressure for it from the public at large. Immediate moves to do so would, in our opinion, tend further to damage the public image of social workers. The substantial opposition which could be expected to such a step would heighten the feelings of rejection which have been implanted in the minds of some social workers by the public enquiries and court cases arising from non-accidental injury to children and the treatment sometimes accorded to them by the media. But a minority of our number feels that it would be appropriate to introduce a General Council immediately.

12.35 We are all agreed that the protection of the public remains the strongest argument in favour of an independent Council in any profession. It would be valid in social work if it could be shown that it was the most appropriate means available to achieve this end. The Working Party as a whole does not consider this to be so at the present time.

Possible alternatives

12.36 As regards the maintenance of standards of practice and conduct we believe that two particular developments would, if introduced, accomplish as much as would the setting up of a General Social Work Council and be more generally supported.

12.37 The first development, which we endorse most strongly, would be a probationary period for each social worker. We urge that the award of a qualification in social work should be made only on successful completion by the social worker of at least one year's probation. During this time the newly-appointed worker's ability to practice social work would be subjected to rigorous scrutiny, preferably by an independent assessor working with senior staff of the employing agency, in accordance with nationally agreed criteria. (The Central Council for Education and Training in Social Work would be an obvious candidate for the setting of such criteria.) Social workers in the probation and after-care services are already appointed subject to confirmation after a probationary period. We believe this arrangement should be extended to include all social workers seeking a qualification.

12.38 We see this development as eminently practicable and desirable. We recognise that existing courses all contain practical placements and do not, in any way, wish to underrate their importance. What is clear to us is that these placements do not provide a reliable enough basis for assessing how students will react and perform in a full-time social work post. Both in residential and in field work the surest way of evaluating a student's potential is in a prolonged period of experience and responsibility.

12.39 The second development is one we have considered less fully. Though convinced of its importance we are less sure of the way in which it should be operated and we recognise that at least within the short term it has resource implications. There should be, in our view, an independent inspectorate which would monitor the practice of both social workers and their employing agencies. Whatever arrangements are made by individual social workers and their organisations for evaluating their work and effectiveness, we are convinced that this will not be sufficient to ensure that all clients' interests are protected and public confidence in social work maintained. We would welcome immediate discussion on the implementation of this recommendation, but recognise it needs much detailed thinking before it could be given effect. A minority of Working Party members would support an extension of the powers and duties of the Social Work Service giving its officers a comprehensive inspectorial rather than a purely advisory role. The Secretaries of State may wish to consider this. Meantime we would suggest that local authorities and voluntary agencies assign to holders of their senior consultant posts the duty of inspecting the work of their social workers in addition to their advisory duties. A model is offered by the local inspectorates and advisory teachers within some education departments.

OTHER WAYS OF PROTECTING THE RIGHTS OF CLIENTS

The vulnerability of clients

12.40 In addition to the two developments recommended above we believe that steps should be taken to formalise and strengthen the rights of social workers' clients.

12.41 The clients of social work agencies are more in need of protection than most consumers in the sense that the agency is usually a 'monopoly supplier' and market forces cannot operate. They may also, by virtue of disadvantage or handicap, be in a poor position to fight for their rights, and in many instances they may be receiving attention from the agency against their wishes. Many agencies too, have legal and quasi-legal functions and important decisions about peoples' lives are often made within the agency and outside the framework of the courts. It seems reasonable to expect, where such decisions are being taken, that the rules of natural justice should apply in the agency as they would do in the courtroom; that is, that the person affected should have the right to know the grounds upon which the decisions have been taken, to present his own case personally or through a representative, to question any disputed facts, and to appeal against the decision.

12.42 A client is both a client of the individual social worker and of his employing agency, and frequently also a consumer of practical or material services from that agency. If he has a grievance, it may be against the social worker, the agency, or both, and we refer later to the need to identify clearly the true focus of responsibility whenever a complaint is made. Furthermore, a decision taken at field level which impinges upon an individual client may simply reflect a general agency policy made at a higher level. If the rights of clients are to be more than a token then their interests must be represented at the level at which policy is made and not just in the individual case. We discuss below our proposal for 'local welfare advisory committees' through which clients' interests could be brought to bear upon the formation of agency policy.

12.43 Most of the evidence which we received on clients' rights relates to local authorities, and mainly to their activities in the field of statutory child care. It could be argued that much of this evidence paints a negative picture of current practice drawn from extreme and untypical cases, but we note that its conclusions are essentially the same as those of the British Association of Social Workers, and our impression is that both social workers and users' groups in general are uneasy about the current state of policy and practice in the matter of clients' rights.

12.44 Some of our respondents argued that, although social workers are frequently very active in helping their clients to obtain their full rights from other professions and agencies, they are often reluctant to accept in turn that the same considerations should apply to them, and that, however good their intentions, their actions may not always be beyond question. 'A serious flaw in some social workers' thinking . . . is that once they have taken a decision that they consider to be in the best interests of their client, anyone opposing that judgement is deemed to be acting *contrary* to the best interests of the client' (338).

Some criticisms of current practice

12.45 Social workers, it is said, frequently fail to explain the reasons for their decisions, fail to give clients essential information about their rights, and fail to make clear to their clients either the reason for their involvement or the extent of the powers which they possess. It was said, for instance, that a parent might first approach a social worker, perhaps asking for practical help, and be offered what appeared to the parent to be a relationship of mutual agreement and trust, only to find that the social worker had all the time been monitoring the parent's child as being 'at risk' and was now considering statutory action. 'The basis for work with clients should be made explicit from the outset – there should be no "hidden agendas" upon which social work decisions are made' (244). This is not a simple issue, because the social worker must feel his way in establishing a relationship and needs great sensitivity and skill to find the right time and the right context to raise issues which may be threatening or hurtful to a client. The pressures of work, the practice of the department or voluntary organisation, the setting in which the social worker operates will all influence how he handles these matters.

12.46 Social workers are sometimes criticised for blocking their clients' access to management, for instance if they wish to request a change of worker. In general, much social work practice is described as paternalistic, in contrast to the ideal of an equal partnership, with clearly-defined objectives – an ideal which receives strong support from groups which speak for clients, and from social work literature.

12.47 Local authorities are also criticised for failure to make explicit their criteria for allocation of resources (for example, in deciding whether or not an elderly person should have a telephone), for reluctance to allow access to files, and for failure to observe the rules of natural justice when taking statutory action. There is further resentment that this failure may be compounded by gaps in the system of legal aid: 'Clients who feel aggrieved . . . usually find that the law does not provide for their fair representation . . . and the vast majority of parents in care cases find that, although they stand accused of being incapable parents . . . there is no legal aid for them' (338).

12.48 It is for reasons such as these, some respondents said, that vulnerable groups of people (for instance, single parents) have come increasingly to regard social workers with fear and suspicion, believing that they now have excessive powers which they may use in an arbitrary and unpredictable fashion. Gingerbread, for instance, told us that they would be reluctant to involve social workers in some problems. Judged by the whole of our evidence it is clear that this fear and suspicion is far from universal. As we note in Chapter 11, there are differences of attitude and of concern about 'rights' between different client groups.

The inadequacies of current arrangements for redressing grievances

12.49 It was a frequent contention in the evidence that current channels for making a complaint or for lodging an appeal were at best inadequate, and that it often appeared that social worker and local authority acted as 'judge and jury in their own cases'. An aggrieved client might proceed in one of two ways: he might pursue his grievance himself, or he might ask someone with better access to the system to act on his behalf. In either instance, it was suggested, he faced a number of hurdles. If he pursued his case himself, he would have no guaranteed access even to the social worker's immediate manager (who might well be the person who had actually taken the decision), and a letter to the director might get him no further: 'In many cases letters are sent unread to the original case worker' (266). Nor would he have any right of access to information (for instance, the contents of his casefile). Even if he could establish the facts, it would be difficult for him to prove that the social worker's or the authority's action was unreasonable as he would not be able to point to any generally-accepted standards of reasonable practice: 'There appear to be considerable variations between social services departments in the handling of cases . . . (complaints have arisen) concerning the betrayal of client confidence, sometimes unwittingly and at other times due to local or individual codes of practice . . . a common national code of practice for social workers would be useful' (313). Nor would he be able, in most circumstances, to obtain a 'second opinion' from an impartial social worker.

12.50 A representative might fare no better. Councillors and Members of Parliament, it was said, often fail to resolve complaints, either because (in the case of councillors) they have a vested interest in defending the authority, or because, like the client, they are denied access to information and in the last resort have difficulty in questioning 'professional judgement'.

12.51 If, having complained through the channels provided by the local authority, the client is still dissatisfied there are, it was pointed out, few other avenues open. The courts, as many users' groups have found, offer limited opportunities to challenge the decisions of a local authority, the Ombudsman is restricted to the investigation of maladministration (albeit the boundary of professional judgement is ill-defined) and there is no other external body to which appeal can be made.

12.52 A common theme of the evidence is that there should be a right of appeal to a body independent of the local authority and able to review all aspects of a case.

Criteria for improvement

12.53 It seems to us, on the basis of this evidence, that any steps taken to improve matters must aim to satisfy the following five criteria:

● First, the client should, as far as possible, be enabled to participate in the making of important decisions about himself or should be consulted before they are made.

● Secondly, he must be made aware of his rights, and how and where to set about obtaining them.

● Thirdly, he must be given an essential minimum of information, including information from records, as to what decisions have been taken about him, by whom and why.

● Fourthly, if he is aggrieved, he (or his representative) must have direct access to a person or body with the power to make redress.

● Finally, again if he is aggrieved, he must have access either to an independent professional opinion, or to some other objective yardstick as to what constitutes acceptable practice.

Factors limiting the full application of these criteria in all cases

12.54 It must be acknowledged that the 'social control' functions of local authorities and of some voluntary agencies do impose certain limits upon the extent to which clients can reasonably expect to be able to participate in the making of decisions about themselves. There is also a limit upon free access to information imposed by the need for social workers to work closely with members of other professions (in particular, doctors) who have strong traditions of confidentiality. The British Association of Social Workers in their publication *Clients are Fellow Citizens* makes a distinction between 'counselling' and 'social control' activities. In the former, where the relationship is voluntary, the social worker should share information freely and should respect his client's right to self-determination; in the latter, where self-determination may have to be denied, he should at least ensure that all his actions are 'open and above board', that his client is aware of what rights he has, and that he knows who is making decisions about him and why.

12.55 There are other circumstances in which client and social worker cannot be on an equal footing. Through disadvantage or handicap many clients of social workers will be unable either to understand their rights or to argue their own case, and amongst the most vulnerable will be young children, whose interests may be very different from those of their parents. These people may have rights denied to them unless there is someone able both to recognise their need and to press their case, and in the case of the most isolated and stigmatized clients there is often no one but their social worker. In these circumstances, however good the practice the relationship between social worker and client must be unequal and paternalistic to some degree. For the sake of these people it is essential that any complaints or appeals procedures should be sufficiently flexible to accommodate appeals made on behalf of individuals by other individuals and organisations, including, it may be, organisations who might not enjoy the best of relations with the local authority – some welfare rights groups, for instance, who might be the only people to whom the most stigmatized clients could turn.

12.56 It must be acknowledged, however, that there are some very isolated clients who will always be to some extent at the mercy of bad social work practice, and for whom no complaints procedures will offer much safeguard. For these people the greatest protection must continue to be the internal monitoring procedures of the employing agency, and the steps which it takes to ensure competence.

Local welfare advisory committees

12.57 Any steps taken to strengthen the safeguarding of clients' rights are likely to be of greatest benefit to those individuals (or organised groups) who are best equipped to argue their case, and this carries the inevitable risk that agency policy will become biassed towards the interests of those groups who are most effective in the pursuit of complaints. We do not see this as sufficient justification for witholding opportunities to make their case, either from clients in general or from particular groups; but it will place a heavy burden upon agency management to ensure that the less articulate groups receive fair and equal treatment. We suggest that local welfare advisory committees might provide a valuable means of ensuring that a proper balance is kept, and recommend that this idea should be explored.

12.58 In coming to this conclusion we are not suggesting something altogether novel. The Seebohm Committee recommended advisory bodies in their report (paragraph 506). One of their concerns was that large new social services departments would by their bureaucracy and advocacy of 'professionalism' shift the balance of power away from clients and communities. The local bodies were one way of seeking to secure a more healthy balance. We are envisaging a wider remit for local welfare advisory committees, but our overriding concern is the same. We have not had the time (nor did we have the brief) to explore this proposal in detail. We have reached certain general conclusions however: there cannot be a blueprint for such committees in terms of size, population and area covered, constitution, or relationship with voluntary agencies working in the area; they will need to be developed in such a way that the interests of recognised organisations and groups do not predominate over those of the inarticulate and deprived; they must find a source of funding such that they are not dependent on social services departments for their continuation. They cannot be imposed from above but need to be encouraged to form from below.

12.59 There is now a wealth of information available about the setting up and functioning of similar groups and we recommend that the experience of the Community Councils in Scotland and the Community Health Councils in England and Wales be studied carefully in arriving at the best way forward. (We recommend specifically the Scottish Development Department document: *Community Councils: Some Alternatives for Community Council Schemes in Scotland*, HMSO, 1974, for consideration because of its imaginative handling of the need for flexible yet accountable organisation. This discussion document sets out several options for local, representative bodies. It recognises the need for local people to define their community, the differences between urban and rural areas, and the importance of communication between individuals, voluntary organisations and local authorities.)

12.60 Local welfare advisory committees would be designed to provide a forum in which representatives of clients, employers and social workers could discuss agency policies with respect to the rights of clients, including such issues as confidentiality, access to information, and criteria for resource allocation. They would also, among other things, test out new ideas and policies, and comment on the structure and operation of social services agencies. The aim would be for each agency, in consultation with the advisory committee, to adopt a formal policy on clients' rights, together with clearly-stated procedures for dealing with complaints or appeals. The advisory committee would not itself act as an appeals body but should be responsible for monitoring the implementation of appeals procedures. Links between an independent inspectorate if established and these committees would need to be carefully worked out and arrangements made for the committees to receive relevant reports from inspectors.

Examples of procedures to be agreed by the advisory committees

12.61 Although the detail of complaints and appeals procedures should be a matter for local agreement we think that it is possible to identify some general issues.

12.62 There is a need (as we have acknowledged already) to distinguish between complaints about the performance of the individual social worker, and those which question an action or a policy of his managers or of the agency as a whole. The individual client may – as our evidence suggested – have difficulty in finding out, by whom, and on what grounds, a decision about him was actually made, and this may lead him to make a complaint about the individual social worker when the social worker was simply acting in accordance with an agency directive. It is important too, to distinguish between an appeal (where the client wants a decision to be reversed) and a complaint (where the client simply wants an apology or an assurance that it 'won't happen again'), and, perhaps, most important, between those issues which may be decided by objective criteria (for instance, an application for a telephone) and those which involve a large element of subjective judgement by a social worker (for instance, a request by a parent for more access to a child).

12.63 There must be different procedures for resolving each of these different types of issue. If the question is one of agency policy, or of the application of objective rationing criteria, then it may be most appropriately dealt with by the social services committee (or the council of a voluntary agency) or by an appeals sub-committee, who may in turn seek guidance on the general issues from the local advisory body. If, however, the question is about a social worker's professional judgement, or if there are allegations of incompetence or misconduct, then it will probably be inappropriate to refer the matter directly to a lay committee, and the initial and primary responsibility for resolving the issue must rest with senior management.

12.64 It is not, however, consistent with the rules of natural justice that the senior managers in the agency concerned should be the sole judges of what they describe as 'professional' issues, given that they may have a strong vested interest, and it is essential that there should be some provision for obtaining an independent second opinion in cases of serious disagreement. In a local authority, it is possible for the social services committee to require the director to commission a second opinion; if this opinion is in variance with that of the director and his staff then the committee must eventually be the final arbiter. As far as we know this course of action rarely occurs.

We see it as a helpful device in providing for clients' interests, with claims to be more widely considered as an option in future.

12.65 At present, although we note the growth in number of independent social workers involved in child care court cases, there is no formal machinery for obtaining a second social work opinion other than the various local and regional schemes which exist to provide reports to solicitors in contested care proceedings. Perhaps local authorities and the major voluntary organisations might come together on a regional basis to agree upon the reciprocal provision of second opinions; but it would be open to local welfare advisory committees, if they were to be set up, to consider this issue and make recommendations.

Some possible consequences of the above recommendation

12.66 We think that the formalisation of clients' rights is a necessary development, and that our proposals amount to no more than the public is now increasingly coming to expect of any occupational group or publicly-funded agency which has entensive powers over the lives of individuals. It says much for social work that some of the most radical proposals for the protection of clients' rights have come from social workers themselves, rather than from pressure groups urging reforms on a suspicious and defensive profession. We recognise, however, that many consequences will flow from the introduction of 'consumerism' to the personal social services, and that some of these might be unintended and potentially harmful to the quality of service to the public.

12.67 Inevitably, the formalisation of rights can be a complex and expensive business. It is simpler and quicker, in the short run, not to explain your actions to your client or involve him in decisions, the more so if explanation may lead to your actions being challenged. Written notification of decisions is time-consuming; appeals and complaints procedures soak up further staff time and slow the process of decision-making; and any arrangement to provide 'second opinions' inevitably means that valuable staff will be seconded to neighbouring authorities or agencies on work which brings little or no apparent benefit to the employer.

12.68 On the other hand, there will be a counterbalancing gain if the strengthening of clients' rights promotes better working between agency, social worker and client. It is hard to predict the effect on the nature of social work practice, but, if the evidence is to be believed, there ought to be some improvement in the level of trust and confidence placed in social workers by some vulnerable groups, if social work practice moves 'emphatically away from paternalism towards partnership' (136). This is also consistent with the direction in which we believe social work should move as explained in Chapter 13.

12.69 It could be argued that the increased risk of a complaint, together with the need to provide the client with more information and explanation, would impose a healthy discipline on social work practice which would require both social workers and their agencies to think more clearly about the purpose and the value of their intervention, to be more specific about what they were offering (and when they were ceasing to offer it) and to ensure, where appropriate, that the client was a full and consenting partner from the outset.

12.70 On the other hand, there is the risk that an 'adversarial' element would creep into many transactions between worker and client, as is now the case in many welfare agencies in the United States, and there might be an increase in 'defensive practice', with social workers and agencies reluctant to take actions which are necessary in the community's or the client's interest but which might lay worker or agency open to a complaint.

12.71 If the effects on practice are difficult to forecast, it is certain that an increase in clients' rights will make both social workers and their agencies more vulnerable. When agencies codify their standards and practices, and give public guarantees that they will conduct themselves in a certain way then they inevitably lay themselves open to public censure if they are seen not to have lived up to these standards.

12.72 Social workers will be more vulnerable in the sense that they may find themselves, to a much greater extent even than now, sandwiched between the expectations of their agency and the demands of their client; a client who will be in a position to make a complaint which, even if unjustified, could be very distressing and damaging to the social worker. On the other hand, the social worker's position may be enhanced by the existence of explicit standards and codes of practice, which bind his employer equally as himself, and he may welcome an appeals procedure as a means of resolving the tensions and conflicts which can arise if he is required by the employer to impose upon his client a policy with which he does not himself agree.

SUMMARY OF CONCLUSIONS

1. A majority of the Working Party believes it would be premature to set up a General Social Work Council; some members oppose the proposal entirely; some favour its immediate implementation (12.3, 34).

2. Newly-trained social workers should serve a probationary period and have their competence assessed before receiving a qualification (12.37).

3. The independent monitoring of the practice of social workers and their employing agencies is of great importance; on one possible means – the establishment of an independent inspectorate we would welcome immediate discussion (12.39).

4. Pending the setting up of any independent inspectorate, agencies should assign inspectorial functions to senior consultant staff (12.39).

5. Steps should be taken to formalise the rights of clients who should, as far as possible, participate in decisions, be made aware of their rights, receive information about decisions taken, have a channel of appeal or complaint, and access to a second opinion (12.40, 53).

6. We recommend that the concept of local welfare advisory committees should be explored (12.57–65).

7. We recognise that some consequences of formalisation of clients' rights may be unwelcome to social workers and social services agencies and may have unintended effects upon practice. But we think such formalisation necessary (12.66–72).

Chapter 13

Towards community social work

Introduction

13.1 The Working Party believes that if social needs of citizens are to be met in the last years of the twentieth century, the personal social services must develop a close working partnership with citizens focussing more closely on the community and its strengths. A move towards what we are calling community social work is the start of such a development.

13.2 Community social work depends upon an attitude of mind in all social workers from the director of the department or agency to front-line workers which regards members of the public as partners in the provision of social care.

13.3 We believe there is no one way in which partnerships between those involved in using and providing social care should be developed. Each statutory and voluntary agency must consider the geographical area and the nature of the people and the communities it serves before deciding upon the particular forms and combinations of community social work which it wishes to develop. Thus what we are suggesting is not a blueprint but the development of flexible decentralised patterns of organisation based upon a social care plan which takes full account of informal care, and mobilises voluntary and statutory provision in its support.

13.4 In this chapter we explore the grounds on which our support for a community social work approach is based, explore some of the forms it may take and consider some of the important questions which must be answered by those who seek to implement it. We are necessarily more speculative in some parts of this chapter than we have been in earlier chapters because the attitudes, forms and structures which we are considering have not yet been widely tested.

13.5 The community approach we are advocating seeks to share more fully with citizens the satisfactions and the burdens of providing social care. We are concerned only with social work and its place among the personal social services but a community approach logically knows no such boundary, nor can it be fully implemented in just one sector of the social services. Other services such as housing, health and education are equally, if not more, important. The limits to improvements which can be won by changes within the personal social services alone are obvious when viewed from this wider perspective. Nevertheless, we can consider only the personal social services since we would be going far beyond our capacities, let alone our remit, were we to attempt to go further.

The case for community social work

13.6 The case rests upon our understanding of the nature of community and the meaning and form of social care. We defined community as a network, or networks, of informal relationships between people connected with each other by kinship, common interests, geographical proximity, friendship, occupation, or the giving and receiving of services – or various combinations of these. The Seebohm Report, which recommended that social services should be community-based, defines community in similar terms: 'The notion of a community implies the existence of a network of reciprocal relationships which, among other things, ensure mutual aid and give those who experience it a sense of well-being' (paragraph 476).

13.7 An important feature of community is the capacity of the networks of people within it to mobilise individual and collective responses to adversity. Among the adversities that may afflict us, and prove beyond our powers to manage alone, are those for which the personal social services have accepted a degree of responsibility, often, but not always statutory: difficulties associated with ageing or sickness; dependency in young people resulting from family disruptions or inadequacies; mental disorders and physical disabilities; the personal agonies of bereavement, loneliness and broken relationships. The sum of helping (and, when need be, controlling) resources available to people in adversity, whether provided informally by community networks or formally by the public services, are what we mean by *social care*.

13.8 The bulk of social care in England and Wales is provided, not by the statutory or voluntary social services agencies, but by ordinary people (acting individually or as memebers of spontaneously formed groups), who may be linked into informal caring networks in their communities. Care of this kind is often maintained only at great personal cost to the carers. For example, a substantial proportion of those receiving help, and in particular the very old and people with chronic physical handicaps, are largely or entirley dependent upon one caring person – often an unmarried relative and usually a woman. The demands made on the individuals concerned can become enormous, and it is scarcely surprising that some break down under the stresses and strains involved. The informal caring networks, in other words, are vulnerable and fragile, and it is precisely when they give way that large numbers of referrals are made to social services departments and voluntary agencies. If social work policy and practice were directed more to the support and strengthening of informal networks, to caring for the carers and less to the rescue of casualties when networks fail, it is likely that the need for such referrals would be reduced.

13.9 It is difficult to over-estimate the importance of the social care that members of communities give each other. The majority of people in trouble turn first to their own families for support. If this is lacking or insufficient, the help of wider kin, friends or neighbours becomes a valued resource – first because people we know are often (though by no means always) easier to talk to and confide in than workers in public agencies, secondly because seeking help from our informal networks is, within limits, socially acceptable. Doing so is usually less of a blow to our self-esteem than approaching official-dom. Even when our need for resources is on such a scale, or our difficulties so complex, that they outstrip the capacity of our informal networks to help us cope with them, the continuing concern of those we know and trust is often a vital factor in maintaining morale.

13.10 These statements are borne out by research. In the last two decades studies of various dependent groups living in the community, such as the frail elderly and the mentally and physically handicapped, have consistently shown the importance of kinship networks. The large majority of people, in the categories served by the personal social services, who are unable to care for themselves, receive their principal support from relatives. Friends and neighbours also often play a significant role in caring networks. It is also becoming evident that informal caring systems can be adaptive. For example, some retired elderly are able to move closer to supportive kin as they grow older. Or where family care is weak or absent altogether, other relationships may develop to supplement or replace them. In sum, it is clear that the centre of the caring arena is occupied by the community, not the statutory services.

13.11 Research also suggests, however, that informal networks are complex and not always benign. Friends and relatives are not necessarily helpers although they may serve as links to help, nor do people wish to consult their friends or their families about all problems. Some, because they are too sensitive or are felt to be too complex, can only be talked about outside the family or social network. Localities vary greatly in the extent and nature of informal networks and some communities seem better able to develop and use them than others. Warren, for example, in a study of networks in Detroit (1981), found that black neighbourhoods were most likely to have and to use local informal helping systems. It is facts of this kind which lead us to believe that social services departments may have much to learn about the networks existing in their areas and that if links with informal carers are to be effected, many different approaches must be explored.

13.12 There is also some evidence to suggest that the statutory services may, however unintentionally, undermine care by friends, family and neighbours. Where such care is available statutory social services may be withheld. Recent studies of the carers of elderly and handicapped people living in the community, summarised by an Equal Opportunities Commission report (1981) provide an illustration of the problems such carers face. The report comments:

'There is evidence to suggest that services are withheld on the grounds that the disabled person is living with relatives and has therefore a support system in operation. In Moroney's words: "If the elderly person is living with relatives, especially children, the service is withheld on the assumption that the family will provide needed care." In other situations, it would appear that even when family members cannot or will not provide care, the service is refused on the basis that they should do so. This policy is defended on the grounds of economic efficiency – in times of recession, services have to be restricted to those in "greatest need", usually interpreted as those living alone. The state, therefore, is not operating a community care policy which *complements* the family and informal caring networks. On the contrary as Moroney says, "it is possible that in making this policy distinction (i.e. withholding services when support is believed to exist) the state is actually penalising those families who are willing to retain the primary caring function. By not offering support, existing social policy might actually force many families to give up this function prematurely." (Moroney, 1975)'

13.13 It is for such reasons that we think it essential for the personal social services providing social care on a formal basis to work in close understanding with informal caring networks and not in isolation from them. Social workers, as the spearhead of the personal social services, need to find ways of developing partnerships between informal carers (including self-help groups), statutory services and voluntary agencies, in which each partner is regarded as a partner whatever the level of resources each brings to their collaborative efforts. Caring networks in a community need to have ready access to statutory and voluntary services and to contribute their experience to decisions on how the resources contributed by these services are used within their community. Citizens who give and receive services should have opportunities to share in decisions which affect their lives. This partnership is the essence of what we mean by community social work and depends upon an *attitude of mind* in those in the statutory and the voluntary sectors.

13.14 Such an attitude may not be easy to develop since some social trends seem to be running against it. Despite the fact that a high proportion of social care is provided by community networks, neither central nor local government policies appear always to have given weight to the value of preserving or developing local communities. On the contrary, policies have often had the effect of weakening them. They have done this in three ways: first, through the physical destruction of old housing and scattering of those who lived in established communities; secondly, through the more long drawn out process of slow strangulation when transport links are cut, or a major source of employment is lost and not replaced; thirdly, through the emphasis in planning and administering services on the individual, rather than on the communities in which he lives. Thus housing has been planned in individual units, based on the nuclear family, and provision rarely made for grandparents or other members of the extended family. New employment has often been planned on the assumption that workers should be ready to move home to obtain it. The citizen has more often been encouraged to think of his rights as an individual than of his responsibilities as a member of a community.

13.15 A community approach for the personal social services may help to reverse this trend. At all events, we believe that a partnership between citizens and the statutory and voluntary services offers the way most likely to meet the needs of citizens with social problems. Our reasons for this belief involve both practical and ethical considerations. Sharing social caring is a way both of promoting better care and more care in the community and of distributing the burden of caring for the disadvantaged more fairly. At present, as we have noted, if often falls most heavily upon close relatives. A partnership can also allow services to be provided in ways which contribute to the feelings of self-respect and well-being of those who receive them, as well as using scarce and expensive resources to their best effect.

13.16 Individual members of the Working Party would put particular stress on different reasons for recommending this community approach. For some it is self-evident that professional services carry a moral obligation to be fully accessible to the people they wish to serve. They must avoid both physical and psychological barriers which deter potential clients from seeking help. It is difficult for social workers to achieve such accessibility. Their clients are often particularly disadvantaged, suffering as many of them do from the effects of poverty. They often lack the confidence which is needed to seek help. A community approach offers ways of making social workers more readily available to people who may need help.

13.17 Other members of the Working Party would want to emphasise the ideas of equality and participation which are a feature of the kind of partnership we are suggesting, and for some of us the fact that more citizens may be recognised as, or come to be, givers as well as receivers of care, is particularly important.

Why the approach might succeed now

13.18 We are aware that, in recommending community social work and a partnership which requires the recognition of the strengths and potentialities of many different networks, we are doing little more than repeat the recommendations made by the Seebohm Committee in 1968 for a community approach. We make no apology for this since we believe that the Committee was right when it stated: 'Our interest in the community is based on the practical grounds that the community is both the provider as well as the recipient of social services and that orientation to the community is vital if the services are to be directed to individuals, families and groups within the context of their social relations with others. . . Implicit in the idea of a community-oriented family service is a belief in the importance of the maximum participation of individuals and groups in the community in the planning, organisation and provision of the social services' (paragraphs 475, 491).

13.19 What we must do, however, is to make clear why we consider that social services departments and voluntary agencies may now be able to orient themselves towards communities when they have had only limited success in moving in this direction in the ten years between 1971 and 1981.

13.20 Our main reason for believing that such an approach is now possible is that there has been a very general movement away from centralism and towards a belief in the capacity of ordinary people. This trend is seen already, or there is pressure for it to occur, in such diverse areas as party politics, discussions within trade unions, a disaffection with the older professions, the way some police forces are organised, in the management of rundown housing estates and in the move to decentralise authority in large industrial undertakings. People themselves are very generally less willing to tolerate the taking of decisions by remote authority which does not take account of circumstances affecting their neighbourhoods or communities of interest.

13.21 We believe that social services departments may now be ready to follow a community social work approach – and in fact many have already started. It must be remembered that when the Seebohm Committee reported social services departments had yet to be created. When they were established in 1971, as a result of the Local Authority Social Services Act, it was perhaps only to be expected that the energy of senior staff would be devoted largely to establishing structures for work and in learning to respond to the demands from their committees for the accountability which is expected in a representative democracy. At the ground level staff experienced what was often felt as bombardment from potential clients, and social workers were near to being overwhelmed by the sheer quantity of need which came to their doors. Like their managers, they had no time to look beyond the immediate demands which faced them each day. Gradually systems of management and service delivery have been developed, vacancies have been filled, now usually with qualified staff, and many departments have already started to build partnerships with the various communities they serve.

13.22 It also appears to us that the present difficult financial situation provides an opportunity for a change of approach. Clearly social services departments have to find ways to respond to what is likely to be increasing demand with constrained resources. At such a time an approach which offers co-ordinated use of both formal and informal resource must, we believe, make sense. In saying this we repeat the point made in Chapter 6 that this cannot be achieved on the cheap: our point is that only by such co-ordination will it be possible to respond to the demands we foresee. This, we believe, should counterbalance any reluctance felt by elected members or social services staff to relinquish, as this approach implies they must, some of their established ways of working and share some of their power as well as their responsibility. The will to change will be necessary if established ways of working are to be relinquished.

What is community social work?

13.23 Community social work is concerned both with responding to the existing social care needs of individuals and families and with reducing the number of such problems which arise in the future. Its actual form will vary greatly from place to place and time to time, but its underlying rationale is more enduring.

13.24 It rests, as we have made clear, upon a recognition that the majority of social care in England and Wales is provided, not by the statutory or voluntary social services agencies, but by individual citizens who are often linked into informal caring networks.

13.25 This recognition leads to a widening of the focus of social work attention. The individual or family with problems will of course remain the primary concern of social services agencies. The solution, easing or prevention of individual or family problems is and remains the reason for the existence of personal social services agencies. But the focus will be upon individuals in the communities or networks of which they are part. There has been a tendency for social workers to see their own clients in sharp focus against a somewhat hazy background in which other people were somewhat less than life-sized. Community social work demands that the people who form a client's environment are seen for what they are or may be – an essential component of the client's welfare.

13.26 Social workers have already moved from a focus upon individuals, or mothers and children, to seeing people as members of families. What community social work demands is that the circle of vision is extended to include those who form, or might form, a social network into which the client is meshed. Social workers have to be able to take account of a variety of different kinds of networks. These will vary in size and in the bonds which hold them together. There are many ways of describing these groupings but we have found it useful to consider the different ways in which social workers may need to view them. We think there may be three ways which are particularly important.

13.27 First, social workers need to stand, as it were, in their client's shoes and see the various people with whom that person is in touch. For example an elderly person in Haringey may have a personal network whose most important members are her neighbours on either side, with whom she talks, a son in Brighton who sees to her finances, a daughter in Enfield who comes over twice a week to do a bit of cleaning and who always brings a casserole with her, and a friend in Camden who comes over to play cards once a week. The example is of a fairly restricted network; many families are involved in much more complicated ones. None the less the aim in either case is the same: to see the people who make up the human contacts in a client's life whether they consist of five people or a hundred, whether they are local or more distant, based on relationships in leisure time or at work.

13.28 The second way social workers need to view networks is by focussing upon the actual or potential links which exist or could be fostered between people who live either in the same geographical area or in the same residential home or long-stay hospital or attend the same day centre. Staff in residential homes, day centres and hospitals need to understand and promote relationships between people who live or spend their days together, as well as between them and the people of the locality. This they often do already but it does not always receive the time and thought required.

13.29 Finally, social workers ought to keep in mind the communities of interest which develop between people who share similar interests, sometimes because they suffer from the same social problems. An example of a group who tend to be closely linked are parents of mentally handicapped children. The size of such groupings may vary. In this example they might be expected to consist of a hundred or more people who will certainly be spread across a wide geographical area.

13.30 These ways of viewing networks are not mutually exclusive. Each takes, as it were, a picture from a different angle. The first looks outward from an individual or family, the second looks down on a neighbourhood or group who live or spend time together, and the third traces the links created by a shared interest or concern. Comparing the first with the other two viewpoints may suggest possibilities for enriching individual networks.

Examples of community social work

13.31 We have been given many examples of the ways in which some social services departments and some voluntary agencies are encouraging, developing, supporting and sometimes giving resources to social care networks. They indicate possibilities for development. They are however often somewhat isolated attempts which have yet to be built into a planned whole by senior management in social services departments or voluntary agencies.

13.32 The examples we have been given fall into two broad categories. In the first, the focus is upon locality. Each social worker, together with other social services staff, serves a particular geographical area. In the second, the distinguishing feature is a shared concern or problem. Social workers and social services staff focus upon the needs of a particular client group. There is, of course, overlap between locality and client group but the categories help to suggest the kinds of network which may be of primary importance in each case.

Examples of community social work based upon locality

13.33 Local or patch teams. These vary in character but all include the allocation of social work staff to a limited geographical area. Preferably they have a base within the area and include other social services staff, such as home helps and street wardens, whose clients live 'in the patch'. The 'team' here may refer to a single social worker and the social work assistants, home helps and wardens who work together or may refer to a number of such groups and one or two team leaders who have overall responsibility for several patches and the staff who work in them. In the latter case each group of staff may work from a sub-office on their patch; where this is not possible, they may have the use of rooms on the patch where people can call in to see them.

13.34 We refer here only briefly to these particular examples based upon locality because some of our number have written extensively about them in their own addition to this report (Appendix A). We refer readers to this account since we share with them a belief that patch-based teams are an important development. They part company from us only when they suggest that locally based services are the only possible form for community social work.

13.35 A variant is the idea of **resource centres** which may be set in a residential establishment such as a children's home, an elderly persons' home or a day centre, and which provide a calling point for clients and a centre for clients, volunteers, home helps and street wardens to meet each other. Such centres may offer facilities for individual clients, perhaps day care for some elderly people or clubs for adolescents, and also for voluntary groups who may, for example, need rooms for their meetings or the use of office equipment.

13.36 Attachment of social workers to, for example, health centres and schools is another means by which they can come closer to groups of people who usually live in the same locality and, especially in the case of schools, have a shared concern. In both instances they are also involved with other professions as well as with groups of the general public.

13.37 **Social workers in hospitals** provide another example of groups who serve a particular community, in this instance made up of patients and members of various other disciplines. As the examples of hospital social work given in Chapter 1 illustrate, an understanding of the many social and professional networks, within the hospital and without, which cross-cut and interlock with each other is essential if patients' social needs are to be met.

Examples of community social work which emphasise shared concerns

13.38 The so-called 'specialist team' seems to fall into the category of development which emphasises shared concerns among groups of people rather than their geographical proximity. We have noted what on the face of it seem to be two divergent trends in the organisation of fieldwork services. One is towards localised patch arrangements and the other towards specialist teams. We discuss later the implications this may have for the skills social workers will be called on to use. First we touch on the scope for a community social work approach by different types of specialist teams.

13.39 Some local authority area teams have been divided into, usually, two sub-groups. One group works mainly with the elderly and the handicapped and is known by terms such as 'social care team', 'domiciliary care team', 'home care team'. The other group works largely with families and children and carries out the department's statutory duties towards children at risk, those committed to care and those who are subject to supervision orders. So-called 'specialist teams' of this kind provide an opportunity for their members to develop close links with the various social care networks which support their particular client groups and with the voluntary and statutory agencies involved with them. We are aware that such 'specialist teams' can, and often do, operate without a community orientation but we do not believe this is a necessary feature of this form of organisation.

13.40 A variant of the specialist team is the multi-disciplinary community team established most frequently, we have found, in relation to the mentally handicapped, and less often, following the Warnock Report, to serve physically handicapped children. Such teams may serve the whole of a local authority area. They have the opportunity to develop particular links with the relevant hospital services, with voluntary organisations concerned for their client group and with self-help and parents' groups throughout the authority. Again such teams do not always have a community orientation, but their service to their clients is greatly strengthened if they develop an approach resting upon a concept of partnership in caring with members of the communities concerned.

13.41 Use of a day centre or residential home as a base for a resource centre, which we noted might provide one variant of a locally-based community social work service, may equally be a feature of work based on specialist teams. Since the centre or home will often itself provide a specialist service and have specialist staff this may be even more appropriate.

What a community approach demands of the social worker

13.42 We consider that community social work can only be achieved if social workers are enabled by their training and by the organisation in which they work to espouse certain attitudes, master particular fields of knowledge and develop particular skills. None of these attitudes, knowledge fields or skills is new to social work but we consider that their importance needs to be emphasised.

13.43 Community social work requires of the social worker an attitude of partnership. Clients, relations, neighbours and volunteers become partners with the social worker in developing and providing social care networks. We have already referred to the description of the relationship by one respondent as one of people 'equal but different' (15); we might be prepared to go further and describe social workers as upholders of networks. This may make clear our view that the function of social workers is to enable, empower, support and encourage, but not usually to take over from, social networks.

13.44 Such attitudes cannot be expected unless the organisational structure supports them. We consider later the role of management but here wish to note that attaining such attitudes cannot be left simply to the good intentions of the social workers.

13.45 We have sketched in Chapter 10 what we see as the knowledge base for social work. Community social work does not change this base but may require a shift of emphasis. Understanding the internal worlds of individuals and families will remain important but increasing attention may need to be given to theories which help to explain the interaction of individuals in groups, localities, organisations and communities. A start may be made in initial training but social workers in post will need to be helped to know their own community be it a locality or a group of people with a shared concern.

13.46 It has been suggested that social workers who are organised into local or patch teams need to be generalists while those serving communities with shared concerns need to be specialists. We think this distinction may be misleading. Both kinds of social workers, if they are to operate with a community orientation, must have knowledge of communities and how they function. Each may require a specialist component. For the patch social worker it will be knowledge of a particular locality. For a so-called 'specialist team' member it will be knowledge of a particular disability or social problem or method of working. We are also uncertain whether patch social workers are necessarily required to be as generalist as might at first appear. Some existing teams seem to concentrate heavily upon particular client groups – notably the eldery and physically handicapped. People with other kinds of difficulty living in the patch may be referred to specialist workers.

13.47 We have suggested in Chapter 3 that social workers require the skills for two kinds of work: direct counselling and social care planning. We believe that both methods of work are required in community social work.

13.48 On some occasions the social worker will be the only person who is available or acceptable to the client to offer a counselling service. As and where community networks strengthen, this skill in social workers may be drawn upon less frequently but it is difficult to envisage its never being needed. In fact, even if counselling, in its traditional form of continuing meetings in which worker and client attempt to change the client's attitudes or feelings, decreases as a social work activity, the skills of counselling will still be needed in full measure in assessing clients' needs and enabling them and others to accept and provide social care.

13.49 So we are not suggesting that skills in counselling will no longer be required, but we do suggest that other skills need to be developed. Social workers will need to increase their capacity to negotiate and bargain, to act as advocate for groups and individuals and to teach others how to find their way within the social services system. These skills however must be used in ways which take into account the feelings of others. In working through others and in establishing a development role social workers will need to extend the attitudes they have traditionally expressed towards clients to a much wider group of people. Some of the research carried out by the National Institute for Social Work (see Crosbie and others, 1982) suggests ways in which social workers are working with caring networks. They enable networks to grow by setting up schemes within which friendships can develop and by introducing people to each other. This, the researchers comment, 'is a skilled task which some do beautifully' and which depends upon an understanding of the kinds of interests, needs, concerns and skills which might serve to bind people together. Social workers also supplement and relieve those who carry the main burdens of care and sometimes carry out tasks which others around a client cannot do. For example some people cannot talk to their families about grief and some people find it difficult to take a firm line with a child or an elderly relative at risk. We support the view that working with networks is a highly skilled job.

Implications for management

13.50 A community approach by front-line social workers will be seriously hampered if it is not accompanied by a similar attitude at all managerial levels of the social services department, or voluntary agency, and by a willingness to translate this attitude into action by devolving as fully as possible decisions about resources and decentralising organisational structures.

13.51 The key management role in the delivery of services is that of team leader, and in a community approach to social work, the team leader's job will be a particularly crucial one. Whether the team he manages is working with a 'patch' or a specialist client group, he will need to be able to help his staff in developing social networks as well as in direct work with clients. He will have to acquire entrepreneurial skills himself to bargain for the resources his team, community or client group require and to negotiate with mutual aid groups, voluntary organisations and other statutory organisations for a co-ordinated approach to the problems in the communities served by his team.

13.52 The team leader in a community social work team may be responsible for a mixed group of workers which includes, perhaps, home help organisers, occupational therapists, ancillaries, street wardens and family aides, and their development will be partly his responsibility. He will also have to allocate work between different kinds of worker and may have to co-ordinate the resources of the department – including day and residential as well as field work services – in a locality or for a client group.

13.53 The delegated structure of management that is essential to community social work makes other demands of the team leader. He may be required to manage an area or client group budget and will certainly need to contribute to overall agency planning. Since a community orientation requires a 'bottom-up' rather than a 'top-down' approach to planning, team leaders will be taking part in priority setting and resource allocation on an agency-wide level as well as at the level of their own teams.

13.54 Team leaders – or officers in charge – in hospital social work departments and in residential and day services, may also need to adjust their role, particularly when their establishment forms a resource centre for a particular client group or a locality. They may need, like fieldwork team leaders, to help their staff understand and work with networks amongst the patients, residents or day centre users, and in the wider community in which the hospital or establishment is a part. This may include encouraging clients to give care and support to each other as well as ensuring that the facilities of the establishment are used flexibly.

Issues to be considered

13.55 It seems to us that if local authorities and voluntary agencies seek to move towards community social work, as we hope they will, they need to give particular consideration to the following issues.

Management issues

13.56 Our argument so far (despite the caution expressed in paragraph 13.11), risks conveying the false impression that informal community networks are invariably perceived as helpful and supportive by members of the community. This is by no means the case. Some people in any community, among them the most 'difficult' and the most vulnerable, are scapegoated or ostracised by neighbours and even by their own kin. Others may have become for various reasons a serious social menace, wholly beyond the capacity of the community to contain or control. It follows that a proportion of social work resources will always have to be devoted to protecting certain individuals from the antagonism of their local communities, and to preventing other individuals from threatening community peace and integrity. This draws attention to the point, in danger of being obscured by our emphasis upon the value of informal networks, that they are not all universally benign and that they may be arenas of conflict between their members as well as sources of social care.

13.57 Social workers will therefore be involved in decisions not to take action when neighbours and relatives demand it, in intervening when no one in the client's circle wants anything done and in working with people who have totally opposed views as to what would be the best way to solve a social problem. These possibilities show how community social workers will still necessarily exercise considerable powers of action and control over resources, and will need considerable courage in taking action unwelcome to people in the community they serve and considerable skill in maintaining the underlying relationship with the community. In these circumstances particularly social workers will look to management for support. Managers have a responsibility to make clear to the public that social workers have certain over-riding duties and must be expected from time to time to take unpopular action in fulfilling them.

13.58 It has also been made very clear in our evidence that some people do not want help from their neighbours but are willing to accept it from social workers. For example the Family Services Units' evidence (320) stated that some families considered there were clear limits to what neighbours and friends could do. We also heard of elderly people who held that certain aspects of personal care were acceptable only from female relatives or a paid employee. Similarly, people sometimes suffer from feelings so painful that they can be shared only with an outsider. In principle, citizens are entitled to choose the person or people from whom help is most acceptable; while some may be unable to express a view and some may have a choice between informal care or none, nothing we are recommending should be taken to imply that clients generally should have informal caring networks imposed upon them.

13.59 The community social work approach may create or expose tensions between a local community and a social services department: not only because the department has duties of control, protection and surveillance, but also because it rations access to scarce resources. It can be argued that this only makes need more apparent. This may be desirable but carries with it the possibility that social workers will be seen not as upholders of community endeavour but as street level bureaucrats whose constant answer is 'No'.

13.60 On the other hand, there are arguments in favour of the view that it is precisely a community approach which gives some hope of surmounting the resource problem. For a social work team using such an approach is not dependent solely upon the agency resources it controls directly, but is in a strong position to tap into the much wider range of personal, community and state resources that are potentially available. The team and its community support each other in bargaining for, demanding and bringing into play these resources.

Political issues

13.61 The resource problems touched on it the preceding paragraphs raise the first of a number of issues with political in addition to their management implications. The first has to do with equity, or 'territorial justice'. There are already differences in the level and quality of service in different parts of each local authority area. The community approach may make such discrepancies greater and more noticeable. It may also increase disparities in service for particular client groups, for to some extent the resources allocated and the services received will depend upon the pressure which a particular network can create. There are examples of particular 'communities of interest' obtaining what might, by other groups or areas, be regarded as an unfair share of local authority resources. The most disadvantaged members of society are also those least able to create informal networks and to compete for resources. Adding their voices to those of front-line social workers, elected members and senior managers will increasingly need to act as spokesmen for such groups as well as arbiters in the process of allocation.

13.62 A community approach, with its principle of partnership between informal caring networks and formal social services organisations, entails, as we have already pointed out, conferring some share in decision-making on local communities, and mutual help and self-help groups. Under our system of representative democracy at central and local government levels, ultimate authority is vested in elected members. It is the general practice for elected members of local authorities to delegate authority on a day-to-day basis to chief officers in charge of departments, and they in turn to managers at various levels. We have argued in Chapter 9 that powers to take decisions in all but a minority of matters affecting clients ought to be delegated to area teams or, as appropriate, to experienced social workers individually and have noted that with authority goes accountability. Development of community partnership makes social workers, however, answerable in some degree to the community and its informal networks. Social workers, their managers and elected members must appreciate this and be prepared to agree to the implications. These will include in some circumstances allowing informal carers and communities direct influence on how resources are used.

13.63 In any form of community social work, social workers will be subject to multiple accountability. Primary accountability will remain to the elected members (or the council members of voluntary agencies) who employ them and can call them to account; but they will also have a duty to give an account of their actions and decisions not only to individual clients or client-groups, but also to informal carers with whom they are in partnership. It will need to be made as explicit as possible who is accountable to whom, and in what sense, for which aspect of his work; but no one can remove from social workers the burden of managing ensuing tensions. This is not a new problem for them. Social workers have always had to maintain a balance between conflicting interests, and their role as advocates and negotiators requires them to do so.

13.64 Teams which develop a community approach will tend also to develop a blurring of roles between team members. The community approach recognises that many kinds of people have or can acquire skills in social care and this is as true for paid workers as for volunteers and neighbours. There is therefore a tendency for roles to become blurred. This may be an extremely positive development for the individuals concerned and for the people they serve. Where posts in social services departments, however, have nationally negotiated job descriptions and pay scales attached to them, the blurring of roles may raise difficult issues for employers and Trade Unions to resolve.

13.65 There is an additional question about the devolution of local authority financial resources – how much can in practice be devolved to small front-line units of social workers? Some authorities we know have devolved revenue budgets to the areas and the Kent community care scheme has given social work teams the responsibility for deciding how to meet the needs of elderly people in their area within given budgetary limits. Further moves of this kind may be possible and experiments would be of value. It would be more difficult to delegate any capital spending or the allocation of staff. Indeed it would be impossible to give teams complete control over their own staffing level, since situations might occur in which priority had to be accorded to the needs of other areas.

13.66 It has been suggested in some quarters that the community is an untapped source of social care and that, once fully engaged, it would make social services departments unnecessary. We do not believe that families and the community can or should take over all the functions of a social services department. We consider that some of the ideas about the capacity of the community to care are confused by a failure to distinguish types of care which can be provided by social networks from those which need to be provided either jointly or entirely by formal agencies. While, for example, we have no doubt that loneliness could be greatly alleviated by social networks, we are equally sure that, even where elderly mentally infirm people have families, it is unreasonable that families should be expected to care alone for relatives who need virtually constant attention all day and much of the night.

13.67 We think it is vital that a social services department should carry the ultimate residual responsibility for seeing that social care networks are maintained. It has also a number of mandatory duties entrusted to it by Parliament, which it cannot neglect or repudiate. Many of these (such as protection of children at risk and arranging compulsory admissions to hospital under the Mental Health Act of 1959) consume much social work time and cannot be undertaken by informal carers. Social services departments wishing to promote a community approach to social work have the unenviable task of working out the distribution of their scarce resources between the maintenance of their statutory duties and the support of informal caring networks.

13.68 More immediately, we fear that by promoting a community approach we may tempt politicians to believe that the community can do everything and can do it without funds. We cannot emphasise too strongly that a community approach is not cheap, although we believe it will give good value for money. But it will only give value if it is well enough resourced. To underfund a community approach is to run the risk of discrediting the entire notion of shared care.

Concluding comments

13.69 At the beginning of this chapter we stated that its contents would necessarily be more speculative than those of other chapters. We do not seek to provide a blueprint for the future, and we have deliberately tried to avoid a degree of precision in our description of community social work that could only be spurious in our present state of knowledge.

13.70 A blueprint is undesirable because we still know too little about what determines the shape and style of informal networks or what constitutes a 'healthy' community – or, for that matter, a 'healthy' social services organisation. Local communities and informal caring networks are strikingly different one from another. The Personal Social Services Research Unit, University of Kent, reporting on the Thanet Community Care Project, comment: 'The mobilisation of human resources is an aim that with the evidence we have at the moment . . . does not necessarily lead to a preference for one structure rather than another. . . Much of the evidence, like our experience, suggests that . . . the patch approach is only one among several which appear to mobilise human resources successfully' (Challis and

Davies, 1981). The evidence reaching us, similarly, abundantly attests that there is no one way of knowing or serving communities.

13.71 We have therefore, sought in this chapter to do no more than indicate a direction in which we believe social work should be moving. In doing so we wish to encourage the flexibility that will be needed to adapt to new circumstances and new pressures as they develop – and above all we wish to encourage experiment.

13.72 We do not believe the changes we seek will be easy to achieve. Few, if any, social services departments have done more than take the first step towards community social work. We say this because we do not wish the response to our report to be 'we are doing that already'. Our evidence suggests that this is not the case, but it also makes clear that the goodwill, imagination and commitment to caring which exist among statutory and voluntary agencies make a move towards community social work a real possibility.

13.73 We believe that changes in attitude, organisation and practice are essential if social work is in the future to be able to respond to the needs of those whom it exists to serve. Our final recommendation (and it is the most important single recommendation we make) is that all who have responsibility for social work in England and Wales should use this report as a basis for the discussion that is needed to ensure that changes do in fact take place.

SUMMARY OF CONCLUSIONS

1. The personal social services need to develop a close working partnership with citizens (13.1, 22).

2. This requires of social workers an attitude of mind which will provide the basis for what we have called 'community social work' (13.2, 13).

3. No blueprint for partnership is possible: a social care plan must take account of the differing informal, voluntary and statutory resources of the communities served (13.3, 69–71).

4. The bulk of social care is provided by informal carers: if social work were directed at their support it is likely that the need for formal services to take over would be reduced (13.8).

5. In recommending a community approach the Working Party is repeating a recommendation, made by the Seebohm Committee, to which social services departments generally have not hitherto been able to give more than limited effect (13.18–19).

6 There is now a general trend to decentralisation of authority, and already a move within many social services agencies in the direction we recommend (13.20–21).

7. Community social work implies a focus on individuals and families set in the context of all the networks of which they do, or might, form part (13.26–27).

8. Community social work may be based upon locality (centred on patch teams, on resource centres, or on social workers working in hospitals or attached to general practices or to schools) or upon shared concern (centred on specialist teams at area level or multi-disciplinary teams serving a wider population) (13.31–41).

9. Community social work requires of social workers changes of attitudes; increased understanding of the interactions of people in groups and communities; and an increased capacity to negotiate and to bring people together to enable networks to grow; skills of counselling are still needed; however community social work is based, each social worker may have a specialist component in his work (13.42–49).

10 Elected members and managers need to be ready to devolve, as fully as possible, decisions about resources (13.50, 62).

11. The team-leader's role as negotiator and manager is crucial in a community-oriented service (13.51–54).

12. Community social workers remain responsible for functions which may set them at odds with the communities they serve (13.56–59); they have a complex accountability to their employers, to their clients and to informal carers with whom they are in partnership: the nature of their accountability to each should be made explicit (13.63).

13. Community social work is likely to lead to a blurring of staff roles which may raise issues for employers and Trade Unions to settle (13.64).

14. Families and communities neither can nor should take over all the functions of social services departments (13.66–67).

15. A community approach is not cheap. It will only give value if well enough financed (13.68).

16. Those responsible for social work in England and Wales should use this report as a basis for discussion to ensure that changes in attitude, organisation and practice do take place (13.73).

Appendix A

A case for neighbourhood-based social work and social services

A note by Mrs P. Brown, Professor R. Hadley and Mr K.J. White

Introduction

We welcome and endorse the support given throughout the Report to the development of community-oriented social work. We believe this represents a major shift in thinking on the nature of social work and its relationships to society.

However, in our view, the case for this development and its implications for the roles and tasks of social workers and the social services organisations within which it is located, have not been spelt out clearly enough in the Report. Nor has there been sufficient acknowledgement of the extent to which community-oriented social work represents a significant departure from current practice. In consequence, there is a danger that the impact of the Working Party's proposals will be lost and that community-oriented social work will be interpreted as being any package of vaguely innovatory developments which have a 'community' flavour or label. In this form they may readily be tacked on to existing structures and procedures without effecting either the fundamental changes in attitudes and practice which we believe the Working Party as a whole is seeking to encourage, or the fundamental organisational reforms we believe such changes require.

We believe there are significant and radical differences between the welfare state approach and the community approach described in Chapter 7. They start from different assumptions and tend to lead to different organisations and practice (197). We do not believe that the one can evolve gradually into the other. In this note, therefore, we set out first to re-examine the implications for social services and social work of adopting a focus based on the support of systems of informal care; we consider the limitations of existing practice in this context and propose certain principles which might help to guide the development of more appropriate structures and methods. To distinguish our emphasis and approach from that of the main report, we use the term 'neighbourhood', although we recognise it is not entirely satisfactory as a description of our ideas. Although we have minor reservations relating to other sections of the main report, we have concentrated our attention here on the arguments developed primarily in Chapter 13. We have also restricted our attention mainly to the statutory social services, although our recognition of the importance of the whole voluntary sector should be self-evident from our arguments. We do not restrict our comments to front-line social workers because we cannot see how they can be considered in isolation from the organisational structures and policies of the personal social services.

The Working Party has received much contradictory evidence on many points we make, but we are convinced that there is a substantial amount of evidence in support of our major conclusions; much, but not all of it, from outside social services departments.

Informal caring networks and conditions for their support

In Chapters 5 and 13, the central importance of informal caring networks of family, friends and neighbours in providing help for dependent people living in the community is fully acknowledged as is the need for social services departments to accept greater responsibility for helping to support these networks. The Working Party rightly points out that not all these networks are local in character and that some are more properly regarded as 'communities of interest' which may be spread over a wide area. However, in our view, the account of informal networks presented in Chapter 13 fails to recognise the over-riding importance of locally-based informal relationships in providing care for most dependent people and the significance of locally-oriented social services in strengthening and reinforcing such networks when they need support.

We recognise that many areas and estates seem to have very little community spirit or identity; we also realise that a community can be very hostile to individuals or groups within it, and that areas which seem to have the greatest social needs often seem to have the weakest informal networks (181). Our view of neighbourhoods is, in short, far from a rosy or sentimental one.

What we are emphasising is the fact that most dependent people whose needs come within the remit of the personal social services (the frail elderly, the mentally and physically ill and handicapped living in the community, families with children at risk, and others) are tied because of frailty, illness, fear, handicap, low income or habit to their local area, whether or not it has any sense of community. Unless they are going to be rehoused or admitted to residential establishments, they are going to continue living in these confined geographical neighbourhoods. The kinds of action the more dependent of them require to continue to live any sort of fulfilled existence in their own homes and neighbourhood are likely to involve practical help, advice, friendship, emotional support, or some form of monitoring. This may, for example, involve such activities as helping a frail old person or a handicapped person to get up in the morning, assistance with washing, going to the toilet, providing meals, cleaning, shopping, and giving them advice and support in coping with the problems arising from their dependence. Or, to take another example, where a single parent family is involved and the parent is encountering serious difficulties in coping, it may require support which combines practical help with domestic chores and advice on child rearing.

Ideally, this contact will come from family, friends and/or neighbours (informal networks). In practice, many such people are isolated from others. For social workers or their assistants to see all these people personally and regularly is neither possible nor desirable. (Some of our evidence shows that the needs of the elderly, in particular, have been 'seriously neglected' (66; also 50, 232, 239).) The scale of the task in relation to formal social work resources is demonstrated in Chapter 2. In certain cases, skilled social work assessment, counselling and advice will be needed, but in the vast majority of cases, it is frequent, reliable, practical, sensitive contact that is called for. We can see no viable alternative to locally-based carers. In practice this is what happens in most informal support systems. Although informal networks often spread over large distances, and are maintained by letter, phone and visits, the bulk of help required on a frequent, routine basis appears to be provided by people living with or close to the dependent person.

For the same reason, when personal resources and informal caring networks come under strain and are in danger of breaking up, they need access to and support from social services which are capable of intervening reliably and regularly at a local level. In any case, what is needed from the social worker is, first, a detailed knowledge of local informal networks, and, second, the willingness and ability to develop such networks where they are weak (or even non-existent). It is our view that any social services organisation seeking to locate and work alongside such networks, must meet at least four requirements:

● **Ability to locate and be accessible to local networks.** The social services department should be organised to enable its staff to locate informal caring systems that exist in the areas it serves. This process is likely to require that at least some personnel have knowledge of particular neighbourhoods; that different staff can readily pool the knowledge they acquire; that good communications are established at local level with other statutory and voluntary agencies working in the same localities. Equally important is the other side of this coin; that the organisation is accessible to clients and their supporters.

● **Responsiveness and flexibility.** Supporting informal caring systems is likely to require a range of inputs as we have indicated. Informal carers may, for example, need relief from part of the daily round of caring by the input of additional practical help, night-time 'sitters', laundry or meals services. Again, they may need advice and counselling. The statutory services can provide help in many of these cases through home helps, ancillaries, meals services, etc. But the 'packages' of support required are likely to vary from one informal caring system to another, and from one day to the next. Effective service, therefore, implies a highly flexible and sensitive response at the local level and willingness on the part of workers to adapt their roles accordingly. It also implies close and detailed collaboration with other local agencies (such as the primary health care team who will often be working with the same clients), and that specialists are known by and available to local social workers.

● **Developing additional resources.** However well the existing resources of statutory (and voluntary) agencies are deployed, the development of a proactive, preventive policy backing informal caring systems in the community is likely to make demands for additional caring resources. Some of these will rightly be sought from the public purse. But others may be found by encouraging the wider involvement of informal helpers, formal volunteers, and voluntary organisations. Given the nature of the informal caring systems described, the main focus of this development will need to be local if the kinds of routine daily intervention so central to the care of more dependent people is to be provided.

● **Understanding people and groups, identifying with them.** Clearly a knowledge of local cultures, problems, thought patterns and structures is important. If the social worker (and his organisation) is ignorant of these, is seen as an outsider coming from the 'welfare' and from another class or type of area, the chances of understanding people and their networks are considerably reduced. This will take time and a local presence.

For all these reasons, therefore, it would seem that a strategy aimed to provide a significant measure of support for the informal helping systems that provide the bulk of care in our society, requires a strong local orientation. This perspective in no way ignores the additional contribution that can be made by wider 'communities of interest' referred to by the Working Party but recognises that they cannot usually afford the close, routine daily help that so many dependants require. Nor, of course, does it exclude the role of 'secondary' institutions such as day care, and specialist support, and advice in bolstering informal caring systems in the community. But the best use of these forms of support, it follows, can only be determined when the nature of the needs of the informal systems is properly understood and the availability of additional resources of all kinds has been explored.

We must now turn to ask how well the predominant methods of organising our social services departments and the role and tasks of social workers within them answers the demands of a strategy to support informal caring systems, as we have sketched it here.

Current problems in the role of social services departments and social work in providing support for informal caring networks

In our view, the systems of service provision most commonly found in social services departments today, and the role of social work within it, are not well suited to provide effective support to informal caring networks in the community. Indeed, their deficiencies in this respect are hardly surprising since the task for which most departments seem to have been planned is quite different: they were set up to help individual clients who are already in crisis. The organisation is designed to assess the needs of such clients and provide them with one or more of a range of specialised services such as domiciliary care, aids, counselling, residential and day care.

Consistent with prevailing views of efficiency when the departments were established at the beginning of the 1970s, large-scale centralised structures were favoured, with separate control of the residential and day care, field and administrative sections. Area teams, following recommendations in the Seebohm Report, often covered large populations of 50,000–100,000 or more. The role of social workers in these organisations tended to be firstly to oversee the assessment of clients and their allocation for different services; secondly, the provision of certain of these services more particularly where they involved counselling and other activities with families and children, and mental illness.

Much of the evidence we received, both from social workers and outsiders, was critical of the structure and management of social services departments, and argued that any discussion of roles and tasks which ignored organisational frameworks was likely to be misguided (e.g. 46, 112, 137, 149, 171, 181, 199, 273, 307, 348). Some of this criticism has been reflected in the main report but the fact that such hierarchical and bureaucratic organisations are particularly ill-equipped to locate and work alongside informal caring systems is not spelt out clearly.

The structures were not designed to relate to informal caring systems or the localities in which many of them were lodged. In so far as the community, as opposed to individual clients, was seen as a legitimate target for intervention, it was typically regarded as the business of specially appointed community workers, not social workers and the teams they led.

Whatever the rights and wrongs of the decision to adopt such 'service delivery' structures in social services departments in the early 1970s, their general inappropriateness for the development of supportive work with informal caring systems is not difficult to perceive. If we consider the service delivery model of organisation in the context of the four main requirements for organisations seeking to support informal caring systems listed in the previous section of this note, its specific weaknesses become even clearer.

● **Ability to locate and be accessible to local networks.** Since staff are not deployed to work in particular neighbourhoods or localities, it is unlikely that relevant information about informal care systems (and other local caring resources) will be gathered on a systematic basis in the organisation. Such information as may be picked up by individual workers in the course of their duties about informal carers and their needs is not readily passed on to others in different sections who may be able to use it, since such communications typically have to be transmitted through the hierarchy and are between workers who often do not even know each other (e.g. a home-help and a social worker).

Relationships with workers in other agencies who do operate on a local basis, such as health visitors, district nurses, beat policemen, and clergymen, are unlikely to be close when the social workers and other social services staff cover much wider areas and will have few clients in common.

Typically, social services departments and social workers know little about informal networks at present. They tend to concentrate on individuals, groups of clients or households, usually in a state of upheaval or crisis. Time with others in a locality is limited and the positive features in a local social situation are often overlooked. Social workers do not usually live in communities they serve (even residential ones) although this is desirable from certain points of view (45); they often know less of a situation than neighbours (343) and are out of touch with communities (304).

Similarly, access to the social services department where a service delivery model prevails, is not likely to be easy for clients or their informal carers. Centralised field offices mean that few people live within easy walking distance of their area team. Those who do make contact may find that the staff are only able to help clients who can show that they have no extant informal support networks, and are not geared to preventive intervention.

● **Responsiveness and flexibility.** The division of the 'service delivery' departments into different specialised sections and the absence of any local co-ordination of their work makes it more difficult for staff to organise joint packages of care to support informal care networks, as, for example, through the collaboration of social worker, home-help, housing warden, and district nurse. Similarly, in the absence of local control, it is difficult for any official support systems of this kind which may be established to adapt flexibly to changing circumstances in the informal networks they are serving.

● **Developing additional resources.** The creation of new support networks by the recruitment of neighbours and volunteers and the encouragement of local voluntary organisations would also be impeded by the lack of specific knowledge of neighbourhoods and localities. Community workers employed by social services departments might be better placed to develop such resources but it is hard to see how they could then be interwoven with other statutory services that had no local base.

Many people will require specialists and special services. A lot of evidence to the Working Party has commented on the lack of specialist knowledge and skills of social workers. Clearly no single social worker will know everything, but at present they seem poor at knowing what specialist services exist and where they are to be found. This lack of knowledge seems to be particularly acute in relation to services provided outside the social services department. One of the great ironies of social work at present is that while social workers are known to be under so much pressure, they seem to others to be so reluctant to share their load (15, 64, 69, 112, 123, 171, 181, 185, 197, 243, 275, 303, 304, 321, 343, 349). This point does not seem to us to have been made strongly enough in the main report.

● **Understanding people and groups, identifying with them**. For a number of reasons, social workers are often not seen as identifying sufficiently with clients and neighbourhoods. Some evidence noted the stigma still attached to contact with the social services departments (e.g. 223, 323, 329). Other evidence showed that clients have a different set of priorities in what they see as important in a relationship with a social worker. The social services department and social workers rate knowledge, training, qualifications and skill highly, while clients, not under-rating these, put personal qualities much higher. The main report tends to reflect social work priorities rather than those of clients. Experience, sensitivity, integrity, commitment, are among the most highly-rated qualities clients look for in social workers (72, 239, 243, 278, 306, 321, 326). No amount of role or task clarification and training can make up for a lack of these qualities in clients' eyes.

People need choice if they are to identify with someone. Client-determination is a much quoted principle of social work, but it often means little because most significant decisions have already been made (64)! In our view, the main report underestimates the current in our evidence that questioned the desirability of local authority monopoly of aspects of the social services, particularly because of its effect on the client-social worker relationship (3, 15, 46, 224, 275, 277, 329, 338).

Conditions for the development of a community-oriented approach

The Working Party acknowledges the force of some of these criticisms of current organisation and practice, but places the main emphasis of its recommendation for change on a shift in attitudes. Workers should recognise the importance of informal networks and other aspects of community organisation, and learn to collaborate with them.

In the view of the Working Party, however, there is no one right way of deploying social services and social workers within them to facilitate this approach. Local patch teams staffed by generalists as well as more centralised teams of specialist workers are both cited as examples of community-oriented social work.

While we share the Working Party's views on the importance of attitude changes among social workers and other social services personnel, we believe the main report does not follow through the implications of this approach. It seems to us that certain common organisational features are required if social services are to relate effectively to informal caring networks in the way outlined above. The most important of these features are: (1) localisation, (2) integration, (3) role flexibility and (4) autonomy. In identifying these aspects of organisation, however, we are not, as the Working Party seems to fear, proposing the adoption of a universal blueprint. Rather the reverse. These features open the way for experimentation, flexible responses in relation to communities of very different types, resources and problems. Our proposals, we believe, describe the minimal conditions for an effective service. They would help ensure that personal social services, including social work, were more readily identifiable, easier to approach, and better placed to respond to the needs and problems of the particular localities or neighbourhoods served. Their effect would be to create local primary social care teams at a roughly corresponding level to the primary health care teams of the NHS. But the form of these teams would be likely to vary substantially for the changes we are proposing are aimed at facilitating greater organisational flexibility in response to the needs and potentialities of different localities, not at the imposition of an organisational strait-jacket. In all of this, we believe that clients, neighbours and neighbourhoods should be involved in the planning of the social services provided, and neither we, nor anyone else, can decide beforehand what its final shape will be.

(1) Localisation. If informal caring networks are to be identified and, in turn, to have ready access to the social services department and if there is to be adaptation to changes in informal systems and local voluntary organisations, then the statutory services must be local enough to operate at street or village level (e.g. 304). This does not imply an office in every street or village but a readily recognisable contact person in every neighbourhood, whether a home help, ancillary, or even a volunteer, who has direct links with the local office. This office, in turn, would deploy a local team or sub-team of domiciliary and field services capable of responding to the pattern of needs emerging in its own patch. Clearly, the areas covered by such teams would be much smaller than Seebohm's 50,000–100,000 population. One might think, for example, of area teams covering 20,000–30,000 with a number of sub-teams within each, covering up to, say, 10,000 people. We are quite clear that these local teams will need the back-up of specialists, however. These specialists will sometimes be located with social services departments, often outside them. They will usually serve much wider geographical areas, and often communities of interest.

(2) Integration. Three kinds of integration are implied in the community-oriented strategy: integration *within* the social services department, integration *between* the social services department and other local agencies providing social services, and between the social services department and informal networks.

● *Integration within the social services department.* It is a key part of a community-oriented approach that information and resources should be pooled on a local basis to maximise knowledge, adapt the response of services to the particular problems of the locality and its potentialities for development. This implies, in individual cases, bringing domiciliary, ancillary, and field workers into the same local teams. It also implies working for closer integration of residential, day care and field services on a local basis. This would be a pre-condition for making the greatest use of residential and day institutions in support of local caring networks and, in turn, of generating the active support and involvement of the community in the institutions. We are thinking here of contact between, say, field and residential care, but also between the front-line social workers and the senior management. The social planning component of social work cannot function unless locally-based workers in touch with local resources and problems, influence departmental policy.

● *Integration with other agencies.* The users of the personal social services are also, of course, potential users of a range of other social services, both statutory and voluntary. The principle of pooling knowledge and resources applies as much to relations with these bodies as it does within the social services department itself. Naturally, it is unlikely to be possible to carry integration between these agencies to the same point as internal integration, but the advantages of establishing close working relationships on a local basis with, for example, members of the primary health care team (53), a neighbourhood school, or the local branch of Age Concern are considerable. The main report stresses the importance of inter-agency co-operation; we are underlining the importance of such co-operation at *local* as well as at other levels.

● *Integration with informal networks.* Linking with informal carers is the most important but also most difficult task of the community-oriented team. It can be achieved partly by extending direct contacts with users to their networks, and maintaining links with these even after the initial reason for contact may no longer apply. It can also be developed by fostering contacts with intermediaries or 'gatekeepers' – people such as publicans, corner shop-keepers, lollypop ladies and so on, who often acquire roles as informal advisers. In some projects in the United States, such intermediaries have been offered training to increase their knowledge of resources available and to help improve their counselling skills. Both kinds of contact require delicate handling if the statutory agency is not be in danger of taking over and weakening the informal system.

(3) **Wider Roles.** It follows from the localising, integrative approach, that all staff roles need to be less narrowly defined than in the service-delivery model (123). This does not preclude local workers having particular skills, knowledge or tasks, but it does mean that they will tend to develop their contribution far beyond the sometimes narrow limits of their job descriptions. Non-social work, residential staff, social work assistants, domiciliary workers or administrative workers have all found this to be true in existing teams working at neighbourhood level.

The successful extension of community-oriented services will depend upon the capacity of local authorities to recognise, encourage, and accommodate these developments on a systematic basis. This will have implications for the negotiation of wider job descriptions, for salaries, and for training as well as the construction of career paths for those who have the ability and motivation to move on to more responsible posts. The arguments for broadening the roles of social work staff are spelt out below.

(4) **Greater autonomy.** Finally, the local social services teams will need a larger measure of discretion to develop these approaches than they have been formally accorded in the service delivery model. In particular, they will need some freedom to decide how the team's budget can be best used, what particular balance of staffing is most appropriate, and in what ways relations should be developed with other agencies. Such autonomy is not an end in itself, but should enable social workers to become more responsive to clients and neighbourhoods. It should lead to 'greater participation from the community . . . as partners in formulating policies on service developments and also in criticising and evaluating existing services' (64).

Some examples of existing developments in neighbourhood-based services

This description of the elements of a neighbourhood-oriented approach is not based simply on hypothetical arguments. It is drawn, at least in part, from the practical experiences of a number of social services teams in Britain. Attempts to develop such services are increasing. In many cases these schemes are a result of initiatives taken by staff, within individual area teams and residential institutions. More recently there have been signs that a number of local authorities are looking closely at the possibility of applying community-oriented methods systematically throughout their social services departments. Indeed, one social services department – East Sussex – reorganised its services at the end of 1981 into patch teams covering populations between 8,000 and 20,000, each of which incorporates the local residential and day services as well as field staff.

However, most of the established community-oriented or 'patch' teams have been more restricted in scope and have been confined to field social workers and their assistants. For example, in Southsea, the area team has divided the town into three patches. Each is covered by a sub-team led by a senior social worker and includes social workers and social work assistants. Only a few local areas have been able to integrate more grades of staff into their teams. Normanton, in Wakefield, provides one example. There, home helps, ancillaries, social workers and volunteers are deployed on small patches covering between 5,000–8,000 people each. Recently the street wardens in the town have been further localised within these patches and each now covers a small neighbourhood of about 1,200 people. Inter-agency co-operation has been locally based on a housing estate in Lewisham, at Honor Oak (Kelly and others, 1980). There, social services, housing, a community worker from the ILEA, and a CAB worker work closely together.

Although there is an increasing literature about these and other schemes like them, only the Normanton team and an experimental team set up at Dinnington (Rotherham) have been the subject of systematic evaluation. Even this research is not yet completed and so assessments of outcome must be largely impressionistic. However, it is interesting to note that there is a remarkable degree of consistency in the gains claimed by teams operating more neighbourhood-oriented systems, as there is in the problems which they say they have encountered. Higher referral rates, earlier intervention, fewer unforeseen crises are all listed as gains. It is also claimed that much closer working relationships are usually established with other agencies operating locally – the primary health care workers, teachers, community police, tenants' associations, mutual aid groups, churches, and so on, and that local commercial enterprises such as pubs and corner shops become recognised as important sources of information. Another common feature of the teams appears to be their ability to foster local voluntary initiatives – mutual aid groups, youth clubs, tenants' associations, advice centres and the like. How successfully the teams have interwoven their services with community networks remains to be established by empirical research, but the impressionistic evidence suggests that they have moved a considerable way in this direction (Hadley and McGrath, 1981).

Common gains are matched by common problems. Unions are likely to object where workers' roles become too loosely defined. Some staff find community-oriented methods are not to their taste. Some other agencies, operating over larger areas and from more centralised bases have difficulty in making sense of the new methods adopted by the team. Most teams say they also have problems in explaining what they are doing to their own organisations and in obtaining and maintaining sufficient autonomy to develop community-oriented methods. But this problem should not face locally-based teams when, as in East Sussex, the whole authority adopts a community orientation.

It is worth noting that another common characteristic of most of the teams we have met is their enthusiasm and high morale. Of course, these are by no means the monopoly of such teams but we have seldom encountered them with such consistency elsewhere. We believe that such evidence of the satisfaction many people get from working in community-oriented teams can be attributed in part to the fact that they do usually work as *teams*, with shared decision making and high levels of mutual support. But other factors would appear to be important too, much as has been reported in studies of community policing: staff prize the wider responsibilities they are given and the increased discretion that goes with them, and gain great satisfaction from the evidence that they are recognised and valued by the local communities they serve.

We are aware of many voluntary organisations, centres and projects working in local areas. The work of Bob Holman in 'Edgetown' is one noted in the main report, but there are countless others, quite different in scope and shape, and we see it as vital for social services departments to support and work alongside these whenever possible. Often a local social work team may be based with another agency or project, some areas may be better served by local, non-local authority teams (although social services departments will, of course, retain specific responsibilities within their allotted boundaries). We believe that social services departments seeking to work in neighbourhoods will often find small, but thriving voluntary and independent initiatives already active. It would be silly to ignore them or seek to duplicate their work.

The role and tasks of social workers in neighbourhood-oriented social services

What would the systematic adoption of these neighbourhood-oriented methods imply for the role and tasks of social workers and the wider organisation within which they work?

First it is apparent that front-line social workers would normally need to be generalists. Behind them there would be a second tier of specialists. It is also apparent that the managers of social workers (and other social services staff) would need additional skills to those required in most conventionally organised social services teams today.

As we have already implied, by recommending a two-tier approach to the provision of practitioner services we are proposing a parallel development to that which already exists in the NHS. In our view, every locality should have its own primary social care team of social workers, ancillaries, domiciliary workers and so on, just as it is already served by a primary health care team of general practitioners and community nurses. We believe that as with health problems, the large majority of user problems in the personal social services field can be sorted out successfully at this level by generalist social workers and their colleagues. Those problems which cannot be resolved will be passed on to the appropriate specialist. To enable this system to work, however, it is important to encourage generalist workers to acquire some permanency in their patches just as most GPs stay many years with a particular practice. To this end it should be possible for the community-oriented social worker to be promoted to higher salary grades without having to move to a management or specialist post.

(1) **The generalist: the community-oriented social worker.** The counselling skills which are often regarded as at the core of the training of social workers for work in present day service delivery model organisations would still have a place in the training of the community-oriented social worker but it would be a less central place. In particular, the community-oriented social worker might be expected to have a thorough grounding in the problems of the two major client groups referred to social services departments: the elderly, and family with children at risk. In other fields of specialism they should have the ability to recognise where they need to call in specialist help. In addition, two other kinds of skill would be

called for. First, working at second-hand through lay people. Nancy Hazel in her evidence on 'The Role of the Social Worker' has given a useful account of the way in which this approach differs from traditional social work practice: 'The striving for professionalism and expertise by social workers means that, in order to protect their own professional standing, their work must be differentiated from that of lay people. As a result, volunteers have generally been considered suitable only for the less difficult tasks, to be carried out under the direction of professionals . . . The "equal but different" collaborative mode of working enables lay people to develop their skills and undertake new and demanding roles, either as paid freelancers (e.g. paid foster parents), or as unpaid members of self-help and other groups.'

She points out the impact this change of approach may have on social workers: 'But this mode of working robs the social worker of the power and emotional satisfaction inherent in a one-to-one thera-peutic role, and demands attitudes and skills which are different from those traditionally acquired during social work training. The nature of social work professionalism is also called into question' (15).

As we have already pointed out, much evidence to the Working Party was on this theme. The second skill required is that more usually associated with the community worker. It involves a whole range of entrepreneurial and supportive activities characterised by the National Council for Voluntary Organisations in its evidence as the 'development task': 'We are wary of a narrow professionalism which over-emphasises statutory duties and would recommend, rather, the melting of barriers between professional and non-professional aspects of social work, so that social workers define their job in a broader way that takes in the need to see individual problems in the round, work through community, self-help and voluntary organisations, give proper attention to preventive rather than remedial objectives . . .' (123).

A key part of this broader approach is the development of social planning. While management must have special responsibilities in this respect, covering the larger issues affecting the agency, all community-oriented social workers would be expected to share in the planning process.

The community-oriented worker will be working with individual clients, at second hand through lay-workers with individual clients, with informal networks of family, neighbours and friends, with voluntary groups, and with other statutory agencies. In practise a good number of social workers in locally-oriented teams (and others) already undertake a range of work of this kind. So do many workers in voluntary organisations, the classic example being the parish priest. It is clear, however, that the role calls for different kinds of training from that found in most colleges and universities at present, and that it is likely to be better performed by social workers who have some years of experience under their belts.

(2) **The specialist** is still required to deal with specific client groups whose needs could not normally be met by natural carers, however dedicated, or by generalist social workers (e.g. the assessment and treatment of certain types of mental handicap); the specialist may also be required to undertake tasks which the generalist social worker cannot expect to encounter with any frequency but which, nevertheless, may be of very considerable importance. For example, it is arguable that mental health sections should be handled only by those social workers with specialist training in mental health work. It is important that such specialists as are appointed have a sound appreciation of the methods of working of the neighbourhood teams so that their work can be related closely to that of the particular teams in whose areas their clients live.

(3) **The manager of community-oriented social work organisations** will require a blend of community-oriented social work, social planning, and managerial skills. Entrepreneurial capacities will also be important in adapting team organisation to local conditions and in developing community resources (e.g. 226). While the community-oriented strategy advocated here necessarily involves substantial decentralisation, it is not a proposal for the devolution of everything or for the Balkanisation of the personal social services.

The maintenance of a strong central organisation is essential to the successful development of a decentralising strategy. It is necessary to ensure that standards of service are maintained throughout the different local teams, that clients are treated equitably throughout the authority, and to provide a channel for the accountability of the organisation to the social services committee. It will also be required to establish and maintain appropriate specialist services and training programmes, and to match resources to local variations in need and potential as these are uncovered by the neighbourhood teams.

Political issues
By and large, we share the views of the Working Party on the political issues raised by the development of community-oriented social

services and social work. However, we do not believe that community-orientated teams of the kind we have described are likely to increase inequities in the provision of services, as the Working Party seems to fear. On the contrary, we believe that the improved knowledge the teams are likely to acquire of their areas will make it easier for social services departments to apply measures of positive discrimination to redress gross imbalance in provision which may be uncovered.

On the issue of accountability, we believe that community-oriented teams are likely to be *more* accountable than those in traditional service delivery organisations. Their work is likely to be under closer scrutiny by the areas they serve, by their own colleagues, and by colleagues in other local agencies with whom they collaborate on a regular basis. The local focus of the teams' work may also throw up differences between people in the areas they serve and the local authorities which employ them concerning the priorities which should be pursued by the teams. In the long run such tensions may create pressures for the introduction of more local forms of political representation and control.

Conclusion

The neighbourhood approach sketched here, although it is being developed in a few local authorities, would involve a substantial change in direction for a majority of social services departments. It would mean the evolution of new, decentralised structures and important modifications to the role and tasks of social workers employed by them. The problems involved in shifting direction in these ways are considerable but we believe they can be overcome. One positive effect of the economic crisis has been to make the need for re-evaluation more widely accepted and to increase the willingness of people to consider the case for far-reaching change. The development of neighbourhood-based social services and social work alone will not solve the resource problem. There is a real debate over how large the reservoirs of informal caring networks are. We do not know, but are convinced that social services departments as currently structured and organised are neither in a good position to discover, nor tap, them. The practical approach we describe offers the prospect, as its pioneers have shown, of more effective use of existing resources, a closer working relationship between the citizen and social worker in which both have more significant and responsible roles to play, and a more coherent base from which services can be planned and extended in the future. We see it as a necessary part of any community-oriented social work.

Appendix B

An alternative view

A note by Professor R.A. Pinker

I am not able to sign the Report of the Working Party on the Role and Tasks of Social Workers. I have therefore written this note setting out the main reasons for my dissent. I am equally critical of the community social work model which has the support of the majority of the members and of Professor Hadley's neighbourhood, or patch model. If either model was adopted, I believe it would be detrimental to the quality of social work services in England and Wales.

I shall argue that these two community-based models share a common perspective with regard to the crucial issues of generalism and specialism, and hence with regard to the distinctive features of the role and tasks of professional social work, as well as the nature of accountability and its implications for resource allocation and the exercise of discretion. The two models differ mainly in degree on these issues. The supporters of the community social work model reach their conclusions by default, while the advocates of the neighbourhood, or patch model do so by intent. Both approaches are seriously flawed.

The main observable difference between the community social work model and the neighbourhood model described in the Report is that the former retains the area team as the working unit while the latter does not, and the size of its catchment area lies somewhere between those of the traditional client-centred model and the neighbourhood model. The average number of team members is not specified, but as a rule it would again be on the small side.

The Report states that the community social work approach calls for highly localised and smaller area teams, working more closely with local community networks and with a greater, if limited, degree of control over resources. Both community-centred models, it is argued, would greatly augment the flow of information about local needs. The roles of local authority social services staff would be more openly defined, and each team would have its own budget and a greater degree of autonomy and discretion. Both models recognise the need for some specialised social workers, but in the neighbourhood, or patch model they will be located away from the frontline teams in some unspecified 'second tier'.

In the neighbourhood model it is assumed that there is considerable scope for increasing community participation through the use of more ancillary workers. This model looks forward to the integration of all field staff, including social workers, in small locally based teams. The teams will enjoy a much greater degree of autonomy and discretion in organising their work and managing their own budgets. At the same time we are assured that a very high degree of devolution and decentralisation would be compatible with the maintenance of a strong central organisation.

Defining social work

What then are the essential role and tasks of social workers, and how can social work activities best be organised? Our present model of so-called client-centred social work is basically sound, but in need of a better defined and less ambitious mandate. Social work should be explicitly selective rather than universalist in focus, reactive rather than preventive in approach and modest in its objectives. Social work ought to be preventive with respect to the needs which come to its attention; it has neither the capacity, the resources nor the mandate to go looking for needs in the community at large.

It is more practical to define the role and tasks of social work in terms of the range of activities which social workers undertake in response to certain institutional imperatives. The first set of imperatives derives from the range and variety of needs that confront social workers. The second is contained in the legislation that defines their mandatory local authority obligations and also indicates the range of their permissive undertakings. The third relates to the employers – statutory or otherwise – to whom social workers are accountable, who are themselves accountable in the discharge of their mandatory and permissive undertakings. The fourth set of imperatives derives from the professional standards and values to which social workers may individually and collectively subscribe.

What kinds of knowledge and skill do social workers need in order to do their job, and how should the job be defined? Many social work skills are the normal skills of sociable living, although it would be misleading to labour this point. The crucial difference arises from the distinctive use to which social workers put these skills, the type of clientele they serve, the type of context in which they work, and the nature of the mandate by which their work is authorised. These are the factors that shape the role and tasks of social workers, and accordingly the skills of social work are informed by a great deal of specialised knowledge.

The skills of social workers include the ability to assess needs and situations with insight, efficiency and impartiality, including the ability to make judgements about the capacities and the intentions of clients; the ability to formulate feasible methods of response to clients' problems, preferably with the clients' co-operation, but without it if necessary; and the ability to put such plans into effect and to obtain the necessary resources if they are available. The Report calls these basic skills the 'social care planning' part of social work.

The other part is social casework, which the Report describes as 'counselling'. The term 'social casework' would be more appropriate because it is a broader term, describing a method of work which, as Yelloly points out, takes account of not only the personal but the social aspects of human problems which are so severe that they threaten or destroy clients' capacity to manage their own lives or to function effectively as members of society (Yelloly, 1980, pp.125–30). The basic skills which the Report puts under the heading of 'social care planning' are general skills employed by the entire personnel of the personal service professions. They only become a part of social work when they are related to a process and method of intervention which is distinctive to social workers in response to a distinctive clientele with a particular set of needs.

This is not just a semantic difference; it is one which directly affects the focus and emphasis of concern in social work. The Report appears to attach equal importance to 'social care planning' and 'counselling'. In fact it diminishes the significance of the counselling element in social work by conceptually separating it from the social implications of casework. The Report shows that, contrary to popular belief, social casework is not the chief activity of social workers. Nevertheless social casework is an essential part of social work, and it seems unnecessary to give it a new label.

On the rare occasions on which it uses the term, the Report caricatures social casework. For example it defines social casework in the past tense, as if it were an obsolete practice, and suggests that 'Many social workers now feel somewhat embarrassed or ambivalent about the term' (10.19). In contrast, the Report asserts that social workers should see themselves as '. . . upholders of networks. This may make clear our view that the function of social workers is to enable, empower, support and encourage, but not usually to take over from social networks' (13.43). Since the Report's definition of social casework seems deficient, I shall give an alternative one, which will also make plain the reason why I could not sign the Report.

Social casework is the fundamentally distinctive method of social work which is derived from social work's concern with helping individuals and families with their problems in social living. Social group work is a logical extention of this concern because it pursues the same objectives through different means. Therefore the affinity between social casework and social group work is close. The same cannot be said of community work, which is primarily concerned with needs of a more general kind. The contribution of community work is therefore largely indirect, and the broader its scope of operation, the more pronounced this characteristic becomes. All social workers undertake some indirect work, but that is not what makes them social workers.

In my view, therefore, social work and social casework are virtually synonymous, but my definition of social casework is a broad one which includes counselling and various practical tasks. The counselling part of social casework is carried out through the use of a professional relationship between the social worker and the client (and other people who are immediately affected) as the means of helping the client to manage his own life.

Interviews are a prominent feature of social casework; they are the means by which the relationships are developed and the setting in which support and advice can be offered. The aim of counselling is to help clients to understand the nature and causes of their distress and discover their personal strengths and weaknesses, and to encourage them to find the will and capacity to help themselves – if necessary by changing their attitudes and behaviour. The problems of social work clients have a great variety of causes, including bereavement, illness, handicap, mental difficulty and breakdown, criminal behaviour, and so on.

There is nothing mysterious or esoteric about social casework. It requires certain qualities of character which are common to most people, but which can be developed through training and experience. It would be wrong to dismiss social casework as nothing more than giving help, support and advice to clients, since we all give and receive help from time to time. If social work has a quality of strangeness, it is because social work is concerned with relationships between strangers.

Social workers are professional people. They cannot choose their clients and they certainly should not discriminate between clients on the basis of personal likes and dislikes. They will naturally welcome the gratitude of their clients but they have no right to expect it;

indeed they have to be prepared to put up with a great deal of aggression and exposure to other people's misery. As Davies points out, at some time or other we all take part in interviews, but in doing so we seldom have to 'cope with verbal aggression, threats of violence, tears, total silence or more bizarre behaviour' (Davies, 1981, p.48) as ordinary events in the average day's work.

In addition social workers are accountable to their agencies and employers for what they do. Davies is right in saying that 'social work *can* have no existence independently of the agencies in which it operates.' The powers and responsibilities of social workers cannot be brushed under the carpet of egalitarianism. Davies lists some of their duties, which include supervising children and young persons who are at risk in the locality, or containing them in residential settings; advising courts on children who are the subject of care proceedings; making fostering and adoption enquiries; acting as *guardians ad litem*; making pre-release reports on people in various forms of custody; allocating scarce resources in cash and kind; arranging accommodation for the elderly; and advising on admissions in to psychiatric care (Davies, 1981, p.8 ff). In personal terms this means working with people who are vulnerable, damaged, distressed or dangerous.

The efficient and humane discharge of social work duties calls for specialised legal, psychological and social knowledge. Apart from practice skills, social workers must have clear and detailed knowledge of the aspects of the law which affect their dealings with child protection, care and supervision; mental illness and mental subnormality; and the care and rights of the elderly, the chronic sick and the disabled and separated, divorced or violent spouses; and they must know the relevant court procedures. They need some knowledge of welfare legislation in the fields of housing and rates, educational welfare, income maintenance and health care, and they need to know how their own agencies work, and something about the nature and scope of external local resources in both the statutory and the voluntary sectors. They must also be given the chance to acquire expertise and experience in some particular aspect of human need, and to make this available to their colleagues. Finally they must be able to put all this information to practical use in the service of their clients. Consequently they need to be familiar with the knowledge and insights which academic disciplines can give them concerning human nature and society.

The Report reviews the available evidence on the effectiveness of social work intervention. Davies reminds us how easy it is for social workers – and their critics and defenders – to exaggerate the extent to which people or situations can be changed by social work intervention. Very often the situation of the client is one in which 'The social worker couldn't make it worse, because it couldn't *be* worse' (Davies, 1981, p.116), and it would be unrealistic to expect the social worker to make it better. Some problems have no solution, and all too many tragedies cause permanent grief.

In practice a great deal of social work is a task of 'maintenance', containment, control and support (Davies, 1981, p.137 ff), so it is inevitable that social workers will find numerous examples of misery and injustice in the course of their work, but that does not justify switching the focus of social work from personal to political objectives. They already have at their disposal the normal channels of communication and influence in their agencies through which to get a better deal for their clients, and they have their professional associations through which to inform public opinion about the shortcomings of social policy. Social workers have to accept the fact that demand for their services is connected with the failures rather than the successes of social policy, whatever type of society they may work in. Their view of social life is both a special and a partial one.

Because of the enormous complexity, variety and range of needs calling for social work intervention, the case for specialisation is self-evident. The important question is, can specialisation be developed in such a way that appropriate attention will be given to each individual client as a whole person rather than as a collection of separate problems? There is no reason why the demands of generalist and specialist social work cannot be reconciled within a properly organised system of care based on adequately staffed generic area teams in which there is a sensible division of labour.

The notion of community
Before attention is given to some of the other implications of the Barclay proposals, the notion of community should be briefly considered. It is one of the most stubbornly persistent illusions in social policy studies that eventually the concept of community – as a basis of shared values – will resolve all our policy dilemmas. The very fact that this notion is cherished from left to right across the political spectrum makes it highly suspect. There is no unitary definition of community because, like the concept of equity, it is open to various interpretations. The idea that in a complex industrial society the notion of community could provide a basis for shared values (and hence for consistent social policies) is erroneous.

It seems that when our policy-makers reach an intellectual impasse they cover their embarrassment with the figleaf of community. It happened in the case of the Seebohm Committee, when it failed to discover a specific definition of 'the family' and immediately proceeded to extol the virtues of 'the community', which, for the purposes of that Committee, came to mean everybody and everything. Consequently the personal social services throughout the past decade have had to carry the burden of universalism implied in this definition.

The definition of community given in the Report is neither better nor worse than most of its kind. However, the concept of community can never be sufficiently well defined to serve as a framework for formal and equitable social policies, and consequently policies based on this concept are bound to be inadequate. In fact the Report itself explains why this is the case in its concluding paragraphs, where it admits that 'We still know too little about what determines the shape and style of informal networks or what constitutes a "healthy" community. . . The evidence reaching us, similarly, abundantly attests that there is no one way of knowing or serving communities' (13.70). I agree.

However suspect, it is not surprising that community-based approaches to social work evoke, albeit for different reasons, the approval of radicals and conservatives alike, since the idea of community is both intangible and paradoxical. It is intangible because it has not yet been satisfactorily defined in the setting of an industrial society, and paradoxical because historically it has inspired some of the most paternalist philosophies of social welfare and some of the most libertarian ones. I am aware that my view goes against the current of fashionable opinion. Whether the concept of community should be described as the Coronation Street or the Ambridge complex of sociology depends perhaps on whether the academic concerned is an urban or a rural sociologist.

Accountability

Three main dimensions of accountability are referred to in the Report, but none of them is consistently analysed. The first is accountability in a broadly political sense; the second, deriving from the first, is accountability for the use of resources, and the third is accountability for the exercise of professional discretion.

In Chapter 13 the Report touches on the issue of accountability and political control, stating that there must be a willingness on the part of social service managers to devolve 'as fully as possible decisions about resources and decentralising organisational structures' (13.50). At the same time the Report recognises that social workers may often have to take decisions which conflict with the preferences of local communities, but that 'In these circumstances particularly social workers will look to management for support' (13.57). In addition we are reminded that 'ultimate authority is vested in elected members' (13.62).

The advocates of the neighbourhood model believe that significant movement towards more community-orientated methods of social work can be achieved within the existing political system, but go on to argue that in the longer term it will be necessary to develop new political institutions like neighbourhood councils at a local level, with powers of management. Changes of this order would require new legislation.

The Report states with regard to the political element in the role of social workers that they should have a greater say in policy-making, but it neglects some of the effects it would have on representative local democracy if frontline social workers – or any other occupational group – were given a more authoritative role in policy-making. Local authority councillors are the *elected* representatives of citizens, and they are accountable to the citizens for their decisions. This is not true of social workers, nor was there any detectable enthusiasm in the evidence received by the Working Party for the view that if social workers were made more accountable to their clients and at the same time more influential in policy-making they should then become subject to the ordinary electoral sanctions characteristic of representative democracies.

The Report is generally in favour of giving both clients and local 'communities' a greater say in decision-taking, but it does not adequately analyse the conflict between accountability to clients and accountability to local 'communities'. In the context of the personal social services it is very likely that sharp conflicts would arise between clients and communities because the two groups have differing expectations of social workers.

The following quotation from the Report give some idea of the confused pattern of accountability devised by the Working Party for the community social work model: 'In any form of community social work, social workers will be subject to multiple accountability. Primary accountability will remain to the elected members (or the council members of voluntary agencies) who employ them and can call them to account: but they will also have a duty to give an account of their actions and decisions not only to individual clients or client groups, but also to informal carers with whom they are in partnership' (13.63).

This does not exhaust the complexities of the community social work model, since we are also assured that 'It is vital that a social services department should carry the ultimate residual responsibility for seeing that social care networks are maintained' (13.67). As the Report observes, optimistically, 'It will need to be made as explicit as possible who is accountable . . . to whom for which aspect of his work', although we are reminded that 'No one can remove from social workers the burden of managing ensuing tensions' (13.63).

The neighbourhood model, as mentioned above, is less equivocal about the issue of accountability. Its supporters regret the fact that political authority is vested solely in local authority councils and their committees, and see this as an impediment to greater local autonomy at neighbourhood levels. They favour 'participatory' rather than representative forms of democracy, with social workers – and their clients – as very active participants.

The first duty of a social worker is to do his job within the terms of reference presented by his local authority, and he is solely accountable to his local authority in a legal and contractual sense. If his job gives rise to conflicts of loyalty which make him feel less capable of serving his clients' needs, then he ought to resign, although it is very doubtful whether many social workers spend their working lives moving from one crisis of conscience to another. This would be much more likely if social workers were made significantly more accountable to their clients and their local neighbourhood councils as well as other informal carers.

It is not enough simply to disentangle the various strands of political accountability from the community social work and neighbourhood models; the resource implications of accountability are also important enough to merit further discussion.

In both community-centred models the local communities are presented as the major untapped social care resource. Insufficient account is taken of the likelihood that the capacity of local communities to provide sustained patterns of informal care may be exaggerated, especially in areas where the needs are greatest.

Formal systems of social service delivery developed because the informal networks of mutual aid in local communities were manifestly incapable of meeting the kinds of personal need which arise in complex industrial societies. It is a romantic illusion to suppose that by dispersing a handful of professional social workers into local communities we can miraculously revive the sleeping

giants of populist altruism. The most localised system of 'social'
service in the history of British social policy was the Poor Law. Its
relieving officers and guardians all served localities and
constituencies that were sufficiently small to be intimately known. It
was just this distinctive quality of parochial social service that added a
uniquely hurtful dimension to the experience of stigma among the
recipients of poor relief.

The idea of investing local communities with a measure of real
control over the use of resources and the ordering of welfare
priorities leaves open both the question of general financial
accountability between local communities and their local authorities
and the questions of accountability and equity among the local
communities. By what criteria are resources to be allocated to patch
teams, for example, and by what criteria are they to be distributed
within the patches? By what criteria are the boundaries of the
patches to be drawn, for example in local authorities with marked
geographical variations in social class, including wealth and income?
How many additional bureaucrats will be required to ensure that
justice is done between the various groups of local lobbyists? Are
there any reliable inferences that can be made about the self-interest
or altruism of these local constituencies? And how is a community to
be defined? The literature advocating community-centred models of
social work does not provide satisfactory answers to these questions.

The Report is strongly in favour of giving experienced social
workers more autonomy and more scope for the exercise of their
own judgement and discretion. It is also in favour of enhancing the
rights of clients and carers. How are these two objectives to be made
compatible? The exercise of discretion is primarily required in the
interpretation of regulations in particular cases and in the case of
idiosyncratic needs which have not been anticipated in the
regulations. It is difficult enough when the pattern of accountability
is unequivocal; none the less the Report signally fails to relate its
recommendations about accountability to its recommendations
about social workers' use of their own discretion.

We are asked to accept a model of 'multiple accountability' in
which social workers will remain primarily accountable to elected
members of the local authority, but additionally accountable to
council members of voluntary agencies, individual clients or client
groups, neighbourhood councils or mutual aid associations and
informal carers (13.63). A statement of this kind is too vague for
policy purposes, especially when it is considered in relation to the
Report's appeal to employers to review their management systems in

order to ensure a clear organisational structure with a minimum number of layers of decision-making. In addition the due process of accountability, with the element of consultation it involves, directly affects the speed and cost of service delivery; yet, on top of its failure to differentiate the types of accountability, the Report does not seriously analyse this consideration either, which detracts from its claim that community social work is a viable method for organising the personal social services.

Generalism and specialism

Both community-based models effectively relegate specialist expertise to a residual role. The two models are based on a threefold division of labour between generalists, specialists and managers (team leaders). The generalists would continue to do counselling work, but more of their time would be given to community-orientated work involving negotiation, bargaining, advocacy and teaching others 'how to find their way within the social services' and how to use social care networks (13.49). There would be no increase in the total number of professional social workers – generalist or specialist; none of the increased number of volunteers would undertake statutory work; but more of the professional workers' time would have to be devoted to enlisting and managing volunteers, as part of their broader 'social care planning' remit.

The case for developing community-based social work rests very much on the assumption that proximity will enhance effectiveness. None the less in both variants of the model many of the specialist social workers would be moved further away from the front-line area teams, despite the clear evidence from the Stevenson and Parsloe study, *Social Work Teams* (1978, p. 279 ff), that specialists or 'consultant' social workers who are not active members of area teams are seldom used effectively. In fact very few area team members were able to use them at all. As if in anticipation of this criticism, the Report prescribes that 'Both kinds of social workers, if they are to operate with a community orientation, must have knowledge of communities and how they function' (13.46). Again there is no indication of *how* they would acquire this knowledge. Presumably it would be up to the workers to study their locality while they were working in it; the specialists serving more than one locality would have to study very hard indeed.

The Report gives equal emphasis to the activities of social care planning and counselling in social work. However, the term 'social care planning' is misleadingly grandiose, although it accords with the model of community social work since it implies a range of reponsibility beyond the competence and resources of social workers. If social care planning is intended to complement the task of counselling, which is primarily a one-to-one activity associated with individuals and families, the emphasis on the 'social' aspect is misleading. If it has broader implications, a social worker attempting to work at both disparate levels is unlikely to excel in either job.

None the less the claims and counter-claims that are likely to fall on the basic-grade worker in the community social work model are minimal in comparison with those reserved for the managers, or team leaders (13.51–53). The team leader would be a manager, an entrepreneur, a negotiator, a watchdog over various budgets and a planner. His responsibilities would encompass not only social workers, but a variety of other paid and unpaid workers. There is no serious discussion as to whether or not he would retain a case load. If so, it could well be the last straw; if not, the authority of his supervisory and supportive role in relation to junior colleagues would be seriously undermined.

It is very difficult to follow the Report's analysis of the relationship between social work and community work. The term 'social care planning' seems to subsume large elements of community work. We are told, for example, that 'Community work, in which social workers carry out activities overlapping, but not co-extensive, with those of community workers, includes direct work with local community groups' (10.21), and in the next paragraph the Report states that 'We do not find the distinctions made between casework, group work and community work as methods of social work particularly helpful' because 'these terms identify the client, without telling us anything clearly about social workers' activities or the settings in which they are undertaken' (10.22). In the community social work model all social workers will undertake social care planning and counselling and therefore all social workers will be involved in some aspects of community work.

The neighbourhood, or patch model does not bother with such fine distinctions. It would effectively convert nearly all the social workers into community workers with special responsiblities for the frail elderly and families with young children. Within the patch teams, staff roles would be less narrowly defined than in the service delivery model, and counselling skills would have a less central place.

One of the most serious flaws in the Report is its neglect of specialised skills and knowledge and their role in social work practice. There are several paragraphs on specialisation in the Report which are intended to rebut the argument that the community social work model could not accommodate specialisation (10.34–37), but they are unconvincing for the following reasons. Within the community social work model all social workers would 'undertake social planning and counselling for any client group in a competent but basic way' (10.33), but, at the same time, 'Administrative structures may so relate the work and social workers together as to allocate most work of a particular kind to specially designated staff' (10.35). Specialists would be 'linked with' generalist teams (10.36), but in some cases, particularly where the volume of work is small, there would be centrally based specialist teams (10.37). The Report, however, goes on to insist that 'Whether or not an individual social worker is a specialist . . . the "community dimension" of his practice must always be taken into account and applied by him in carrying out his work' (10.38).

The simplest test of the practicability of these proposals is to treat the list of skills and knowledge which the community social worker would be expected to acquire (10.23–29) as the broad outline of the 'community dimension' mentioned above, and then to ask the following questions. How could a general social worker maintain a basic level of competence as a social worker within the terms of such a broad remit? How could a specialist social worker remain a specialist whilst acquiring and applying more than a token knowledge of these 'community' skills? How would general social workers ever acquire specialist knowledge and expertise? The Report itself gives a partial answer to these questions by acknowledging – albeit half-heartedly – that its recommendations would have profound implications for social work education if they were to be adopted (10.34). Most, if not all forms of specialist training in the CQSW courses would have to be abandoned to make room for more teaching about the 'community dimension'. The main responsibility for specialist training would, by default, devolve on post-qualifying courses. Generic social work training at CQSW level would become a form of generalist community social work training, and specialist training would be consigned to what is currently a very small and highly vulnerable part of social work education.

It should also be noted that any trend towards increasing generalism at the expense of specialism will run counter to present government policy, which is responding to the demand for more expertise. The Mental Health Bill before Parliament at the time of writing, for example, provides for the formal designation of approved mental health social workers and the restriction of this status to those who have followed an *additional* two-year course of training. If this principle is accepted in the field of mental health, it is arguable on grounds of natural justice alone that it should be extended to other highly vulnerable categories of need. It seems unlikely, for example, that the central government can long delay taking similar action with regard to children at risk who are under the age of 5. But the mentally ill and small children who are at risk are not the only special groups whose needs might well be neglected in a community-centred model.

The most vulnerable, disadvantaged and stigmatised clients will be at greatest risk in the community-based models of social work since they give greatest offence to local norms of behaviour and are often rejected by their local communities. The Report itself refers to the evidence submitted by the Family Service Unit, which revealed 'the great difficulty' with which certain families accept 'any notion of reliance on informal networks of family, friends or neighbours, their vivid fear of being victims of gossip and the importance they attach to confidentiality' (11.36). In addition the social worker's lack of special expertise is a recurring complaint from a variety of user groups, including a high proportion of physically handicapped people and ethnic minorities.

This is not to recommend reversion to a pre-Seebohm model in which social work is divided into isolated and narrow specialisms which, in turn, are separated from the other main social services. That is emphatically not the answer. Good social work practice depends on effective co-operation not only with other formal social services, but also with the informal networks of social care. The community social work model might well strengthen the links with the informal networks, but only at the expense of co-operation with the other formal social services and efficient discharge of statutory responsibilities.

The argument here rests on a number of considerations. First, a preciser definition of the role and tasks of social work is essential to the improvement of understanding and co-operation between social work and other social services. Secondly, the organisation of social work must make provision not only for an orderly internal division of labour based on generic team practice, but also for liaison with external services to be based on specialised expertise. Specialists within the area team should be the main co-ordinators of care when other services are involved.

Thirdly, the Report admits that 'several points were made repeatedly in evidence from those whose work brings them into close and regular contact with social workers. Without exception they argued for specialisation by social workers in a particular range of work' (8.31). This point was made by the courts, the medical services and many voluntary agencies. The Report responds with the statement that 'We recognise its importance but are also acutely aware that . . . we have not given this subject all the attention it requires. Others, however, have done so' (10.30).

Fourthly, the Report recognises that if a community social work model were to be adopted, new problems of co-operation with other social services would arise if they did not reorganise themselves on similar lines. The Report states that 'arrangements for collaboration need to be planned, and factors which affect relationships to be understood and not allowed to give rise to tensions . . . in the relevant agencies' (Chapter 8, conclusion 4). The Report says nothing further about this issue, apart from suggesting that 'A new balance will be called for between the skills we have considered . . . if social workers are to work in close partnership with other social services staff and with social networks, be these within local communities or within communities of interest which cross over geographical boundaries' (10.38). These are very vague recommendations from a committee that has been deliberating for over a year.

Co-operation and communication between social services departments and other social services are vital to the welfare of the most vulnerable clients. This was one of the issues which compelled Professor Stevenson to write a minority report to the Maria Colwell enquiry. In her covering letter she wrote that 'Time and again we have had to refer to failures in communication. However, as our comments section demonstrates, responsibility for effective communication in our welfare state is a two-way affair. . . It is most disturbing to contemplate the amount of concern and anxiety about Maria which never reached Miss Lees' (the social worker who was in charge of the case) (Department of Health and Social Security, 1974, pp.8, 88–115).

A model of social work which accentuates the organisational and operational differences between social work and other social services is unlikely to improve co-operation, and in all probability both community-based models would have that affect. The experience of the Maria Colwell enquiry and similar events since then must have contributed to Professor Stevenson's insistence that we get a sensible balance between genericism and specialism, and also uphold the specialist nature of liaison work with other social services. Clearly there is scope for improvement in the present system of liaison between social work and other social services, but it will not be achieved either by reducing the average size and increasing the number of area teams or by abolishing them altogether in the search for 'community'.

Specialism can be organised around particular activities such as adoption, fostering, welfare rights, and so on, around particular client groups such as the deaf and the blind, or around methods such as social casework, group work, community work and family therapy. The type of setting in which social workers are employed hardly seems to be a criterion of specialism in its own right, although it is sometimes the case that particular settings are developed on the assumption that special needs and skills are involved. Hospital-based social work is an obvious example. Similarly, residential work has specialist features partly because of the nature of its setting and partly because distinctions between its formal and informal aspects are neither possible nor desirable. Community work remains a vexed issue. It is one of the few specialisms which are definable largely in terms of method, although the method entails an orientation and focus differing markedly from those of social casework. Each different method of organising social work services will impose its own orientation and focus on all the workers involved.

In brief, the concept of specialism is a highly relative one, since it implies a variation from some understood norm of generic or general practice. Organisational change, if it is sufficiently radical, can therefore alter the whole frame of reference, and hence the meaning of the terms used.

Organising social work
To a very large extent the expectations that employers have of their social workers are directly determined by legislative imperatives. The autonomy of the employing bodies derives from the freedom with which they can organise their own social services not only to meet their mandatory duties, but also to provide for the permissive undertakings which they think are important.

For the past five years at least, the employers – local authorities in particular – have been discharging these responsibilities in conditions of intensifying disadvantage. The volume of legislation has grown steadily and it has outpaced the supply of resources required to meet newly recognised needs. Under such circumstances the inherent weaknesses in any system of organisation are bound to become more apparent, and even its best features will eventually be compromised. It is therefore a particularly difficult time for sorting out the intrinsic and the extrinsic causes of intra-organisational conflict. If there was adequate scope for specialisation as well as team work, social workers would be less likely to feel 'deskilled' and socially isolated, and more likely to cope effectively with the dilemmas of obligation and choice which characterise their job.

The questions facing us – what is social work and what should it be? – embrace the nature of the needs confronting social work, the kinds of resources required to meet these needs, and the modes of organisation best suited to service delivery within the framework of mandatory and permissive legislation.

Several themes recur throughout the mass of evidence received by the Working Party. .First, with regard to the needs of social work clientele, there is little doubt that professional social workers are or ought to be mainly concerned with the welfare and interests of people who in general are rejected, vulnerable, disadvantaged and sometimes a danger to public safety. In addition to this minority of complex and difficult cases there are many other needs – largely material and advisory ones – which can be met fairly quickly and effectively by other professional, non-professional and untrained workers, with the help of volunteers – given the necessary resources.

The second theme is the issue of genericism and specialism in social work which, in principle, is far less contentious than might be supposed. It should no longer be seen as an 'either/or' issue, but as one of finding the best ways in practice of combining the two types of activity. Professor Stevenson's assertion that 'there is a common core of knowledge and skill which should be acquired on basic qualifying courses' (Stevenson, 1981, pp.13–28) is well supported by the evidence. None the less, in turning her attention to the relationship between the complex needs of a minority of difficult clients and more straightforward requests for help, Professor Stevenson goes on to recommend that 'ways are found of better utilising specialist expertise *outside* teams for the benefit of the team. But this does not dispose of the case for specialisms *within* teams [my italics].' She continues with the question, 'are people's diverse problems so straightforward that we do not need expertise in face-to-face dealings with them?' and she proposes that 'If social work is *only* about promoting, stimulating and supporting community networks, then some other occupational group will have to move in, or be invented, to offer service to those with specific and complex social and psychological difficulties' (26).

Expertise, however, develops through continuous experience on a basis of specialisation. Co-ordination and co-operation in social work depend on the development of a shared core of generic knowledge and skills. Where needs are complex, the tasks of co-ordination and co-operation extend from the social work team, in field or residential settings, to other social services. Whatever deficiencies there are in the current pattern of social work organisation in area teams, it seems improbable that an alternative system which is more geographically dispersed than present ones will improve levels of co-operation and efficiency in *both* the formal and the informal contexts of social care.

Thirdly, we know that traditional systems of organisation based on area teams have not always succeeded either in getting the best allocation between their generic and specialist workers or in harnessing the services of local communities. In part this is because the preventative, practical and community-orientated activities of social services departments do not give rise to the really intractable problems of organisation and resource deployment. It is the hard-core minority of families and individuals with longstanding and recurring problems that imposes a 'residual' status on the Departments and compels them to assume a reactive and contingent function which can never be justified on grounds of cost-efficiency alone.

In her impressive submission to the Committee and her related book, *Specialisation in Social Service Teams*, Professor Stevenson outlines a way of both generalism and specialism. Her proposal is based on the so-called 'client-centred' model, with area teams and a formal, hierarchical system of administration. It also accepts and accommodates the need to improve liaison and co-operation between professional workers, volunteers and local communities. Professor Stevenson argues that 'every team should have within it a worker whose role is thus defined and whose remit is at once to sensitise the team to community need and to offer specific and concrete advice in relation to particular problems in a given locality. The links of such a worker with a range of voluntary and self help groups would be invaluable' (26, cf. Stevenson, 1981, pp. 130–6).

But Professor Stevenson is insistent that this is only one part of the work of an area team, one specialism within a team of specialists, and her model shows how the total resources of the team can be divided and deployed not only by reference to the skills and resources of the team, but with regard to maintaining good working relations with *other* social services which may be needed by the clientele of the team.

Her model also allocates to one of the team's six sub-units the primary responsibility for intake work and work with clients whose main problems are material and financial. All team members would serve the intake team on a rota basis, which would ensure that the most skilled and experienced staff played a part in this vitally important work and at the same time did not become over-specialised in their own work. There would also be close co-operation between the community-based sub-unit and the other sub-units.

The job of the team leader would still be an onerous one, but he would be working with a team of experienced specialists, and he would be able to concentrate on a finite number of tasks, including liaison with the team's social services department. This model was seriously considered by the Working Party and then rejected on the grounds that it gave insufficient emphasis to informal community networks of social care.

Social work values

As suggested earlier, it is unpopular and stigmatised people who are at greatest risk in a community-centred model of social work, and reference has already been made to the reluctance of FSU clients to accept help from informal local networks and their 'vivid fear' of gossip. The Report reassures us on this matter by declaring that 'Citizens are entitled to choose the person or people from whom help is most acceptable . . . nothing we are recommending should be taken to imply that clients generally should have informal caring networks imposed upon them' (13.58). Yet the whole preventive rationale of community social work seems bound to lead to exactly this outcome. Scarcely any attention has been given to the ethical (as distinct from the economic) implications of preventive social work – or to its compatibility with the principles of respect for persons and confidentiality.

In localities where a community social work model was adopted it would be much more difficult to protect the privacy not only of clients, but of other citizens who have no intention of becoming clients. The dangers would be greatest in the case of the neighbourhood, or patch model whose advocates insist that their method of operation will greatly augment the flow of information about local needs into the local offices. At a time when profound public disquiet is being expressed about the indiscriminate and often *unreported* collection of information about ordinary citizens by public and private bodies, we are now invited to endorse the creation of a proliferation of local data banks based largely on hearsay, gossip and well-meaning but uninvited prying.

It is argued that in a patch system social work staff would be able to build up a detailed knowledge of the local patterns of informal care and that this knowledge will be augmented by fostering contacts with intermediaries or 'gatekeepers', including people such as publicans, corner shop-keepers, lollypop ladies, and so on, who often acquire roles as informal advisers. In some of the areas operating a patch system it appears that local commercial enterprises such as pubs and corner shops would become recognised as important sources of information.

Respect for persons must entail respect for people's privacy and, in turn, for their right to confidentiality. The idea of preventive social work on a local basis would seriously threaten the right to privacy, since it would licence strangers (including volunteers) to enquire into the personal circumstances of citizens who may neither have asked for help nor committed any offence. The best way of preventing breaches of confidentiality is to collect as little confidential information as possible, and to confine the collection of it to professional workers.

David Billis has pointed out that 'the preventive umbrella permits an unbounded variety of work to creep into the original sanctioned agency function. That body of issues for which the organisation was set up in the first place can be steadily increased.' He states that 'the abandonment of pseudo-prevention may be a step towards the clarification of departmental boundaries based on the analysis of problems rather than the attainment of ideal states. It may take us towards not only "workable limits to social work", but trimmer, more muscular, and defensible, social service departments' (Billis, 1981, p. 379). However, a move towards community-based social work would almost certainly take us in the opposite direction.

Is there any justification for the indiscriminate collection of information that would appear to be envisaged for the community-based system of social work? According to the Report, this information would help social workers to foster a general sense of community, and would also help them to detect needs at an early stage. Not to over-dramatise the issue, a system simultaneously governed by the concepts of community and prevention would be potentially lethal to our civil liberties. In totalitarian societies the imposition of community – in the form of a unified network of local loyalties which are subservient to the state – is one of the basic political aims of government. Democracies tolerate the coexistence of many different loyalties. It is important that some rapport exists between the formal and informal systems of social care. It is equally important that the state is not allowed to intrude too far into the private worlds of individuals, families and local communities.

The right to privacy in one's personal life is one of the hallmarks of a free society. Justification must always be made before that right is violated. Preventive social work is an insidious threat to privacy because it can always be 'justified' on grounds of social welfare. In this matter I am reminded of Lord Melbourne's remark made after he had listened to an evangelical sermon on the consequences of sin: 'Things have come to a pretty pass, when religion is allowed to invade the sphere of private life' (Russell, 1898, p. 79). The same could be said of today's secular welfare evangelicals, who wish to advertise their services in every pub, pulpit and private residence in the country.

In the case of the professional social worker there is an important difference between learning about a suspected case of child abuse, for example, in the ordinary course of his duties and intentionally helping to create an informal network of information. The difference is one of good manners and forbearance. There is already considerable disquiet about the existence of 'at risk' registers in our present system. Imagination quails at the thought of their possible scope in a community-based model of social work.

The desire to locate and provide for unexpressed needs is not a defensible reason for jeopardising people's right to be left alone. The minority of those with unreported needs would be properly protected if social services were more efficiently publicised.

A general council and local welfare advisory committees

The Report reviews all the main arguments on the subject of a general council. Some of the arguments against are serious ones, but none of them is conclusive. For example it is pointed out that the boundaries of social work are imprecise and that 'social work is concerned with social control as well as with caring for people' (12.8). It is not disputed that the boundaries of social work ought to be more clearly drawn; this minority report is submitted partly for the very reason that the implementation of community social work would undoubtedly add to their obscurity. On the question of social control, the same situation exists in other professions, including medicine and nursing, and it is precisely because social control is an element of most professions that antipathy to professionalism is generally expressed as part of a wider sociological critique of the allocation of power in society.

Again, the fact that 'the knowledge base [of social work] is not readily understood by the public at large' (12.8) is true of most forms of professional knowledge, and appears to be a reasonable argument *in favour* of according professional status to an occupation. Other factors have to be considered, but it is misleading to imply that the public accord high status only to knowledge and skills which they 'understand'. They do so not on the basis of understanding, but on the basis of trust, and trust becomes important when people's lack of certainty and knowledge makes them dependent on another person.

The argument that social workers are not entitled to professional status because the majority of them are employed in large-scale public bureaucracies and so few are engaged in private practice is also open to question. Are we to believe that architects in the employment of local authorities behave less professionally than their colleagues in private enterprise? And are we to assume that there has to be an extensive private market for a service before it can be professionalised? Paradoxically both arguments find support among collectivists, in spite of their belief in the moral superiority of the social market.

The Report correctly states that 'Bureaucratic development has also inevitably resulted in a division between management and worker which provides the basis for the influence of the Trade Unions. The move towards full professional status and the introduction of an intermediary in the shape of an independent professional body must constitute a threat to that influence' (12.10). This statement describes the crucial issue in the future status of social work. If it does not become a profession it will become fully unionised; it will certainly not retain its present ambiguous status.

The Report includes, 'without prejudging the issue', the argument that there is a tide of opinion in 'community action and community involvement' which is highly critical of professional authority and professional knowledge in most occupations (12.11–12). Social work, however, is in a singular position, since the greater part of its specialised knowledge and skills is focused on a minority of the public, most of whom are very poor and not very articulate. It therefore goes unchallenged when intellectuals and activists who are largely middle class condemn the elitist nature of professionalism, and debunk the status of 'esoteric' knowledge (in the pejorative sense of the term).

If the characteristic patterns of risk and dependency confronting social workers were to spread to the majority of the population, the general public would very soon demand services of the highest quality from professional social workers of the highest calibre, and the idea of applying egalitarian principles to standards of knowledge and skill would be laughed out of court.

The British Association of Social Workers is in no doubt that a general council would make a positive impact 'on the definition and actual performance of social work' (12.17). It would not be possible for a general council to be set up in the very near future, but the British Medical Association is right in implying that, without 'a properly structured profession', social work will never have the incentive to set its own house in order (12.22), and there is no reason why 'blanketing in' should be an insurmountable obstacle, as the Report acknowledges (12.26). The majority of field social workers are now qualified. The majority of residential workers are not qualified, but the position is beginning to improve with the changing state of the labour market and CCETSW's policy of encouraging courses to develop specialist options in residential care. Agreement on a suitable target date, say in three years, would give us a little time to reinforce what is best in social work and get rid of some of the most glaring anomalies.

In principle this note accepts the view advanced by BASW that a council should be set up to assume general responsibility for the regulation of professional conduct, licensing and accreditation. Whether or not the council would also be responsible for the regulation of education and training is another matter. There is a good case for the appointment of a small working party to advise the Secretary of State both on the advisability of having a general council of social work and on its relationship to CCETSW. The arguments for and against keeping the two organisations separate are fairly evenly balanced, and a decision at this stage would be premature. Madelaine Malherbe has already carried out a substantial amount of excellent work on the issues of accreditation, but there are other related matters which have still to be considered (Malherbe, 1979).

These include the problems of assigning personal responsibility in a profession which is predominantly a public service, and in which the law does not specify which duties have to be carried out by qualified workers (12.9); the problems which might arise in residential care, where as yet only a minority of staff are professionally qualified; the extent to which a general council would be concerned with the activities of non-social workers in the personal social services; and whether or not the probation and after care service would come under the aegis of a general council.

These are complex and highly sensitive issues requiring careful and impartial consideration. They are all related to two basic questions. The first concerns the extent to which local authority management structures can be made compatible with the degree of professional autonomy and accountability that would accompany the creation of a general council. The second concerns the present standing of BASW. The recent history of the Association has been troubled by a loss in membership and a serious financial crisis. Its policies have not always been consistent with those of a professional body. However, there are signs that BASW is beginning to put its house in order, and this is greatly to be welcomed.

Since the Working Party did not receive a substantial body of evidence to the effect that clients' rights are generally being put in jeopardy, it seems quite unnecessary to set up an expensive network of local welfare advisory committees. In many cases this would make it impossible in practice to distinguish between the responsibilities of local authorities and those of their social work employees – a point which is equally relevant to the case for having a general council. The introduction of advisory committees would be bound to encourage the growth of an 'adversarial' element in 'transactions between worker and client', and stimulate an increase in 'defensive practice' (12.69). It is difficult enough to administer speedy, efficient and cheap appeals systems in the field of income maintenance, where the distinction between mandatory and discretionary powers is relatively clear cut; it would be an impossible exercise in the field of local authority social services, where the distinction is harder to make.

The proposal for a system of local advisory committees and an inspectorate will only distract attention from the need to resolve the conflict between 'elitists' and 'egalitarians' in social work. If elitism means seeking to promote and maintain the best possible standards of public service, I am an elitist, and I see the eventual formation of a general council and the professionalisation of social work as useful means to that end.

Implications for social work education

The Committee is unduly confident – if vague – in its recommendations on the future of social work education. It accepts, for example, that 'social work training has concentrated too exclusively upon direct counselling-type support work with individuals and groups' (3.46). There were some assertions in the submitted evidence that this emphasis on counselling does dominate social work education, but not sufficient to justify such dogmatic endorsement by the Report. In fact the Working Party never looked at the curricula of social work courses, because education and training were not within its terms of reference. Nevertheless there is no lack of evidence to the effect that there is a *variety* of emphasis in the courses, and it could be argued that in some courses there is too little emphasis on basic social work skills such as counselling.

The Report, however, proceeds to invite CCETSW to 'consider how it can assist training courses to develop the social care planning aspect of social work, without detracting from the training needed by social workers to fill their other direct counselling role' (3.45). Yet our present curricula for social work education are already in danger of sinking under the weight of so many disparate training expectations.

Short of lengthening the duration of basic training for the CQSW or stripping the curricula of all contributory disciplines, the only practicable way of introducing additional community-orientated training would be to drop a considerable proportion of training in other methods. This would naturally benefit community social work, but it could not be done without damage to training for social casework and for duties which are directly connected with statutory work.

The Report also fails to explain how the qualified social worker would find time to undertake statutory duties and maintain a basic level of competence in community-based activity. Yet it is on the basis of these proposals that CCETSW and the Colleges are seriously asked to develop a drastically revised model of social work training.

This is not to imply that 'promoting community self-help' is unimportant, but social workers are not necessarily the best people to carry out this function, and it should certainly not be expected of all social workers. The Working Party's solution to this problem is to recommend a drastic change in the training of social workers, without asking whether or not the expensive end product would still be professional social workers.

If the Working Party's arguments are accepted at face value, there should be a powerful shift in emphasis, away from highly specialised, skill-intensive work to more generalised tasks with a high 'entrepreneurial' content. Differences between paid workers and unpaid helpers should be minimised in the interests of greater equality and more 'participation'. All but a minority of social work clients should be helped by unqualified volunteers.

There is a good case for reviewing the balance of social work training between courses leading to the CQSW and those leading to the CSS. CCETSW is currently seeking the advice of interested parties on this matter, including the Colleges and employers. The Working Party considered proposals that there should be opportunities for CSS-holders to convert their qualification into a CQSW, which would be sensible under the present system, but pointless if, in deference to egalitarianism, the roles, tasks and status of the two qualifications were to be made virtually identical. That is exactly the effect that community social work would have. It may already be true that over the whole range of the personal social services social casework occupies only a small proportion of the time of a minority of CQSW-qualified social workers in area teams. If so, a more explicit division of labour between social workers and social service workers would release a proportion of CQSW-holders for more specialised post-experience training. This already seems probable in the field of mental health, and it is a welcome and long overdue development. Its logical outcome under the present system of social work would be a stratified profession with a fairly circumscribed range of roles and tasks, a number of which would have legal status. The alternative paths of community social work and neighbourhood social work would lead to more diffusion and more equality all round, but also to the eventual disappearance of professional social work altogether.

Conclusion

Any general move towards a model of practice and organisation based on community social work or neighbourhood-based, or patch social work will put the future of professional social work in jeopardy. There are at least two ways in which the community-based enterprise could go, because its two groups of advocates support it for totally incompatible reasons. First, there are those who believe that it would provide the ideal framework in which local communities could be mobilised into political pressure groups to obtain a massive increase in statutory resources. The danger here is that, if this expectation was not fulfilled, the consensual face of community would be transformed into one of open conflict between social workers as 'advocates' of 'community needs' and their employers.

Secondly, there are those who believe that the community model would generate a sufficient volume of informal care services to justify drastic cuts in statutory funding. This expectation is as questionable as the first, and equally liable to generate local conflict.

It would be foolish to make general predictions about anything as heterogeneous as local authority social services. None the less it is likely that in some local authorities, under the proposed new model, sustained efforts would be made by activists to put community social work to radical political use. Should this become widespread, the inevitable conflict would probably result in professional social work going the way of the ill-fated community development projects; then, by default, the gap left by the departing professionals would have to be filled by volunteers.

Lastly, there is the prospect of the neighbourhood, or patch version of community social work which I find most disturbing. It conjures up the vision of a captainless crew under a patchwork ensign stitched together from remnants of the Red Flag and the Jolly Roger – all with a licence and some with a disposition to mutiny – heading in the gusty winds of populist rhetoric, with presumption as their figurehead and inexperience as their compass, straight for the reefs of public incredulity.

Yet there is nothing fundamentally wrong with the ship in which we sail today, and certainly nothing that cannot be put right with common sense and cautious reform. It is not the present state of social work that gives cause for alarm, but the proposals for radical change in its nature and direction. I have submitted this note because I believe that the time for equivocation has passed.

Appendix C

List of works referred to in the text

Abrams, P., Abrams, S., Humphrey, R. & Snaith, R., *Action for Care*. The Volunter Centre, 1981.

Adams, S., *Evaluative Research in Correction: Status and Prospects. Federal Probation*, XXXXIII, 1, 14.

Association of County Councils, Association of Metropolitan Authorities, National Council for Voluntary Organisations, *Working Together*. ACC/AMA/NCVO, 1981.

Association of Directors of Social Services and Commission for Racial Equality, *Multi-Racial Britain: The Social Services Response*. ADSS, 1978.

British Association of Social Workers, *Clients are Fellow Citizens*. BASW, 1980.

Berg, I., Consterdine, M., Mullin, R., McGuire, R. & Tyler, S., 'The Effect of Two Randomly-Allocated Court Procedures on Truancy', *British Journal of Criminology*, 18, 3.

Bernsten, K. & Christiansen, K., 'A Re-socialisation Experiment with Short-Term Offenders' in *Scandinavian Studies of Criminology*. Christiansen, K. (Ed), Tavistock, 1975.

Billis, D., 'At Risk of Prevention', *Journal of Social Policy*, 10, 3, July 1981.

Brewer, C. & Lait, J., *Can Social Work Survive?* Temple Smith, 1980.

Brody, S.R., *The Effectiveness of Sentencing: A Review of the Literature*. HMSO, 1976.

Brunel Institute of Organisation and Social Studies, *Professionals in Health and Social Services Organisations*. BIOSS, 1976.

Carter, J., *Day Services for Adults: Somewhere to Go*. Allen & Unwin, 1981.

Challis, D. & Davies, B., 'Matching Resources to Needs in Long-Term Care'. Gower (forthcoming).

Cheetham, J., *Social Work Services for Ethnic Minorities in Britain and the USA*. Dept. of Social and Administrative Studies, Oxford, 1982.

Cooper, C., Harwin, B., Detla, C. & Shepherd, M., 'Mental Health Care in the Community. An Evaluation Study', *Psychological Medicine*, 5, 1975.

Crosbie, D., O'Connor, P. & Vickery, A., 'Working with an Area Team: Research and Development in Networks for the Elderly' in *Care in the Community: Recent Research and Current Projects*. Glendenning, F. (Ed), Beth Johnson Foundation, 1982.

Corney, R., 'Social Work Effectiveness in the Management of Depressed Women: A Clinical Trial', *Psychological Medicine*, 11, 1981.

Corney, R., 'The Views of Clients New to a General Practice Attachment Scheme, and to a Local Authority Intake Team'. Unpublished.

Davies, M., *The Essential Social Worker: A Guide to Positive Practice*. Heinemann Educational Books, 1981.

Department of the Environment, *Report on Urban Programmes*, Inner Cities Directorate. DoE, 1980.

Department of Health and Social Security, *Manpower and Training for the Social Services: Report of the Working Party*. DHSS, 1976.

Department of Health and Social Security, *Report of the Committee of Enquiry into the Care and Supervision Provided in Relation to Maria Colwell*. HMSO, 1974.

Department of Health and Social Security, *Report of a Study of the Boarding-out of Children*. DHSS, 1982.

Department of Health and Social Security, *Report of a Study on Community Care*. DHSS, 1981.

Ellis, J. (Ed), *West African Families in Britain: A Meeting of Two Cultures*. Routledge & Kegan Paul, 1978.

Equal Opportunities Commission, *Caring for the Elderly and Handicapped: Community Policies and Women's Lives*. EOC, 1981.

Fennell, G., Emerson, A., Sidell, M. & Haine, A., *Day Centres for the Elderly in East Anglia*. Centre for East Anglian Studies, 1981.

Fischer, J., *The Effectiveness of Social Casework*. Charles C. Thomas, 1976.

Fisher, M., Newton, C. & Sainsbury, E., 'Social Work Support to People Suffering Mental Ill Health, and to their Families'. Unpublished.

Geall, R., *The Social Services Client*. London Borough of Lambeth, 1981.

Gibbon, J., 'An Evaluation of the Effectiveness of Social Work Interactions Using Task-Centred Methods After Deliberate Self-Poisoning' in *Evaluative Research in Social Care*. Goldberg, E. & Connelly, N. (Eds), Heinemann, 1981.

Glastonbury, B., Cooper, D. & Hawkins, P., *Social Work in Conflict*. Croom Helm, 1980.

Glendinning, R. & Bradshaw, J., *Resource Worker Project: Final Report*. DHSS, 1981.

Glendinning, R. & Bradshaw, J., Paper on Resource Worker Study. Unpublished.

Goldberg, E., Mortimer, A. & Williams, B., *Helping the Aged: A Field Experiment in Social Work*. Allen & Unwin, 1970.

Goldberg, E. & Fruin, D., 'Towards Accountability in Social Work: A Case Review System for Social Workers', *British Journal of Social Work*, 6, 1, 1976.

Goldberg, E. & Warburton, R., *Ends and Means in Social Work*. Allen & Unwin, 1979.

Goldberg, E., Warburton, R., McGuiness, B. & Rowlands, J., 'Towards Accountability in Social Work: One Year's Intake into an Area Office', *British Journal of Social Work*, 7, 3, 1977.

Goldberg, E. & Connelly, N. (Eds), *Evaluative Research in Social Care*. Heinemann, 1981.

Gostick, C. & Scott, T., 'Brief Survey of Intake Teams', unpublished.

Hadley, R. & Hatch, S., *Research on the Voluntary Sector: Some Proposals for Exploring Alternative Patterns of Welfare Provision*. Social Science Research Council, 1980.

Hadley, R. & McGrath, M., *Going Local: Neighbourhood Social Services*. Bedford Square Press, 1981.

Harlesden Community Project, *Community Work and Caring for Children*. Owen Wells, 1979.

Holman, R., *Kids at the Door*, Blackwell, 1981.

Holme, A. & Maizels, J., *Social Workers and Volunteers*. Allen & Unwin, 1978.

Illich, I., *Disabling Professions*. Marion Boyars, 1977.

Johnson, N., *Voluntary Social Services*. Blackwell, 1981.

Jones, M., Neuman, R. & Shyne, A., *A Second Chance for Families: Evaluation of a Program to Reduce Foster Care*. Child Welfare League of America, 1976.

Kelly, J. *et al, Great Oaks from Little Acorns Grow*. London Borough of Lewisham, Social Services Department, 1980.

Knight, B. & Hayes, R., *Self-Help in the Inner City*. London Voluntary Service Council, 1981.

Leonard, P., 'Professionalisation, Community Action, and the Growth of Social Service Bureaucracies', *Sociological Review*, Monograph No. 20, Keele, 1973.

Malherbe, M., *Accreditation in Social Work: Principles and Issues in Context*. Central Council for Education and Training in Social Work, 1979.

Mattison, J. & Sinclair, I., *Mate and Stalemate: Working with Marital Problems in a Social Services Department*. Blackwell, 1979.

McCormack, M., *Away from Home: the Mentally Handicapped in Residential Care*. Constable, 1979.

Moroney, R., *The Family and the State: Considerations for Social Policy*. Longman's, 1976.

Mullen, E. & Dumpson, J., *Evaluation of Social Intervention*. Jossey-Bass, 1972.

National Children's Bureau, *Who Cares: Young People in Care Speak Out*. NCB, 1977.

National Council for Voluntary Organisations, *Improving Effectiveness in Voluntary Organisations*. NCVO, 1981.

Payne, M., *Power, Authority and Responsibility in the Social Services*. McMillan, 1979.

Personal Social Services Council, *Setting a Target Date*. PSSC, 1980.

Phillimore, P., *Families Speaking*. FSU, 1981.

Pinker, R., *The Enterprise of Social Work*. London School of Economics, 1981.

Reid, W. & Hanrahan, P., 'The Effectiveness of Social Work: Recent Evidence' in *Evaluative Research in Social Care*, Goldberg, E. & Connelly, N. (Eds), Heinemann, 1981.

Report of the Committee of Enquiry into the Education of Handicapped Children and Young People (Warnock Report). Cmnd 7212, HMSO, 1978.

Report of the Committee on Local Authority and Allied Personal Social Services (Seebohm Report). Cmnd 3703, HMSO, 1968.

Report of the Departmental Committee on the Probation Service (Morison Report). Cmnd 1650, HMSO, 1962.

Report of an Inquiry by the Rt Hon Lord Scarman, *The Brixton Disorders 10–12 April 1981*, Cmnd 8427, HMSO, 1981.

Report of the Wolfenden Committee, *The Future of Voluntary Organisations*. Croom Helm, 1977.

Rose, G. & Marshall, A., *School Counselling and Social Work*. John Wiley, 1975.

Rowe, J. & Lambert, L., *Children Who Wait*. Association of British Adoption Agencies, 1979.

Russell, G.W.E., *One Who Has Kept a Diary: Collections and Recollections*. Smith, Elder & Co., 1898.

Sainsbury, E. & De Alarcon, G., 'The Cost of Community Care and the Burden on the Family of Treating the Mentally Ill at Home' in *Impairment, Disability and Handicap*, Lees, D. & Shaw, S. (Eds), Heinemann, 1974.

Scottish Development Department, *Community Councils: Some Alternatives for Community Council Schemes in Scotland*. HMSO, 1974.

Shaw, M., *Social Work in Prison: Home Office Research Studies No. 12*. HMSO, 1974.

Shaw, M., Lebens, K. & Cosh, A., *Children Between Families*. University of Leicester School of Social Work, 1975.

Sinclair, I., Shaw, M. & Troop, J., 'The Relationship Between Introversion and Response to Casework in a Prison Setting', *British Journal of Clinical Psychology*, 13, 1974.

Sinclair, I., *Task-centred Casework in Two Area Teams*. Report to DHSS, 1981.

Stein, J. & Gambrill, E., 'Facilitating Decision on Foster-Care', *Social Service Review*, 51, 1979.

Stevenson, O. & Parsloe, P., *Social Service Teams: the Practitioners' View*. DHSS, 1978.

Stevenson, O., *Specialisation in Social Service Teams*. Allen & Unwin, 1981.

Tizard, B., 'Relating Outcome to Institutional Settings for Children Taken into Care' in *Evaluative Research in Social Care*, Goldberg, E. and Connelly, N. (Eds), Heinemann, 1981.

Tizard, J., Sinclair, I. & Clarke, R.V.G. (Eds), *Varieties of Residential Experience*. Routledge & Kegan Paul, 1975.

Toren, N., *Social Work: the Case of A Semi-Profession*. Sage Publications Inc, Beverley Hills, 1972.

Townsend, P., *The Family Life of Old People*. Routledge & Kegan Paul, 1957.

Warren, D.I. *Helping Networks*. University of Notre Dame Press, Indiana, 1981.

Webb, A., Day, L. & Weller, D., *Voluntary Social Services Manpower Resources*. Personal Social Services Council, 1976.

Westland, P., 'The Year of the Voluntary Organisation,' *Community Care*, 19.11.81.

Wetton, K., *The Cheltenham Intake Team: an Evaluation*. Clearing House for Social Services Research, 1976, No. 2.

Wood, R., 'Casework Effectiveness: A New Look at the Research Evidence', *Social Work*, 23 (6) 1978.

Wootton, B., *Social Science and Social Pathology*. Allen & Unwin, 1960.

Yelloly, M., *Social Work Theory and Psychoanalysis*. Van Nostrand, Reinhold & Co, 1980.

Appendix D

List of members of the Working Party

Mr P.M. Barclay   Chairman

Dr D.I. Acres, OBE, JP, DL
Mrs P. Brown
Mr T. Cook
Mr W.D. Davies
Mr E.R. Day, JP
Miss A. Elton
Professor R. Hadley
Mr R. Hargreaves

Miss A. Jones
Mr A.F. Jones
Mr T.B. Owen
Professor Phyllida Parsloe
Professor R.A. Pinker
Mrs R. Prime
Mrs M. Sienkiewicz
Mr K.J. White
Mr B.R. Worster-Davis, JP

Appendix E

List of respondents

E. 1   Miss E.M. Goldberg
E. 2   British Medical Association
E. 3   Miss N. Hazel
E. 4   Walsall Area Health
        Authority: Dr G.M. Singal
E. 5   Miss G. Swire
E. 6   Prof P. Mittler
E. 7   Miss J.D. Cooper
E. 8   Dr B.F. Whitehead
E. 9   Mrs B.A. Tower
E. 10   J.W. Peppitt
E. 11   Mrs J. Woodward
E. 12   Local Authorities' Social
        Services Study Group
E. 13   R. Bessell
E. 14   Depressives Associated
E. 15   Miss N. Hazel
E. 16   Dr H.W. Fladée and partner
E. 17   Dr M. Rapoport, Dr W.
        Rapoport and Dr A.
        Rapoport
E. 18   The National Society for
        Autistic Children
E. 19   Mrs D. Silberston
E. 20   Eileen Stacker
E. 21   R.J. Willis
E. 22   A.G. Lacayo
E. 23   W. Jordan
E. 24   Cheshire County Council,
        Social Services
        Department
E. 25   D.B. Wadland
E. 26   Prof Olive Stevenson
E. 27   J.E. Blacksell
E. 28   Susan Chilton
E. 29   Miss M.A. Day and Miss S.M.
        Mowat
E. 30   D. Eastham
E. 31   D.J. Brazier
E. 32   Dr J.K. Anand

E. 33   International Glaucoma
        Association
E. 34   Royal National Institute for
        the Blind
E. 35   A. Gorst
E. 36   D.F.J. Piachaud
E. 37   Prof T. Brennan
E. 38   P.A. Bloxham
E. 39   British Medical Association
E. 40   Central Council for
        Education and Training in
        Social Work
E. 41   Mr Peters
E. 42   The Lions Club of Chester
E. 43   J. Shember
E. 44   Suffolk County Council,
        Suffolk Coastal Social
        Services Division (Miss E.
        Noller)
E. 45   National Council of
        Voluntary Child Care
        Organisations
E. 46   Alan Cohen and Margaret
        Richards
E. 47   D. Mathieson
E. 48   M.S. Veail
E. 49   University of Lancaster,
        Department of Social
        Administration: Directors
        of the Centre of Youth,
        Crime and Community
E. 50   Prof T.H.D. Arie
E. 51   Devon County Council,
        Social Services
        Department (J.D.
        Hamson)
E. 52   Riva Miller and Christina
        Tolaini
E. 53   Medical Practitioners'
        Union, Manchester
        Branch

E. 54 Mrs C. Robertson

E. 55 City of Birmingham Education Department, Family and Child Advisory Services

E. 56 London Borough of Barnet, Social Services Department Area Team D, in conjunction with the Research & Development Section

E. 57 Northamptonshire Area Nursing and Midwifery Advisory Committee

E. 58 Benedict Kennedy

E. 59 Mid-Glamorgan County Council, Social Services Department (Silverbrook Community Home)

E. 60 Marlborough Hospital Social Work Department

E. 61 Welsh Secondary Schools Association

E. 62 Dr W. Johnson

E. 63 The National Council for the Single Woman and her Dependants

E. 64 Mrs H. Snidle and Dr R. Walton

E. 65 Dr S. Ramon

E. 66 The Centre for Policy on Ageing

E. 67 C. Whittington

E. 68 A. Leissner

E. 69 Standing Conference of Voluntary Social Work Organisations in Staffordshire

E. 70 R.T. Needham

E. 71 S. Rolfe

E. 72 Association of Teachers in Social Work Education

E. 73 Senior Registrar, Family Division of the High Court

E. 74 Dr C.A.J. Macafee

E. 75 Dr G. Blessed

E. 76 Cherry Rowlings

E. 77 The Leukaemia Society

E. 78 Church of England Children's Society

E. 79 The Family Welfare Association of Manchester Ltd

E. 80 Institute of Marital Studies, The Tavistock Institute of Medical Psychology

E. 81 Barnardo's

E. 82 Surrey Social Services Department, Woking District Social Work Office: three members of the Intake Team

E. 83 L.G. Wilder

E. 84 Northumberland County Council, Social Services Department, Castle Morpeth Area Office

E. 85 Social Services Committee of the West Sussex County Council

E. 86 Association of Hospital and Residential Care Officers

E. 87 R. Benjamin

E. 88 Marion Paxton and Marion Russell

E. 89 Miss N. Warne

E. 90 Miss J.R. Fells

E. 91 Association of County Councils and the Association of Metropolitan Authorities

E. 92 National and Local Government Officers' Association

E. 93 A.E. Leeding

E. 94 Restormel Council for Voluntary Service

E. 95 R.J. Clough

E. 96 M.S. Jeans

E. 97 M.A. Clifton

E. 98 Bristol Council for Voluntary Service

E. 99 The National League of the Blind and Disabled

E. 100 Elizabeth A. Sclater

E. 101 British Association of Social Workers: Special Interest Group – Social Work in Education

E. 102 Northumberland County Council, Social Work Department Prudhoe Hospital

E. 103 Brittle Bone Society

E. 104 Miss V. Johns

E. 105 E.T. Kelleher

E. 106 Tuberous Sclerosis Association of Great Britain

E. 107 University of Manchester, Psychiatric social work section of the Department of Psychiatry

E. 108 City of Manchester, Social Services Department, North District Hospital Social Work Service

E. 109 Preston Polytechnic, Division of Social Work

E. 110 Association of Chief Police Officers of England, Wales and Northern Ireland

E. 111 City of Liverpool Social Services Department: District 'J' Office – P. Billingsley

E. 112 The National Children's Home

E. 113 Dr P.E. Brooks

E. 114 Prof C. Pritchard

E. 115 City of Westminster, Area Social Services Office 4, Team A

E. 116 Health Visitors' Association

E. 117 Cambridge House and Talbot

E. 118 City of Manchester Education Committee – School Psychological and Child Guidance Service, Withington Child Guidance Centre

E. 119 Elizabeth Crawley

E. 120 Family Service Units (Part I)

E. 121 Association of Community Workers

E. 122 University of Leeds, Applied Anthropology Group, Centre for Social Work and Applied Social Studies

E. 123 National Council for Voluntary Organisations

E. 124 Harlow Council, Community Services Department

E. 125 The Remploy Advisory Panel

E. 126 Marlborough Hospital Social Work Department

E. 127 Hampshire Group of Child Psychiatrists (Winchester and Central Hampshire Health District)

E. 128 The Family Welfare Association

E. 129 Jan Dryden and Malcolm McCarthy

E. 130 London Borough of Enfield, Social Services Department

E. 131 Association of Independent Children's Households

E. 132 Islington Age Concern

E. 133 The Royal College of General Practitioners

E. 134 West Sussex County Council, Social Services Department

E. 135 A.P. Oakley

E. 136 British Association of Social Workers

E. 137 Residential Care Association

E. 138 G.L. Bromley

E. 139 London Borough of Sutton, Social Services Department

E. 140 Council for the Education and Training of Health Visitors

E. 141 MIND – The National Association for Mental Health

E. 142 The Tavistock Clinic

E. 143 University of Leicester, School of Social Work

E. 144 University of Leicester, School of Social Work: Working Party to study teaching of Psychology on Social Work Courses

E. 145 Behavioural Social Work Group

E. 146 St Bartholomew's Hospital, Social Services Department

E. 147 The Royal Leicestershire, Rutland and Wycliffe Society for the Blind

E. 148 M.E. Dieppe

E. 149 Dr C. Brewer and June Lait

E. 150 Soldiers', Sailors' and Airmen's Families Association

E. 151 Chelsea College, Department of Social & Psychological Studies, Social Work Studies Course

E. 152 R.H. Deepwell and Alexina M. McWhinnie

E. 153 The Volunteer Centre

E. 154 The Hospital for Sick Children, Medical Services

E. 155 Bethlem Royal and Maudsley Hospitals' Social Workers

E. 156 Cornwall County Council, Social Services Department

E. 157 National Association of Probation Officers

E. 158 London Borough of Camden, Social Services Area 5 Kentish Town

E. 159 Guild of Catholic Professional Social Workers

E. 160 Croydon Guild of Voluntary Organisations

E. 161 Rochdale Voluntary Action

E. 162 Group for the Advancement of Psychotherapy and Psychodynamics in Social Work – Northern Branch

E. 163 The Southern and Western Regional Association for the Blind

E. 164 The Renal Special Interest Group of British Association of Social Workers

E. 165 British Union of Social Workers

E. 166 National Childminding Association

E. 167 Miss A. Forbes

E. 168 Hyper-Active Children's Support Group

E. 169 'Mothers and Toddlers' Group, Leyland

E. 170 I. Kemp-Tucker

E. 171 National Children's Bureau

E. 172 Mrs J.M. Burgess

E. 173 National Council of Social Workers With the Deaf

E. 174 Age Concern Westminster

E. 175 Devon County Council, Social Services Department, Newton Abbot

E. 176 British Association of Social Workers – Essex Branch

E. 177 Birkenhead Council for Voluntary Service

E. 178 Essex County Council, Social Services Department, Chelmsford

E. 179 The Muscular Dystrophy Group of Great Britain

E. 180 Conference of Chief Probation Officers

E. 181 Stevenage Council for Voluntary Service

E. 182 Committee on Student Placements in Voluntary Agencies

E. 183 Joan M. Barton

E. 184 Federation of Community Work Training Groups

E. 185 J. Goldup, Ann Hamblin, G. Hamblin, Maureen Henderson, Sue Lewis, Helen Phillips, Anne Rice and J. Taylor

E. 186 Gill Butcher

E. 187 The Salvation Army Social Services

E. 188 London Teaching Hospitals' Principal Social Workers Group

E. 189 Invalid Children's Aid Association

E. 190 The National League of the Blind and Disabled, Scottish Area

E. 191 Surrey County Council, Social Services Department, Woking District Office

E. 192 British Association of Social Workers, Obstetrics and Gynaecology Special Interest Group

E. 193 Brenda Nally

E. 194 Motor Neurone Disease Association

E.195 North Regional Association For The Blind

E. 196 The National Deaf Children's Society

E. 197 Members of a residential workshop organised by the Central Council for Education and Training in Social Work and The Volunteer Centre, March 1981

E. 198 Child Guidance Training Centre, Camden and Islington Area Health Authority (Teaching)

E. 199 J. Pottinger

E. 200 Norfolk Area Health Authority

E. 201 Worcester District Community Health Council

E. 202 V. Hall, D. Jamieson, B. Lyall, D. Robinson, M. Tennant, M. Timothy, E.J. Wight

E. 203 Guild of Psychiatric Social Workers

E. 204 Rugby Voluntary Services Association

E. 205 D.R. Monk

E. 206 Community Service Volunteers: A. Taylor

E. 207 Leicester Royal Infirmary, Obstetric/Paediatric Unit

E. 208 British Association of Social Workers, Special Interest Group on Ageing

E. 209 Jewish Welfare Board

E. 210 Child Poverty Action Group

E. 211 Northumberland County Council, Social Services Department, Morpeth

E. 212 Kent County Council, Social Services Department Development Group

E. 213 National and Local Government Officers' Association, Nottinghamshire County Branch

E. 214 Elstree & Borehamwood Council for Voluntary Service

E. 215 Association of Directors of Social Services

E. 216 Camden Committee for Community Relations

E. 217 Ann Orledge

E. 218 Miss L.M. Ashley

E. 219 Socialist Medical Association

E. 220 A.B. Thomas

E. 221 G.N. Andrews, T.E. Myers, Mrs J. Rogers

E. 222 Social workers at the Hospital for Sick Children, Great Ormond Street and the Wolfson Centre

E. 223 Association of Professions for the Mentally Handicapped

E. 224 Social Work Education Committee of the Joint University Council

E. 225 University of London, Bedford College tutors

E. 226 Doncaster Council for Voluntary Service

E. 227 Liverpool Welfare Organisations Committee

E. 228 National Union of Teachers

E. 229 Council for Voluntary Service – Dacorum

E. 230 Leeds City Council, Department of Social Service

E. 231 Cambridgeshire Area Health Authority (Teaching), Peterborough Health District (Community Physician)

E. 232 Institute of Home Help Organisers

E. 233 The Patients' Association

E. 234 Dr R.S. Britton

E. 235 King's Health District (Teaching) Dulwich Hospital

E. 236 The psychologists in the Department of Psychological Medicine at the Hospital for Sick Children

E. 237 The Multiple Sclerosis Society

E. 238 G.L. Ridgewell

E. 239 Age Concern England

E. 240 The Association for Multi-Racial Social Work

E. 241 Sister N.M. Nelson

E. 242 Trent Polytechnic, Social Work Tutors' group

E. 243 Redditch Council for Voluntary Service

E. 244 The Children's Legal Centre

E. 245 Cheshire County Council, Chester District Social Services Office, Chester

E. 246 The Society of Area Nurses, Child Health, Newcastle

E. 247 The Campaign for Mentally Handicapped People

E. 248 A. Hayhurst and Isobel M. Morton

E. 249 Thelma Fisher

E. 250 Miss K.B. Richards

E. 251 C.H. Jones

E. 252 Professional Staff Committee of the Child Guidance Training Centre and Day Unit, Camden and Islington Area Health Authority (Teaching) North Camden District

E. 253 University of Warwick, Department of Applied Social Studies

E. 254 Yorkshire and Humberside Region Social Services Research Group

E. 255 Birmingham Tribunal Unit

E. 256 West Sussex County Council, Social Services Department, Chichester

E. 257 Bath Centre for Voluntary Service

E. 258 York Community Council

E. 259 City of Sheffield, Family and Community Services Department

E. 260 The Institute of Health Service Administrators

E. 261 Bristol Courts Family Conciliation Service

E. 262 J.G. Anderson and V. Gallagher

E. 263 Newcastle upon Tyne Council for Voluntary Services

E. 264 Harlow Council for Voluntary Service

E. 265 Lincolnshire County Council, Social Services Department

E. 266 National Council for One Parent Families

E. 267 Frances Sheldon

E. 268 National Society for the Prevention of Cruelty to Children

E. 269 The Police Superintendents' Association of England and Wales

E. 270 The National Council of Women of Great Britain

E. 271 The Spastics Society

E. 272 Royal County of Berkshire, Department of Social Services, Reading

E. 273 Mrs A. Cawkwell

E. 274 Institute of Consumer Advisers

E. 275 National Institute for Social Work Staff Members and Associates

E. 276 Nottingham & District Society for Mentally Handicapped Children and Adults

E. 277 C. Gwyntopher, P. Beresford and Suzy Beresford

E. 278 A Voice for the Child in Care

E. 279 Clwyd Health Authority, North District, Principal Social Workers

E. 280 Dr J.S. Rodgers

E. 281 London Borough of Hillingdon, Hillingdon Hospital Social Work Department

E. 282 Prof G.F. Zollicoffer

E. 283 Brenda Trimmer (The Compassionate Friends)

E. 284 British Association of Social Workers (Langstone Branch)

E. 285 G. Hill

E. 286 President of the Family Division, Royal Courts of Justice

E. 287 P. Hood

E. 288 D. Anderson-Ford

E. 289 British Association of Social Workers (Hammersmith and Fulham Branch)

E. 290 British Association of Social Workers (Camden and Islington Branch)

E. 291 Child Custody Consultation Team, Department of Psychological Medicine Hospital for Sick Children

E. 292 Justices' Clerks' Society

E. 293 Royal County of Berkshire, Department of Social Services, Bracknell Division

E. 294 Mrs S. Bullock

E. 295 National Association of Chief Education Social Workers

E. 296 The Third Hand

E. 297 L. Essex

E. 298 University of London, the Board of Studies in Social Administration

E. 299 Bexley Voluntary Service Council

E. 300 British Agencies for Adoption & Fostering

E. 301 National Association of Specialists in Community Medicine (Social Services)

E. 302 City of Newcastle upon Tyne, Social Services Department

E. 303 June Warner

E. 304 J. Cowan for the London Voluntary Service Council

E. 305 Leeds City Council, Social Services Department

E. 306 T.H. Gent

E. 307 The Royal College of Psychiatrists

E. 308 British Association of Social Workers – The

Haemophilia Society Special Interest Group

E. 309 F. Clinch

E. 310 Royal County of Berkshire, Department of Social Services Slough Division

E. 311 Dr Jean Harris and G.L. Mills

E. 312 C.J. Perry

E. 313 National Association of Citizens Advice Bureaux

E. 314 Institute of Local Government Administrators, Humberside Branch

E. 315 Social Work and Homelessness Group

E. 316 J.R.C. Saunders

E. 317 Nottinghamshire County Council, Social Services Department

E. 318 S. Hinks

E. 319 Metropolitan Borough of Wirrall, Department of Social Services, Birkenhead

E. 320 Family Service Units (Part II)

E. 321 Voluntary Christian Child Care organisations: Mr Fegan's Home Inc, Tunbridge Wells Mill Grove, London The Mission of Hope, South Croydon The Muller Homes for Children, Bristol Spurgeon's Homes, Bedford

E. 322 The Magistrates' Association: Sentencing of Offenders Committee

E. 323 Lord Chancellor's Visitors' Office

E. 324 Vivienne Coombe and Shama Ahmed

E. 325 National Union of the Deaf

E. 326 British Paediatric Association

E. 327 Miss D. Hawkins

E. 328 Mrs R.H. Corney

E. 329 Federation of Independent Advice Centres

E. 330 Apex Trust

E. 331 Prof R. Baker

E. 332 J. Hopkins
E. 333 Alison M. Wynd
E. 334 Prof S.J. Rees
E. 335 Group for the Advancement
of Psychodynamics and
Psychotherapy in Social
Work
E. 336 Mrs J.C. Lee
E. 337 Wendy Gilbert
E. 338 Family Rights Group
E. 339 Hillingdon Area Health
Authority, Michael Sobell
House
E. 340 Mrs F. Martin
E. 341 Lynn Wetenhall
E. 342 Mrs C.M. Kennedy
E. 343 Community Information
Centre, Wantage

E. 344 The Baroness Lane-Fox,
OBE
E. 345 K. Redgrave
E. 346 The British Psychological
Society
E. 347 Southwark Diocesan
Council for Wel-Care
E. 348 Students on the Certificate of
Qualification in Social
Work course at the Suffolk
College of Higher and
Further Education,
Ipswich
E. 349 COPE
E. 350 National Welfare Rights
Officers Group
E. 351 The Council of Her Majesty's
Circuit Judges

Appendix F

Areas visited by members of the Working Party or its secretariat

Hampshire   12 December, 1980
Barnsley   16 January, 1981
Newcastle upon Tyne and neighbouring areas   27 March, 1981
Lewisham   24 April, 1981
Derbyshire   8 May, 1981
Maybank area of Redbridge   22 May, 1981
Hertfordshire   5 June, 1981
Sefton   19 June, 1981
Camden   3 July, 1981
Cornwall   17 July, 1981
Coventry   30 July, 1981
Wolverhampton   18 September, 1981
Gwynedd   16 October, 1981
Oxfordshire   11 November, 1981
Warwickshire   18 November, 1981
Wakefield   25 November, 1981

On these visits informal discussions were held with many social workers and others working in statutory and voluntary agencies and in other services, with elected members, magistrates, foster parents, volunteers and clients. Discussions held elsewhere with particular groups included meetings with groups associated with Age Concern, Brent, members of the National and Local Government Officers' Association, Liverpool, a black women's centre, Brixton, and staff and residents of a voluntary home for the elderly, Braintree.

Appendix G

Principal statutory enactments relevant to the tasks of social workers

Children and Young Persons Act 1933
National Assistance Act 1948
Nurseries and Child Minders Regulation Act 1948
Sexual Offences Act 1956
Adoption Act 1958
Disabled Persons (Employment) Act 1958
Mental Health Act 1959
Mental Health (Scotland) Act 1960
Health Visiting and Social Work (Training) Act 1962
Children and Young Persons Act 1963
Health Services and Public Health Act 1968
Social Work (Scotland) Act 1968
Children and Young Persons Act 1969
Family Law Reform Act 1969
Local Authority Social Services Act 1970
Chronically Sick and Disabled Persons Act 1970
Guardianship of Minors Act 1971
Local Government Act 1972
Employment of Children Act 1973
Guardianship Act 1973
Matrimonial Causes Act 1973
Legal Aid Act 1974
Children Act 1975
Nursing Homes Act 1975
Criminal Law Act 1977
National Health Service Act 1977
Housing (Homeless Persons) Act 1977
Domestic Proceedings and Magistrates Courts Act 1978
Child Care Act 1980
Foster Children Act 1980
Residential Homes Act 1980
Education Act 1981

Appendix H

Papers available from the Librarian of the National Institute for Social Work, 5 Tavistock Place, London WC1H 9SS

Summary of the Findings and Recommendations of the Reports of Inquiries into sixteen Child Abuse cases.

Review of Studies of the Public and Users' Attitudes: Opinions and Expressed Needs with respect to Social Work and Social Workers.

Both by Mr Gordon Craig

Index

Abortions, 28, 34
Adoption, 154
Age Concern, 25, 74, 87, 89, 288
Alcoholics Anonymous, 75, 76
Alcoholism, 31
Area teams, work of, 3–6, 13, 137, 154
Assessment, 12, 13, 16, 151, 172, 174 *et passim*
Association of Chief Education Social Workers, 121
Association of County Councils, 86
Association of Directors of Social Service, vii, 25, 84, 141, 142
Association of Hospital Almoners, 179
Association of Metropolitan Authorities, 86

Bereavement, 34, 43
Bernado's, 70
Billis, David, 255
Birch Report, 24, 25, 75
Blind people, 161
British Association of Social Workers (BASW), 177, 188, 191, 258, 259
British Medical Association, 118, 241
bureaucracy, 56, 179–80, 257

Carter, Sir Charles, 96
Central Council for Education and Training in Social Work (CCETSW), 24, 25, 26, 44, 75, 139,
179, 181, 258, 260
Certificate in Residential Care of Children and Young People, 26
Certificate in Residential Social Work, 26
Certificate in Social Service, 26, 139, 181, 261
Certificate of Qualification in Social Work, xviii, 25, 139, 181, 248, 260, 261
Certificate of the Nursery Nurses Examination Board, 26
Children, 17–20, 28, 30, 128, 162–3:
abuse of, 28, 47, 48, 121, 123
'at risk', 15, 28, 189, 216
care orders, 19, 30, 161–2, 167, 195
handicapped, 30, 53, 55, 161, 163, 167, 168
supervision orders, 19
Children Act 1948, 105
Children and Young Persons Act 1969, 150
Citizens Advice Bureaux, 28, 89
Clients:
age of, 13
appeals, 194
as resources, 111
choice of carers, 83, 213, 226
complaints of, 188, 190, 191, 193, 194, 196
confidentiality of, 146–7, 155, 254, 255
consultation of, 148–9, 155, 187–8, 191
definition of, xii
financial problems, 28
numbers of, 31
public attitudes to, 129, 149
referral to social workers, 114–15
respect for, 145, 147, 254, 255
rights of, 146–7, 187–96, 254–6 *passim*
social workers, opinion of on, 37–8, 158–65 *passim*, 167–70 *passim*, 189, 249
survey of views, 158–9, 176
types of, 11
views of, 37–8, 62, 147–8, 158–65, 167–70 *passim*, 172, 189, 249
volunteer work of, 78
vulnerability of, 187–8
Commission for Racial Equality, 141, 142
Community:
definition of, xii–xiii
nature of, 231–2
Community development *see* Social care planning
Community mental handicap teams, 140, 154
Community of interest, xiii
Community self-help, 44
Community Service Volunteers, 78
Community social work:
conditions for development of, 226–7, 235
criticisms of proposals for, 236–62
definition of, xvii, 199
examples of, 206–9, 229–33

Community social work *cont.*
  examples of, 206–9,
    256–9
  feasibility of, 203–5
  generalist/specialist
    debate, 259–61
  information collection
    and, 237–8, 251–2
  integration and, 255–6
  management and,
    211–13
  methods needed, 210
  nature of, 205–7
  need for, 198, 199–203,
    216–17, 246–62 *passim*
  political issues, 214–16,
    245, 261–2
  residential care and, 70
  resources and, 100, 213
  social workers, demands
    of on, 209–11
  types of, 207–8
  voluntary agencies and,
    85
  see also Informal carers,
    Patch teams *and under*
    Social services
    departments
Community work, xiii–xiv,
  150–1
Community workers,
  definition of, ix
Conference of Chief
  Probation Officers,
  120
Counselling, x, xiv, 12, 15,
  16, 20, 34, 41–3, 138,
  150, 153, 163, 191,
  222 *et passim*
Courts, 61–2, 113, 117,
  119, 148
Craig, Gordon, ix, 159, 171
Curtis Committee, 121

Day centres:
  approaches used, 57–61
  conclusions on, 70–2
  definition, 53
  description of, 54–5
  effectiveness of, 174
  key-workers in, 69–70,
    71
  need for, 61–2
  provisions of, 62–3, 65–7
  qualifications and, 26
  residential centres and,
    63–4
  resources, 46

  segregation in, 56
  social work in, 52–72
    passim
  stigma attached to, 55–7
  voluntary, 26
Deaf people, 161, 163
Definitions, xii–xviii, 24
Department of Health and
  Social Security, 15, 22,
  28, 77, 117, 119, 159
Divorce, 28
Doctors, 28, 116, 117, 120
  et passim
Drugs, misuse of, 31

Educational Priority Areas,
  89
Elderly people, 11, 16, 30,
  43, 46, 47, 54, 62,
  97–8, 173 *et passim*
Equal Opportunities
  Commission, 75, 201
Ethnic minorities, 84–5, 91,
  141–3, 149, 161,
  163–5

Families, 17–20, 28–30, 57,
  167–8:
  single-parent, 28, 98,
    189
  et passim see also Children
Family aides, 137
Family Fund, 168
Family Service Units, 46,
  74, 87, 159, 162, 167,
  213, 232
Field work:
  nature of, 2–9
  numbers engaged in, 26
Fostering, 20, 23, 55, 90,
  141, 154
Fuel debts, 13, 15

Gallup surveys, 159, 169
General Social Work
  (Social Services)
  Council, 177–9 *passim*,
  182–6, 239–42
Gingerbread, 189
Good Neighbour Schemes,
  77, 82, 90
Group work, 150

Hadley, Professor R., 44,
  219
Handicapped people, 82 *see
  also* Mentally

  handicapped people,
  Physically
  handicapped people
  and under Children
Handy Working Party
  Report, 126
Harlesden Community
  Project, 82
Harlow Council
  Community Services
  Department, 163
Hazel, Nancy, 260
Health visitors, 28, 121,
  124
Home helps, 11, 116, 137,
  207 *et passim*
Hospitals, psychiatric, 30
Hospital social workers,
  6–8, 21, 117, 208
Housing, 13, 15, 23, 28, 43,
  116–17, 118
Housing associations, 82

Illich, Ivan, 184
Informal carers, 73, 75–6,
  78–9:
  importance of, 199–201,
    205, 247–8
  networks of, 86, 200,
    205–6, 209, 214, 216,
    221, 232, 247–50
  social workers and, 198,
    200–2 *passim*, 210–11,
    221, 227–8, 239,
    248–53
  see also under Social
    services departments
Institute of Housing, 118
Intermediate Treatment,
  61–2, 139, 141

Jenkin, Patrick, vii
Jones, David, x

Kent Family Placement
  Project, 90
King, Bob, ix
Kinship networks, 200

Leaper Report, 25
Legal aid, 189
Legislation, vii, 10, 36, 119,
  141, 145, 146, 150,
  152, 185, 234 *see also
  under names of Acts*
Local Authority Social
  Services Act, 107, 204
Local Government Act, 141

Magistrates, 61–2, 117, 119, 120
Malherbe, Madelaine, 258
Maria Colwell case, 250
Marriage guidance councils, 165, 175
Meals on wheels, 11
Media, vii, 160, 165–6
Mental Health Act, 120–1, 124, 216
Mental Health Amendment Bill, 121, 248
Mental illness, 30–1, 49, 76, 97, 129 see also following entry
Mentally handicapped people, 11, 30, 55, 97, 98, 140, 163
Mill Grove, 82
Morison Committee, 148
Muscular Dystrophy Group, 80
Mutual aid groups, 73, 76–7, 84, 89 see also Self-help groups

NALGO, 183–4
National Assistance Act, 105
National Association of Young People in Care, 62
National Children's Bureau, 55
National Council for Voluntary Organisations, 24, 79, 82, 86, 99, 184, 223
National Health Service Act 1946, 105
National Institute for Social Work, vii, 159, 210
National Joint Council, 2
National Society for the Prevention of Cruelty to Children, 74, 89, 124
National Union of Teachers, 121
Neighbourhood teams see Patch teams
Nurses, 121, 179

Offenders, 31, 38–9, 49, 82, 140, 148, 170–1, 173

Patch teams, 44, 207, 226, 229–30, 236–7, 245, 247
Personal social services: definition of, xiv see also Social services
Personal Social Services Council, 24, 75
Personal Social Services Research Unit, 216
Peter Bedford Trust, 82
Physically handicapped people, 11, 30, 54, 98, 161, 163
Pinker, Professor, 108
Police, 28, 61–2, 116, 121–2, 124
Poor Law, 52, 55, 105, 245
Poverty, 173
Pritchard, Professor, C., 171
Probation and after-care services, 119–20, 148, 186

Racial issues, 23 see also Ethnic minorities
Reform of Mental Health Legislation, 49
Remploy, 159, 168
Residential Care Association, 56, 57, 177
Residential centres: approaches used, 57–61 clients' opinions of, 162 conclusions on, 70–2 cost of, 54, 106–7 day centres and, 63–4 definition of, 53 description of, 54–5 effectiveness of, 174–5 elderly people in, 30 functions of, 64–7 passim importance of, 111 key-workers in, 69–70, 71 need for, 61–2 qualifications of workers in, 26, 57 resources, 46 segregation in, 56 social work in, 52–72 passim stigma attached to, 55–7 strikes in, 149
Resource centres, 207, 209

Resources, 14, 16, 27, 40, 43, 46, 96, 98, 99–101 passim, 143, 173, 213, 225, 235, 245: allocation of, 89, 99, 134, 189, 212, 214, 236
Resource Allocation Working Party, 89
Restormel Council for Voluntary Service, 86
Righton, Peter, ix
Royal Commission on Criminal Procedure, 122

Scarman Report, 98
Seebohm Report, 106–9, 111, 122, 153, 179, 192, 199, 203, 204, 223, 227, 242
Self-help groups, 75, 84, 142, 202 see also Mutual aid groups
Sinclair, Dr Ian, x
Social care networks, 39–40, 43–5
Social care planning, x, 21, 33, 36–41 passim, 153, 233: community networks and, 43–5 definitions of, xv, 33, 246–7 education and training and, 44 informal carers and, 75, 200 'Social casework', 150, 238–9
Social policy: approaches to, 35, 103–5 conclusions on, 111–12 political role of social workers and, 109–11 resources and, 46 social work and, 102–12 social workers and, 45
Social services departments agency agreements, 87, 88 communications and consultation, 129–30, 132, 133–4 community social workers and, 155, 198–218 passim contracting out, 91, 93 criticism of, 189

Social services dept. *cont.*
  delegation in, 128–34
    passim, 143, 225–6
  difficulties of, vii, 130–1
  ethnic minorities and,
    141–3, 163–5
  informal carers and, 198,
    200, 201–2, 210–11,
    221, 227–8, 239,
    248–53, 254
  innovation and, 81–2
  levels of work, 136–9
  management, 26, 34,
    116, 133, 134–5, 143,
    194 *see also* Team
    leaders
  need to maintain, 131–2,
    144, 215–16
  numbers employed by,
    127
  organisation of, 10,
    126–44, 153, 154,
    234–7, 242, 250–6
    passim
  other agencies and, 12,
    15, 28, 44–5, 113–25,
    232, 233–4, 236, 255,
    257
  planning, 86–7
  resource allocation, 89
  roles, distribution of,
    87–8
  special needs and, 141–3
  stigma attached to, 55–7,
    83, 149–50, 165
  variation in provision of,
    99
  voluntary agencies, 23,
    85–92, 99, 126
Social services:
  definition of, xv
  development of, 105–9,
    127
  expenditure of, 96–7,
    127
  kinds of, 36–8
  need for, 99, 123–4
  see also previous entry
Social services committees,
    2
Social services workers, xv
  see also Social workers
Social work:
  chronic conditions and,
    15–17
  community and, 111 *see
    also* Community social
    work

components of, x, 12–13,
    23, 34, 151 *see also*
    Counselling, Social
    care planning
  definitions of, xv–xvii,
    220–4, 235
  economic factors, 38,
    96–101, 108, 262 *see
    also* Resources
  groups and, 15, 20, 21,
    206
  indirect, 12, 20–3, 43
  local knowledge and, 40
  long-term, 15–20
  private sector, 91, 183
  research into, 24–6, 27,
    75–6, 159, 167–71
    passim, 200, 201
  setting of, 9–11
  short-term, 13–15, 56
  standards in, 177–87
  statute, non-regulation
    of by, 179, 182
  time available for, 10,
    31–2
  values and, 145–9, 237–9
  see also following entry and
    Community social
    work
Social workers:
  accountability of, 88,
    184, 214–16, 219, 223,
    225–9 *passim*, 262
  accreditation, 181–2, 241
  age of, 25–6, 107–8
  allocation of, work,
    137–8
  attachment to other
    agencies, 207–8
  career structure for,
    135–6
  clerical support for, 49,
    50, 139–40
  Conditions of Service,
    National Scheme of,
    136, 183
  criticisms of, 122, 172,
    160–4 *passim*, 166–72
    passim, 182, 188–9
  definition of, xvii–xviii,
    25
  designations of, 137
  direct practice, 135–6
  education and training,
    xvii, 44, 91, 177, 182,
    209, 231–2, 241–4
  effectiveness of, 170–4,
    175, 223–4

expectations of, vii, 123–
    5, 127, 160
  failures of, 36, 37, 113
  functions of, xi, 2–23,
    33–4, 51, 78, 92,
    109–11, 220–4, 250 *et
    passim*
  generalist/specialist
    debate, 210, 219,
    229–34, 235, 236,
    259–61
  informal carers and, 76,
    77
  inspectorate for, 187
  knowledge of, 35, 152–3,
    167, 220–1, 252
  monitoring by, 50–1
  National Scheme of
    Conditions of Service,
    136, 183
  need for, 33–51, 175
  numbers of, 24–32
    passim
  other agencies and, 115
  political role of, 109–11
  probationary period for,
    186
  problems coming to,
    26–32
  professionalism, 177,
    178–80, 222–3, 240–2,
    260
  promotion away from
    direct, 135–6
  public opinion on, 37–8,
    60, 159, 160, 165–6,
    167–70, 186
  qualifications of, 26, 139,
    181, 182, 186, 241,
    244 *see also under names
    of qualifications*
  rationing by, 46–7, 213
  registers of, 179, 181–2,
    184
  role, uncertainty of, 127,
    130
  skills of, 151–2, 220–1
  social control by, 47–9,
    148, 191, 239–40
  social policy and, 109–11
  specialisation of, 37, 51,
    122, 153–5, 163,
    230–1, 252, 261
  strikes of, 124, 149
  supervision of
    inexperienced, 131
  see also Informal carers
  Social Work in Conflict, 128

Specht, Professor Harry, ix, 159, 171
Stevenson, Professor, 44, 153, 233, 235, 236
Street wardens, 207
Study of the Board of Children, 109
Suicide, 31

Team leaders, 132–4, 139, 144, 211–2, 230, 237 *see also* managers *under* Social services departments
Teams, 132–4, 154, 215, 229, 250, 254 *see also* Area teams, work of, Social services departments
Tending, 62, 65–6, 67
Thanet Community Care Project, 216
Tooting Project, 84
Trade unions, 136, 149, 180, 215, 240, 258

Unemployment, 77, 10
Urban aid, 89
Utting, W. E., 91

Voluntary agencies:
accountability of, 88–9
definitions of, 73–4
ethnic minorities and, 84, 141–3, 165
income, 74, 80, 85
innovative role, 81–2, 127
legislation and, 36
nature of work, 9
numbers of, 74–5
paid staff in, 26
planning, 86–7
preventative role, 81
recruitment, 23
roles, distribution of, 87–8
social services departments, comparison with, 79, 83, 99
social services departments, partnership with, 85–92, 126
social workers in, 78–92 *passim*

specialisation and, 80–1, 141–3
training and, 91
watching role, 80
see also Volunteers
Volunteer Centre, 78
Volunteers:
counselling by, 34
numbers of, 74–5
social workers and, 40–1, 77–9

Warnock Report, 208
Welfare advisory committees, local, 192–6, 242
West Indians, 164, 165
Whitwell, Coral, viii
Who Cares, 55, 62
Wolfenden Committee, 75
Working Party:
members of, viii
period of work, viii–ix
response to, ix, 159, 160
terms of reference, vii–viii, 96
visits of, ix, 159
Working Together, 86, 87